AF576798

MICHAEL COSTA:
ENGLAND'S FIRST CONDUCTOR

Michael Costa: England's First Conductor

The Revolution in Musical Performance in England, 1830–1880

JOHN GOULDEN

ASHGATE

Published by
Ashgate Publishing Limited
Wey Court East
Union Road
Farnham
Surrey, GU9 7PT
England

Ashgate Publishing Company
110 Cherry Street
Suite 3-1
Burlington, VT 05401-3818
USA

www.ashgate.com

British Library Cataloguing in Publication Data
A catalogue record for this book is available from the British Library

The Library of Congress has cataloged the printed edition as follows:
Goulden, John, 1941– author.
Michael Costa, England's first conductor : the revolution in musical performance in England : 1830–1880 / by John Goulden.
pages cm.– (Music in nineteenth-century Britain)
Includes bibliographical references and index.
ISBN 978-1-4724-2717-5 (hardcover : alk. paper) – ISBN 978-1-4724-2718-2 (ebook) – ISBN 978-1-4724-2719-9 (epub) 1. Costa, Michael, 1808–1884. 2. Conductors (Music)–England–Biography. 3. Music–Performance–England–History–19th century. 4. Music–England–19th century–History and criticism. I. Title.
ML422.C845G68 2015
784.2092–dc23
[B]

2014026188

ISBN 9781472427175 (hbk)
ISBN 9781472427182 (ebook – PDF)
ISBN 9781472427199 (ebook – ePUB)

Printed in the United Kingdom by Henry Ling Limited, at the Dorset Press, Dorchester, DT1 1HD

Contents

List of Figures

Note: Except where indicated, illustrations are from the author's own collection.

Acknowledgements

I acknowledge in particular the advice and supervision of Professor Bennett Zon. In addition I have received valuable advice and pointers from Professor Bill Weber, Professor Simon McVeigh, Professor Michael Musgrave, Professor Jeremy Commons, Christine Bashford and Beverly Wilcox. My access to sources was greatly helped by generous assistance from Pamela Clark, Registrar of the Royal Archives at Windsor, citations from which are given with the permission of Her Majesty Queen Elizabeth II; Francesca Franchi and the staff of the Royal Opera House Archives; Dr Peter Horton at the Royal College of Music (RCM) Library and the late Paul Collen at the RCM's Centre for Performance History; Susan Gasson, who kindly agreed to the inclusion of material from the personal collection of the late Tony Gasson; Diane Clements, of the London Library and Museum of Freemasonry; Martin Holmes at the Oxford Faculty of Music Library; Katherine Hogg, Librarian at the Gerald Coke Handel Collection in the Foundling Museum; Nicholas Southon and Stephanie Puel at the Université François-Rabelais de Tours, who facilitated access to his thesis on Habeneck; Janet Snowman at the Royal Academy of Music Museum and Collections; Stephen Revell at the Opera Rara collection; Martin Bird, the Editor of the *Elgar Society Journal*; and the staff at the London Theatre Museum and the Theatre and Performance Department of the Victoria and Albert Museum at Olympia. At Ashgate, I have been much helped by Laura Macy, Emma Gallon and Barbara Pretty. Finally, warm thanks to Jennifer Silverstone for offering her insights into Michael Costa's psychology; to Alan Debes, whose two critical readings went far beyond the claims of our long friendship; and to my wife Diana who has faced more proofreading and disruption than any human being should have to endure.

List of Abbreviations

BL British Library.

CG *Correspondence Générale d'Hector Berlioz,* ed. Pierre Citron, Yves Gérard and Hugh J. Macdonald, 4 vols, (Paris: 1872).

Ella John Ella Collection, Faculty of Music Library, The Bodleian Library, Oxford, Mss 163.

Enciclopedia Italiana Alberto Maria Ghisalberti. *Dizionario Biografico degliItaliani* (Roma: Istituto della Enciclopedia Italiana, 1960–), vol. 30 (1984).

Feuilleton *Feuilleton du Journal des Débats,* http://www.hberlioz.com/feuilletons/debats.index.htm.

Goulden, John 'Michael Costa, England's first conductor: The revolution in musical performance in England 1830–80' (PhD diss., Durham University, 2012).

Grove *A Dictionary of Music and Musicians. Grove 1* (1879–89); *Grove 2* (1904–10), *New Grove 1* (1980), etc.

Gye Diary of Frederick Gye, ROHC and the Victoria and Albert Museum Collection, London).

ILN *Illustrated London News.*

MW *Musical World.*

QMMR *Quarterly Musical Magazine and Review.*

QVJ Queen Victoria's Journal, Royal Archives, Windsor.

RA Royal Archives, Windsor.

RCMA Royal College of Music Archives, London.

Ringel Matthew Ringel, 'Opera in the Donizettian Dark Ages: Management, competition and artistic policy in London 1861–70' (PhD diss., University of London, 1996).

Ringel and Dideriksen Matthew Ringel and Gabriella Dideriksen, 'Frederick Gye and "the Dreadful Business of Opera Management",' *Nineteenth-Century Music*, vol. 19, no. 1 (Summer 1995), 3–30.

RAM Royal Academy of Music.

RMU *Record of the Musical Union.*

ROHC Royal Opera House Collections.

SHS Sacred Harmonic Society.

Southon, Nicolas 'L'émergence de la figure du chef d'orchestre et ses composantes socio-artistiques: François-Antoine Habeneck (17811–849). La naissance du professionnalisme musical' (PhD diss., University Francois Rabelais, Tours, 2008).

Spitzer/Zaslaw John Spitzer and Neal Zaslaw, *The Birth of the Orchestra* (Oxford: Oxford University Press, 2005).

V&A Theatre and Performance Department, Victoria and Albert Museum, London.

For simplicity, the theatre at Covent Garden, which performed many functions and was also known as the Theatre Royal and the Royal Italian Opera, is here referred to as Covent Garden.

General Editor's Series Preface

Music in nineteenth-century Britain has been studied as a topic of musicology for over two hundred years. It was explored widely in the nineteenth century itself, and in the twentieth century grew into research with strong methodological and theoretical import. Today, the topic has burgeoned into a broad, yet incisive, cultural study with critical potential for scholars in a wide range of disciplines. Indeed, it is largely because of its interdisciplinary qualities that music in nineteenth-century Britain has become such a prominent part of the modern musicological landscape.

The series explores the wealth of music and musical culture of Britain in the nineteenth century and surrounding years. It does this by covering an extensive array of music-related topics and situating them within the most up-to-date interpretative frameworks. All books provide relevant contextual background and detailed source investigations, as well as considerable bibliographical material of use for further study. Areas included in the series reflect its widely interdisciplinary aims and, although principally designed for musicologists, the series is also intended to be accessible to scholars working outside of music, in areas such as history, literature, science, philosophy, poetry and performing arts. Topics include criticism and aesthetics; musical genres; music and the church; music education; composers and performers; analysis; concert venues, promoters and organizations; the reception of foreign music in Britain; instrumental repertoire, manufacture and pedagogy; music hall and dance; gender studies; and music in literature, poetry and letters.

Although the nineteenth century has often been viewed as a fallow period in British musical culture, it is clear from the vast extent of current scholarship that this view is entirely erroneous. Far from being a 'land without music', nineteenth-century Britain abounded with musical activity. All society was affected by it, and everyone in that society recognized its importance in some way or other. It remains for us today to trace the significance of music and musical culture in that period, and to bring it alive for scholars to study and interpret. This is the principal aim of the Music in Nineteenth-Century Britain series – to advance scholarship in the area and expand our understanding of its importance in the wider cultural context of the time.

Bennett Zon
Durham University, UK

Figure 1.1 Costa in 1835

Chapter 1
Introduction

> It is easy to glide through the first half of the nineteenth century without recognising how massive a set of changes was occurring in the fundamental aspects of repertory, taste and musical values.
>
> William Weber, *The Great Transformation of Musical Taste.*[1]

Until the late 1850s, Michael Costa was the only professional conductor resident in Britain. He was unique also in that he conducted for an unprecedentedly long career – more than five decades – and simultaneously directed London's main opera, concert and choral institutions. The embedding of a new system for directing music in Britain in the period 1830–50 was to a large extent Costa's achievement. He personified the emergence of the professional conductor as an essential part of musical performance and was the first musician to be knighted for his services to conducting. Costa's legacy extended far beyond baton-conducting to embrace orchestral management, rehearsal practice, performance co-ordination, lay-out and acoustics. Together these ingredients made up a new model of orchestral management, which I propose to call that of 'conductor-manager'. Since Costa was the principal architect of this model in England, his career is a good vantage point from which to consider the wider shifts of practice and aesthetics of the period.

But this is not a biography. The emergence of the professional conductor was a long process, which began a generation before Costa's arrival in Britain in 1829. It was the achievement of many musicians and had its roots in many music centres. Foreign visitors like Louis Spohr, Carl Maria von Weber, Felix Mendelssohn and Hippolyte Chélard introduced their own idiosyncratic approaches to conducting in London in the 1820s and 1830s. Even in Britain, which was slow to adopt the techniques of conducting, there were others who took up the baton in the period 1830–50. But the foreign visitors did not stay long enough to impose their models. And the other London-based directors were all primarily engaged in other musical activities: Henry Bishop was principally an arranger, Michael Balfe and Arthur Sullivan composers, William Sterndale Bennett a composer and teacher, Ignatz Moscheles and Julius Benedict pianists and Louis Antoine Jullien and George Smart in their different ways concert-promoters.

Another reason for not adopting a purely biographical approach is that conducting was not an isolated innovation: it needs to be seen in the context of

---

1 William Weber, *The Great Transformation of Musical Taste. Concert programming from Haydn to Brahms* (Cambridge: Cambridge University Press, 2008), 3.

a range of important changes in the early nineteenth century, which revolutionized the way in which music was performed. Orchestras became larger and instruments louder. Compositions became more elaborate, with more frequent changes of tempo and dynamics. The standards of instrumental and choral performance rose. Audiences demanded better finish, larger-scale performances and, sometimes, more novelty. Musical formats and entertainments proliferated, catering to a more diversified audience and gradually widening the gulf between 'classical' and 'popular' music. A canon – or, more correctly, several canons – of works emerged, some of which, because of their complexity, demanded repeated performance and the education of the audience through musical journalism and concert notes.[2] The publication and accuracy of scores received more attention and the notions of fidelity and authenticity began to take hold. Collectively, these changes laid the foundations of the modern music industry, which relied on increasingly specialized support services: set-designers, stage managers, artists' agents, full-time critics and musicologists. As the critic Francis Hueffer observed, musical science saw greater change in the mid-nineteenth century than any sphere except natural science.[3]

In the midst of this musical revolution, the emergence of conducting was a conspicuous and radical innovation. For most of human history, musicians have had no need of a conductor in the sense of someone who stood in front of them and directed without singing or playing an instrument. Musicians were expected to perform adequately without external direction, especially when playing music which they already knew. If direction was needed, it was usually provided by a fellow-performer. This could be done by an instrumentalist (*Concertmeister* or *chef d'orchestre*) or a keyboard-director (*Kapellmeister* or *maitre de musique*). If the performers were too numerous to manage themselves, as in a large choir or an opera chorus, a time-beater (*batteur de mesure*) might provide an audible or visible beat. This à la carte arrangement was both effective and economical in the period prior to about 1780.

The main feature of musical direction at the turn of the nineteenth century was the coexistence of many different models for different genres of music and different contexts and personalities (Chapter 3). What is remarkable is that, within two generations, this plethora of practices gave way in virtually every European music centre to a new system: direction by a conductor. His distinctive quality was that he interposed himself between the audience and the musicians, waving a bow, a scroll or a baton, and was inaudible, except for the occasional beating of his implement against a desk or stamping of his feet. Partly because of their distracting noises and gestures, the early conductors were at first the subject of much controversy. But by 1850, they were seen as an essential part of musical performance, recognizable as conductors in the modern sense of the word.

---

[2] On the early emergence of a canon in England, Weber, *The Rise of Musical Classics in Eighteenth Century England: A Study in Canon, Ritual and Ideology* (New York: Pendragon Press, 2000).

[3] Francis Hueffer, *Half a Century of Music in England 1837–87*, (London: Chapman and Hall, 1889), Ch. 1.

The revolution in musical direction involved an important shift in the meaning of the label of 'conductor'. Dr Johnson's Dictionary (1755) defined a conductor as 'a leader; one who shews (sic) another the way by accompanying him', 'a chief; a general' and 'a manager; a director'. The term was most commonly used in the military context, in the sense of a commander or escort. During a visit to France in 1802, George Smart noted that 'conductor' was used to describe the man who supervised (but did not drive) inter-city carriages.[4] The first hint of a musical connotation comes with an isolated entry in the *Annual Register* for 1774, when Joah Bates was described as conducting, as an organist, at the Westminster Handel Commemoration. There was no entry for 'conductor' in Thomas Busby's *Complete Dictionary of Music* (1806).[5]

As the label began to be used in music in the next three decades, it remained a non-specific term. It could refer to the composer, arranger, rehearser, supervisor, programme-fixer, leader or accompanist. It sometimes identified the person who set the programme, as when Colonel Greville 'conducted' the Amateur Concerts in 1805 and the Earl of Darnley the Ancient Concert in April 1829.[6] It could also be used to describe the organist, the first violin in a quartet, the accompanist at the piano or the chairman of a song-and-supper club. The term was even applied to the manager of the Royal Italian Opera at Her Majesty's Theatre. As late as 1836, Dickens was still using its original sense: 'Following our Conductor, we arrived at a small room.'[7]

The indiscriminate use of the term 'conductor' misled later generations into assuming that it had always meant what it came to mean by the middle of the century. This sort of anachronism is reflected in statements that Mozart 'conducted the second performance and then, in accordance with custom, handed over the baton to another conductor' or that Haydn in England proved himself to be 'not only a capable but a tactful conductor'.[8] It is perpetuated in the music heritage industry: for example the Vienna Mozart Festival Orchestra, which boasts 'concerts in the original Mozart style' and features a 'conductor' on a rostrum, with his back to the audience, using a baton to conduct a bewigged orchestra, arranged in a modern lay-out and with women among the players.[9] Another example appears in Milos Forman's film *Amadeus*, where Mozart 'conducts' operas on a rostrum with his back to the Emperor.[10] Such misconceptions were encouraged by the assumption

[4] H.B. and C.L.E Cox, eds, *Leaves from the Journals of Sir G. Smart* (London: Longmans, Green and Co., 1907), 15.

[5] Thomas Busby, *Complete Dictionary of Music* (London: Gillet, 1806).

[6] Eric Werner, *Mendelssohn: A New Image of the Composer and His Age* (New York: Free Press of Glencoe, 1963), 138. *Fashionable World* (27 Jun. 1805).

[7] *MW* (28 Oct. 1854), 711. Dickens, 'A Visit to Newgate', *Sketches by Boz*, vol. 1 (London: Chapman and Hall, 1910), 236.

[8] Annette Kolb, *Mozart*, trans. Phyllis and Trevor Blewett (London: Gollancz, 1939), 340. Cited in Adam Carse, *The Orchestra in the XVIIIth Century* (New York: Broude Bros, 1969), 91. Haydn in Reginald Nettel, *The Orchestra in England* (London: Cape, 1946), 75.

[9] See http://www.mozart.co.at/Vienna-Mozart-Concerts.

[10] See http://www.youtube.com/watch?v=yIzhAKtEzY0.

that there had always been conductors or that the trend to the modern model of conducting was inevitable, a belief reinforced by its rapid adoption across Europe.

This book seeks to analyse the emergence of conducting and the shifts of practice, organization and aesthetics which accompanied it, through the optic of the early conductors. The men (they were always men) who created the new profession of conducting are largely forgotten, unless they were also successful composers. But the main pioneers included figures who were only minor composers: Hippolyte Chélard in Munich and Weimar, Michael Costa in London, and François Habeneck in Paris. They were eclipsed in the second half of the century by virtuoso-conductors, typified by Hans von Bülow and Hans Richter. Many of the latter were immortalized by the nascent recording industry, which demonstrated how the new profession of conducting could be used to produce performances of great interpretative creativity. But the story of how their inheritance was forged by the previous generation deserves to be told. It is crucial to understanding the origins of the golden age of conducting and the radical shift from a musical world dominated by violin-leaders to one commanded by the baton-conductor, which remains a major feature of today's orchestra.

To appreciate the achievement of the first generation of conductors, it is necessary to look behind the 'Great Composers' narrative imposed by musicologists (mainly German) of the late nineteenth century and the 'Great Conductors' narrative (again mainly German) which accompanied it. This is not to downplay the originality and importance of the great composers and conductors, who still define the music of the period. It seeks rather to locate their genius in what Howard Becker has called the 'art world' in which it flourished. This in turn involves recognition of the 'cooperative networks through which art happens'. It is a concept especially relevant to music, the appreciation of which demands many qualified intermediaries between the composer of the score and the listener: players, singers, directors, designers, teachers, explainers as well as the whole business machinery.[11] It thus calls for an inter-disciplinary view, taking in issues of management, entrepreneurship, social change and institutional politics as well as criticism, aesthetics and repertoire. The contribution of the first conductors to this infrastructure was particularly important. They deserve more than the often dismissive footnotes to which they have been relegated. They played a crucial part in what Richard Taruskin has termed 'the early history of our musical present'.[12] Though overlooked today, some of them were at the time as influential as the composers – and often more visible. They were also among the principal architects of what I argue in Chapter 9 was England's greatest musical achievement in the nineteenth century.

There are two formidable obstacles to excavating the work of the first conductors. First, their emergence was scantily documented at the time. The conductor and rank-

---

[11] For a cogent discussion of this concept, see Howard Becker, *Art Worlds* (Berkeley and Los Angeles: University of California Press, 1982), 1.

[12] Richard Taruskin, *Music in the 19th Century* (Oxford: Oxford University Press, 2010), xxi.

and-file musicians – commonly referred to as 'the accessories' or 'the inferior departments' – were rarely noticed, since audiences and critics focused on the star singers and instrumental virtuosi.[13] Second, they flourished in a cultural climate which was later smothered by what Tovey called the 'the early Wagner–Liszt reign of terror'.[14] Understanding the period prior to 1850 involves entering a lost world in which opera was still dominated by the bel canto composers, where the operas of Verdi or Wagner had barely been performed and where *Fidelio* was rarely heard; where, in the concert hall, Liszt was a piano-virtuoso and not a composer and where Schubert's symphonies were unknown; where modernity meant Mendelssohn's *Elijah* and Meyerbeer's *Robert le diable*; where the prime test of the quality of singers – their bel canto technique – had not yet been declared by Rossini to be a vanished art. It is a period which has suffered perhaps more than any other from the neglect and contempt of musicological positivists for whom the sole tests of creativity are originality and innovation.

Although the new methods of musical direction evolved slowly and piecemeal, 1830 is a convenient vantage point from which to analyse them. It saw the end of Rossini's opera career (*Guillaume Tell* – 1829) and the first mature operas of Donizetti (*Anna Bolena* – 1830) and Meyerbeer (*Robert le diable* – 1831). This period saw the death of Weber (1826) and the first appearance in London of Mendelssohn (1829); the first important theoretical works on the direction of orchestras and choirs; and the emergence of a vigorous musical press. It marked a watershed in singing, with the retirement of the last great castrato, Velluti, and the arrival of new types of leading singer: the heroic tenor (such as Duprez) and the dramatic soprano (in Wilhelmine Schroeder-Devrient). It also marked a social watershed as practitioners became less dependent on aristocratic patrons, who themselves began to lose influence over the management of the opera house, and the traditional half-guinea concert gave way to cheaper ticket prices.

The emergence of the new conductor has to be disentangled from the many confusing variants of musical control which coexisted in the previous two generations. This is the subject of Chapter 3, which leads on to an analysis of how Costa developed existing practice and models into a coherent system of orchestral and choral control (Chapter 4). Later chapters consider what use he made of his system (Chapter 5), his 50 years of operatic conducting (Chapter 6) and his long stints on the concert and choral circuits (Chapter 7). But first it is necessary to summarize briefly his background and his unusual personality, which provides the key to his achievement as a conductor-manager (Chapter 2).

---

[13] 'Accessories', *Morning Post* (18 Jan. 1837). 'Inferior departments', quoted from Mount Edgcumbe by Thomas Love Peacock, 'Mangled operas and the Star System', in Halliford, ed., *Dramatic Criticisms and Translations, & Other Essays*, vol. 10 (London: 1926), 235–50.

[14] Tovey in *Encyclopaedia Britannica*, 14th ed., vol. 15, 244. Herman Klein, *Musicians and Mummers* (London: Cassell, 1925), 232.

Chapter 2
Costa's Background and Personality

Costa was born in Geneva, probably in 1808, and brought up in Naples.[1] His father's family was descended from Jews who had embraced Catholicism at some stage after the expulsion of the Jews from Spain. By the early nineteenth-century both sides of his family were members of the Catholic musical establishment in Naples. His father, Pasquale Costa, was a minor church composer, whose title of 'cavaliere' probably indicated family aspiration rather than aristocratic status. An uncle, Domenico Tritto, was a composer and *maestro di capella* at two major churches in Naples. His mother's father, Giacomo Tritto, was a leading opera composer who later became the Director of the Naples Royal Academy of Music, where Costa received his musical education.

Naples was the biggest city in Italy, with a population of about half a million, more than twice the size of Milan. It offered a far better musical training than was available in England. In later life, Costa urged the Royal Society for the Arts to adopt the regime of the Naples Academy, where pupils from 13 to 21 studied music and the other arts as part of a rounded education.[2] Costa received his earliest lessons from his grandfather, Giacomo Tritto, and later studied composition under Nicolo Zingarelli and singing under Girolamo Crescentini.[3] Naples was still the operatic capital of Europe, providing a base for Paisiello (1813–6), Rossini (1815–1822), Bellini (1819–27) and later Donizetti – and for leading singers who were to play a major part in his London career: Luigi Lablache, Antonio Tamburini and Fanny Persiani. It gave Costa the opportunity to promote his early compositions, notably his opera *La Malvina*, commissioned for the Teatro San Carlo, where he worked briefly as *maestro al cembalo*. The turning point in his

---

[1] *Grove 1* and his obituaries, following Costa's 1871 census declaration and presumably his own account, gave a birth date of 1810. His friend Gruneisen also quoted 1810 in *The Opera and the Press* (London: 1869), 15. Another friend, John Ella, gave 1807. But declarations by Costa (in a July 1847 application to the Royal Society of Musicians) and by his brother Raphael (in June 1847 to Bow St Police Court) gave 1808. The latter is followed by *Grove 2* (vol. 2, 460), the *Enciclopedia Italiana* and *New Grove 2* and seems more credible.

[2] Costa's evidence to the Royal Society of Arts, 16 February 1866, *Journal of the Society of Arts* (1866), 214–16.

[3] Zingarelli (1752–1837) was well-known in his day as the composer of 37 operas one of which, *Giulietta e Romeo* (Shakespeare with a happy ending), was produced at the King's Theatre. He was Director of the Naples Academy from 1814. Crescentini (1762–1846) was a celebrated late castrato, who performed the part of Romeo in Zingarelli's *Giulietta e Romeo*, and teacher. For more see *New Grove 2*, vol. 27, 844–5 and vol. 6, 663.

Figure 2.1 Costa in 1831 (courtesy of the University of Bristol Theatre Collection)

career came when he was chosen in 1829 to supervise an oratorio commissioned by the Birmingham Festival from the 77-year-old Zingarelli (Figure 2.1).

Costa's career in England can be briefly summarized. He began as *maestro al cembalo* at the King's Theatre in the Haymarket in 1829, moving up to become Musical Director, probably in 1831. By the mid-1830s he was in sole control of the musical side of the opera. After a brief golden age at the King's between about 1838 and 1846, he split with the manager, Benjamin Lumley, and left with most of the singers and players to form a new Royal Italian Opera at Covent Garden. Together with Frederick Gye, he established Covent Garden as the leading opera base in London, but a power struggle between them led Costa to leave in 1869, when he returned for a final decade as Musical Director at the Haymarket. In between, he rescued London's leading concert and choral institutions – the

Philharmonic Society (1846–54) and the Sacred Harmonic Society (1849–82) – bringing both to a new level of discipline and polish. As Musical Director at the leading festivals, including the mammoth Handel Festivals, he presided over one of the quintessential achievements of the Victorian period. He died at Hove in 1884 at the age of 76.

Costa was a talented musician, a competent composer and an accomplished pianist, but the key to his impact lay in his long tenure as a conductor and the immense personal authority which he accumulated. Since his influence and authority derived mainly from his unusual character, it is necessary to look at what shaped his personality, before examining the musical structures which he inherited in London and how he developed them into his system.

There is little reliable biographical material of a personal nature about Costa. In contrast to the conductors Charles Hallé and Luigi Arditi or the managers Benjamin Lumley and 'Colonel' Mapleson, Costa left no memoirs. Unlike the other main manager in his career, Frederick Gye, he did not keep a diary. There is no biography, of the kind written by near contemporaries about the conductors Charles Hallé and George Smart, the critic J.W. Davison or the composers Michael Balfe and William Sterndale Bennett. The only primary sources which relate substantively to him are of three kinds. First, there are six opera house contracts and related letters which illustrate the process by which he built up his unprecedented powers.[4] Second, there are three sets of correspondence which put a little flesh on Costa's two-dimensional public figure: with Frederick Gye during their bumpy partnership of 21 years at Covent Garden; with Costa's 'dearest friend', the librettist William Bartholomew; and 45 extraordinary letters from Rossini and one surviving reply from Costa, that throw surprising light on the whole Costa story.[5]

The third key source is the remarkable daily diary of the Covent Garden manager and lessee, Frederick Gye, covering the period from 1847 to 1878.[6] Gye was primarily an entrepreneur, pre-occupied with the business side of the opera house. But his diary provides insights not available for any other musical relationship in England during this period. The richness of this source, which gives Gye's misanthropic perspective on most of his contemporaries and ends on a note of antagonism towards Costa, makes it hard to form a balanced judgement of their respective contributions to the success of Covent Garden. Gye's version inevitably dominates the analyses by Gabriella Didericksen and Matthew Ringel which, though invaluable, tend to overstate Gye's role.[7] Unfortunately Gye's account of events is not balanced by the other side of the story since Costa's friend the prolific critic Henry Chorley destroyed more than 5,000 letters in the days before his death and took care to exclude from his autobiographical material 'any word that can

---

[4] Full texts in Goulden, Appendix A.

[5] Goulden, Appendix B.

[6] Frederick Gye's Diaries are located in the Diary Collection, ROHC. The 1847 volume is held at the Victoria and Albert Museum, London.

[7] Ringel and Dideriksen.

give private pain'.[8] The other main primary source – the prolific Hector Berlioz – calls for careful and in some cases sceptical reading (Chapter 8).

The secondary sources are also unreliable. There are a few reminiscences by well-disposed contemporaries – Henry Chorley, the violinist John Ella, the Leeds-based singer William Spark and the writer John Edmund Cox. Their fond recollections of their younger days and Costa's ground-breaking achievements in the 1830s and 1840s are offset by accounts from less sympathetic contemporaries such as George Grove and the critic J.W. Davison. Grove provided a posthumous reminder of the defects in Costa's system, though this was coloured by his concern to boost the reputation of his sensitive protégé August Manns.[9] Davison came to admire Costa, but much of his critical writing during the 1840s aimed to advance the competing claims of his friend William Sterndale Bennett. Whether favourable or critical, most of these Victorian sources are impregnated with respectability and euphemism. Musical gentlemen are conventionally described as paragons of family life and probity. This is true of the blameless portraits of George Grove (despite his long infatuation with Edith Oldham), Michael Balfe (with his prolonged absences from his family in Paris) and John Ella (with his lady friend in Victoria, London).[10] Costa seems to have avoided such entanglements, but the many encomia on him need to be read against the polite clichés which were conventional in the period.

Nearly all memoirs of the later nineteenth-century treat him as a two-dimensional caricature – autocratic, unimaginative and metronomic. The most frequently re-cycled information about Costa was the joke by Rossini which implied that he was an indifferent composer (Chapter 8). Later sources were heavily influenced by Shaw, for whom Costa was guilty of all the musical sins of the mid-Victorian age. *New Grove* perpetuates the image by stating that Shaw described Costa 'neatly' with the comment that he 'allowed the opera to die in his grasp'.[11] Most of the standard music histories treated him as an essentially performative musician who conducted the big festivals.[12] He is irrelevant to their main concerns – the search for an English Beethoven and the modernization of the repertoire.[13] Historians of the 'Great Composers' school largely (and rightly) omitted him, or briefly

8 Chorley obituary in *Athenaeum* (24 Feb. 1872), 249. Bledsoe, Henry, *Henry Fothergill Chorley* (Aldershot: Ashgate, 1998), viii.

9 *Pall Mall Gazette* of 1884, cited in Charles Graves, *The Life and Letters of Sir George Grove* (London: Macmillan, 1903), 124–5. See Chapter 5, 'Infrastructure and Coordination'.

10 Graves mentioned Edith Oldham only as an alumna of the Royal College of Music, *George Grove*. On Balfe, William Barrett, *Balfe: His Life and Works* (London: Remington, 1882), 199. On Ella, Christina Bashford, *The Pursuit of High Culture: John Ella and Chamber Music in Victorian London* (Woodbridge: Boydell Press, 2007), 262–70.

11 *New Grove 2*, vol. 6, 525.

12 Ernest Ford, *A Short History of Music in England* (London: Sampson Low and Co., 1912).

13 On the quest for an English musical hero, see Bennett Zon, 'Histories of British music and the land without music: National identity and the idea of the hero' in Emma Hornby and David Maw, eds, *Essays on the History of English Music in Honour of John*

alluded to his two oratorios. Perfunctory entries in twentieth-century dictionaries illustrated the rapid eclipse of Costa's reputation after his death (Chapter 9).

There is almost no material on Costa's private emotional life apart from a single hint that he was jilted by the soprano Elizabeth Seguin in the early 1830s and thereafter wanted 'never again [to] be troubled with a woman'.[14] There are few vignettes of Costa away from the rostrum and rehearsal room. A couple of letters to his younger brother Raphael reveal an avuncular, almost obsessive attachment. Grove described the two of them attacking a mountain of macaroni for breakfast on Ischia in 1869 and his distress when announcing that his elderly living-in friend Captain Lyon had broken his leg and was forced to walk 'on crotchets'.[15] The pianist-composer Francesco Berger recalled him hosting Sunday morning receptions at Eccleston Square in 'a dressing gown, no trousers and top-boots worn over his drawers'.[16]

Despite the paucity of the sources, there are several reference points from which his personality can be constructed. In particular, there are three influences that can credibly be assumed to have had a formative effect on his personality after he left Naples and settled in England in 1829: his traumatic introduction to English musical life in Birmingham, his stressful initiation into the Italian Opera in London, and his ambivalent status as an outsider in English society.

Costa's debut at the Birmingham Festival in 1829 was catastrophic. Sent by Zingarelli to 'superintend' his commissioned cantata, the 21-year-old Costa was not permitted to do so, possibly because (unlike the Festival's leading light, Thomas Greatorex), he could not 'conduct' from the organ. He was obliged instead to perform as a tenor in the oratorio and three other concerts. The reviews were scathing. One commented that 'The singer was little, if at all, better than the composition'. *The Harmonicon* observed that Zingarelli 'would have acted with more discretion had he kept both his *sacred* song and his *profane* singer for the benefit of his Neapolitan friends' (emphasis in original). Costa's singing was 'below mediocrity … he does not compensate for his vocal deficiencies by his personal address, which is abundantly awkward'. After he sang, 'Nel furor delle tempeste' from Bellini's *Il pirata,* the same critic commented: 'Had he remained

---

Caldwell: Style, Performance, Historiography (Woodbridge: Boydell & Brewer, 2010), 311–24.

[14] The only source for this is William Spark, *Musical Memories* (London: W Reeves, 1909), 10. Elizabeth Seguin (1815–70), a lesser singer in the talented Seguin family, married a Wallachian baron. Her daughter, Euphrosyne Parepa, had a distinguished operatic career as the wife of Carl Rosa. Costa attended parties at Seguin's house in the 1830s. James Robert Sterndale Bennett, *Life of William Sterndale Bennett by his Son* (Cambridge: Cambridge University Press, 1907), 96.

[15] Cited in Graves, *George Grove*, 123 and 178.

[16] John Francis Barnett, *Musical Reminiscences and Impressions* (London: Hodder and Stoughton, 1913), 82.

but a few moments longer on the stage, he would have witnessed a storm compared to which the roarings of his own Vesuvius would have seemed but a murmur'.[17]

The natural response to this débacle would have been to return home, where he would probably have followed the classic career pattern, with the prospect of performing a steady stream of his own works in the opera houses and churches of Naples. This seems to have been Costa's first inclination until he received a letter of stern advice from Zingarelli not to miss 'a chance which, once lost, never returns'.[18] His decision to stay in England drastically changed the course of his life, by leading him eventually into a career – which would have been improbable in Naples – as a conductor-manager across the spectrum of opera, symphonic and choral music. There is no clear indication why he decided to stay. But three factors were probably at work.

First, he may have wanted to escape from the climate of Naples, which was oppressive both politically and musically. The rule of King Ferdinand and his Austrian wife became increasingly reactionary after they had been expelled twice from the city and her sister, Marie Antoinette, executed in Paris. Costa was less politically minded than some of the Italian singers, notably the tenors Giovanni Mario and Giovanni Rubini, who often struck pro-Republican postures on stage. But he seems to have shared their sentiments, playing a full part during the celebrations to honour Garibaldi's visit to London in 1864. The *MW* later commented that he was 'no prophet … in his own country, nor any great pet of King Bombas' (Ferdinand II).[19] Naples was anyway losing its image as one of the leading music centres in Italy. Several of Donizetti's operas – *Lucrezia Borgia*, *Anna Bolenna* and *Poliuto* – were banned there and Bellini's second opera, *Bianca e Gernando*, was repeatedly blocked by royal protocol. Contrary to the trend elsewhere, the San Carlo orchestra was in decline and the opera itself, according to Donizetti, 'a cage of madmen'.[20] Another drawback was the difficulty of securing a good post in Naples, where Pacini, Donizetti and Bellini were already established and there was a surfeit of local composers.

Second, from a practical angle, he may have needed to find work in London to recoup the heavy costs of his trip to Birmingham. Despite its defects as a musical centre, London promised much higher financial rewards than Naples. He had useful Neapolitan contacts in London, including the tenor Rubini, the soprano Giuditta Pasta, the Vestris family, who ran Covent Garden, and the influential composer Muzio Clementi, who had been impressed by Costa's skilful re-scoring of 'Nel furor delle tempeste' for its inclusion in one of the concerts at Birmingham. These connections put him in touch with the new manager of the Italian Opera at

---

17 Details in *Harmonicon*, vol. 7, no. 4 (Apr. 1829), 91–2. *Harmonicon*, vol. 7, no. 11 (Nov. 1829), 274.

18 Zingarelli to Costa (9 Sep. 1829), *Musical Times* (1 Nov. 1906), 743–4.

19 *MW* (27 Jan. 1855), 56.

20 Spitzer/Zaslaw, 319. Donizetti to Ricordi (3 May 1835), G. Zavadini, *Donizetti: Vita – Musiche – Epistolario* (Bergamo: 1948), no. 164.

the King's Theatre, the French actor Pierre-François Laporte, who offered him the subordinate post of *maestro al cembalo*, probably in late 1829.

Third, family reasons may also have played a part in his decision to stay. His grandfather Tritto died in 1824 and, after the death of his mother, his father remarried in 1826. Although he returned occasionally to Naples, there is no evidence of any connection with his step-mother and half-siblings.[21] The fact that Costa was joined in London in the 1840s by his father and his younger brother Raphael, both of whom were buried in Costa's vault at Kensal Green cemetery, suggests that contact with the rest of his family petered out. At the very least, it is reasonable to assume that his early years in London were profoundly affected by a sense of isolation from his family.

The second formative influence – his painful baptism in the musical world of London – is described in Chapter 4. In essence, he faced a combination of financial insecurity, power struggles and bitter labour relations which help to explain his later obsession with order and authority. When the 21-year-old Costa was introduced to the King's Theatre orchestra, they let out a 'roar of laughter' and, the following day, presented him with a case containing seven miniature razors, for use when he was old enough to shave.[22] In addition to his hand-to-mouth struggle at the King's Theatre, he was failing to establish himself as a composer, trying unsuccessfully to juggle an increasing number of private concerts and keeping afloat by giving lessons to pupils.[23]

It was during those initial years, when he enjoyed neither success nor status, that he was exposed to the third formative experience: the ambivalent position of the outsider in English society. The period around the 1832 Reform Act saw an intense debate about English identity.[24] In this febrile atmosphere, foreign musicians occupied a doubly uncertain position. As foreigners, they were in varying degrees part of the 'Other', against which the English measured their own identity. As musicians they were in a profession associated with emotion, rakishness and effeminacy – all contrary to the emerging self-image of English manliness, restraint and decorum. A *Punch* cartoon underlined the link between foreigners and musicians who should be patronized (Figure 2.2).[25] *Punch* made fun of the entrepreneur conductors, Philippe Musard and Jullien, associating them with flamboyancy and extravagant gestures.[26] Regarded as artisans – or at best as

---

[21] He took a holiday there from August to November 1872. *Graphic* (3 Aug. and 16 Nov. 1872).

[22] John Edmund Cox, *Musical Recollections of the Last Half-Century* (London: Lensley Bros,1872), vol.1, 180.

[23] Pupils in concert programmes at RAM, 205, 572 and 573. Costa leaving concerts early to appear at soirées, *Morning Post* (3 May 1840 and 18 May 1841).

[24] On the issues of English identity see Peter Mandler, *The English National Character* (Yale: Yale University Press, 2006) and Ulrich Pallua, *Eurocentrism, Racism, Colonialism in the Victorian and Edwardian Age* (Heidleberg: Universitätsverlag, 2006).

[25] *Punch* (21 Aug. 1841), 62. Cited by Holly Mathieson, 'Embodying music: The visuality of three iconic conductors in London, 1840–1940' (MusB diss, Otago), 116–25.

[26] *Punch*, Fashions for December, vol. 1 (11 Dec. 1841), 257.

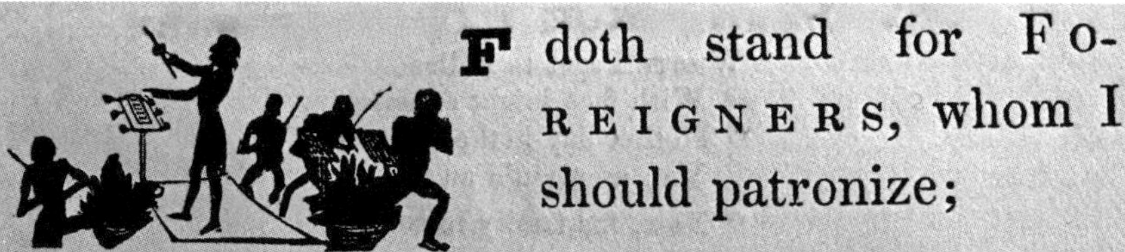

Figure 2.2 'Foreigners' depicted as musicians in *Punch* alphabet (*Punch*, 21 Aug. 1841, 62) (courtesy of Westminster City Libraries)

professionals – foreign musicians struggled to find a respectable position in the complex hierarchies of the middle classes.[27] Costa's experience at Birmingham in 1829 will have alerted him to the powerful nationalistic ethos, which favoured national genres (glees and catches), 'English' opera and British composers. Though influential sections of society were receptive to foreigners in roles which had traditionally been supplied from abroad – singers, composers and virtuosi – this did not extend to the less elevated roles of directing and playing, which were felt to be within the range of local musicians.

Costa was potentially on the wrong side of several important divides – as a Jew, a Catholic, a southern Italian and a musician. He thus occupied a classic liminal position, on the outer fringes of social and moral respectability.

It is not clear whether Costa was considered – or considered himself – a Jew. By the early nineteenth-century, both sides of his family were respectable parts of the Catholic musical establishment in Naples. In London, however, where Costa was a well-known Jewish name, he would have been assumed to be Jewish. This was certainly no barrier to talented musicians: Giuditta Pasta, Maria Malibran and Ignaz Moscheles all enjoyed success in London. Meyerbeer and especially Mendelssohn were on the road to canonization. But social prejudice was still widespread. Lord Ward, the owner of Her Majesty's Theatre, refused to have dealings with Benjamin Lumley because he was 'a bloody Jew'.[28] The 'Jew Bill' of 1836 failed to provide Jews with all the rights recently available to Catholics. Writers such as Dickens and George Eliot were still fostering the anti-semitic caricatures that they would later correct.[29] Racial prejudice may therefore have been a factor in the Philharmonic Society's blackballing of Costa and Moscheles in 1838.

As a Christian, Costa was spared the dilemma that led an estimated 50,000 Jews in England, including his friend the pianist Julius Benedict, to convert prior

[27] Mandler, *English National Character*, 53. Pallua, *Eurocentrism,* 20.

[28] Gye, 29 Jul. 1857.

[29] The harsh references to Fagin in Oliver Twist (1838) were not softened until the revised edition of 1867, by which time Dickens had created the 'gentle Jew' Riah in *Our Mutual Friend* (1864). George Eliot wrote many anti-semitic comments before making a Jew the most admirable character in *Daniel Deronda* (1876).

to 1875. He appears to have distanced himself from Jewish society, organizing his social life round the musical and Masonic worlds. Among the many unpleasant things said about Costa during his career, I have come across only one possible allusion to Jewishness: Mapleson refers to Costa, like Shylock, insisting on his bond.[30] Costa presented himself as a member of 'an old Spanish family'.[31] Grove's story about Costa finding Mendelssohn, Moscheles and Meyerbeer together at Her Majesty's and asking: 'What are these old Jews about?' suggests either that he was relaxed enough to joke about Jewishness or that he saw them as distinctly more Jewish than himself.[32]

His southern Italian background was in some ways a more serious barrier to acceptance in English society, since (unlike his Jewishness) it could not be disowned. There was a prejudice, which remained deep-rooted up to Toscanini's day, that Italians could not conduct symphonic music and came to London only to rob the English of jobs and money (Figure 2.3). After his Birmingham debacle, Costa was told that '… Questo Signor *costa* troppo' and advised to return home since he added nothing to the over-supply of foreign musicians in England.[33] Even when he was well-established in 1848, the *Morning Post* wrote: 'He is not a profound musician – his education being superficial like that of almost all modern Italian professors'.[34]

On the other hand, Italians enjoyed some professional advantages. It was an asset in the opera house that Costa could manage the fractious Italian singers, act as the link to major composers abroad (especially Rossini) and make the often substantial changes necessary to perform French and German works in the Italian Opera. More generally, his superior education at the Naples Conservatoire gave him a distinct advantage over locally trained musicians, especially in the eyes of the xenophiliac opera subscribers.[35] Costa exploited these advantages, especially in his first decade, when the Italian repertoire was still dominant in London. But, as he became established, he increasingly distanced himself from his Neapolitan roots, not only bringing his close family members to London but also, in terms of his travels and repertoire, giving at least as much attention to France and Germany as to Italy.

One of the intriguing aspects of Costa's career is that he did not follow the route opened up by Catholic and Jewish Emancipation to exploit the advantages of his liminal status, but aimed instead to integrate himself in English society as

30 J.H. Mapleson, ed., Harold Rosenthal, *The Mapleson Memoirs (*New York: Appleton-Century, 1966), 138.

31 *Times* (30 Apr. 1884).

32 Graves, *George Grove*, 124.

33 'This gentleman *costs* too much' (emphasis in original), quoted in *Musical Times* (1 Nov. 1906), 743–4.

34 *Morning Post* (4 Nov. 1848).

35 Nicholas Temperley, 'Xenophilia in British Musical History', in Bennett Zon, ed., *Nineteenth-Century British Musical Studies*, vol. 1 (Aldershot: Ashgate, 1999), 3–19.

SIGNOR HAYDYNI MOZARTI CRIBBINI.

Ah! great conductor, what a mighty fuss,
What strange ferocity to wheedle us;
Who would imagine from that brigand look,
That music spoil'd perhaps a decent cook.
Oh! antic muse, who made such men as these,
To finger all our cash, with their false keys;
They rush in shoals their trump'ry notes to play,
And in return, take our bank notes away.

Figure 2.3 Caricature Italian conductor (*ILN*, 30 Dec. 1843, 430) (courtesy of Westminster City Libraries)

an Anglican-Masonic gentleman. In retrospect, his whole career in London can be seen as a campaign to cross the threshold to social acceptability. In common with several foreign conductors (and in contrast with British singers), he anglicized his name from Michele Andrea to Michael Andrew – or, to close friends, 'Mike'. He took English nationality in 1839: the critic Charles Gruneisen announced, when he took over the Philharmonic, that he was now 'Mr Costa – for "signor" with us he shall be no more – he has morally as well as legally naturalised himself'.[36]

He became an Anglican and bought a vault in the new Kensal Green cemetery – though there is no evidence that he was deeply pious. Like many immigrants, he used Freemasonry as a route to status and integration. In 1875, he was appointed Junior Grand Warden, one of the two highest positions below the Grand Master (then the Prince of Wales), later becoming the Order's Grand Organist.[37] He took on an English persona, holidaying at typical English resorts such as Folkestone and Ventnor. In the few surviving letters of a personal nature, he expresses conventionally patriotic sentiments. He wrote from Paris: 'I have to say, nothing to compare with our dear old England'.[38]

Given his austere and strange personality, which will be discussed below, it is remarkable how far he succeeded in assuming the role of an English gentleman. His friend William Spark stated: 'He spoke English well and wrote in a remarkably neat style.' But Gye's Diary parodies Costa's relapse into fractured English in moments of stress. 'You say I do wrong, I do wrong? I cannot do wrong! That is an impertinence to say I do wrong.'[39] His written English is generally correct, sometimes idiomatic, though with lapses: 'what wonderfull fellow is Benedict!!'; 'it is to lat (sic) to go to Sydenham but tomorrow I shall be there'.[40] Although not socially gregarious, he attended Gladstone's working breakfasts and was one of the four witnesses (along with the French Ambassador and the Duke of Manchester) at Adelina Patti's wedding to the Marquis de Caux in 1868. There are anecdotes of him dining at the Marlborough Club with the Duke of Edinburgh and Arthur Sullivan; playing games with Millais and Effie at Ella's Mozart party for children; and being due to dine with Kate Dickens and Lady Devonshire at Chorley's just before the latter's death.[41] In a letter from Paris, he boasted that he was dining out every night and could do so even more often 'if I had a triple stomach and the digestion of an ostrich'.[42]

---

36 *Morning Post* (16 Mar. 1846).

37 Information kindly supplied by Diane Clements, Director of The Library and Museum of Freemasonry.

38 Costa to Bartholomew (13 Nov. 1864), RCMA 3029.

39 Spark, *Musical Memories,* 11. Gye, 14 Jul. 1868.

40 Costa to Bartholomew (2 Sep.1866), RCMA 3037; Costa to Grove, undated, RAM, 2005.1645.

41 Henry Hewlett, *Henry Fothergill Chorley: Autobiography, Memoir and Letters,* 2 vols (London: Richard Bentley and Son, 1873), vol. 1, 334.

42 Costa to Bartholomew (2 Sep. 1866), RCMA 3037; emphasis in original.

He became a regular part of the musical life of the royal family, organizing private concerts and music sessions with them. He first appears in Princess Victoria's diary in 1835, at her sixteenth birthday concert at Kensington Palace, where he accompanied Rubini, Tamburini, Lablache and Ivanoff on the piano '*beautifully*' in her favourite arias.[43] In 1850, a concert involving Pasta was 'The greatest treat for me as I could hear it quietly, there being but few people. I talked to all of the singers and to Costa.' At Osborne House on the Isle of Wight, Victoria slipped into a rehearsal by Mario, Lablache, Castellan and Costa – 'which was a treat'.[44]

Costa provided scores for private music-making by the Queen and Albert. 'Costa and Lablache came [to Osborne House] and we sang with them for a short while. Costa's accompanying is a wonderful support and assistance.'[45] An entry for 1843 records that:

> A little after 6, we had a very nice little amateur concert, Costa coming down from London, and we sang with him (he singing the tenor parts and accompanying us) … We went through the whole of that *beautiful* little *Requiem* by Mozart … and with Costa's powerful accompaniment it really sounded very well and full. It was a great treat. He is such a perfect musician and helps one so much, keeping all so well together. His voice is pleasing though not very powerful.[46]

In addition to acting as the main channel between Queen Victoria and the opera (Chapter 6), he briefed her on musical matters. In 1849, he wrote to inform her that Meyerbeer's *Le prophète* had gone very well in spite of having only two rehearsals: Viardot was 'sublime' and Mario 'excellent'.[47] When she grumbled about a poor piano version of this opera, Costa replied (in French): 'Her Majesty is completely right in finding the arrangement of *Le prophète* for four hands is not very good. But sadly it is the only one that exists' – though he promised to do a better version from the full score when he had time.[48] After Prince Albert's death in 1861, he orchestrated his *Invocazione all'Armonica* and premiered it at the Birmingham Festival. As royal patronage declined during Victoria's long years of mourning, he retained his royal links mainly as a leading mason (with the Prince of Wales) and by giving music lessons to the Princess Royal and Princess Louise. His knighthood seems to have come at the initiative of Victoria, who commented that he well deserved it, 'being a good composer and admirable musician as well as a most respectable man'.[49]

---

43 RA QVJ 18 May 1835.

44 RA QVJ 28 Jul. and 5 Aug. 1850.

45 RA QVJ 6 Aug. 1850; emphasis in original.

46 RA QVJ 21 Oct. 1843.

47 RA VIC/Add C 4/137 25 Jul. 1849.

48 RA VIC/Add C 4/142 31 Jul. 1849. Author's translation.

49 Gladstone replied to the Queen that he was 'aware of no reason against it'. Gladstone to Victoria (5 Apr. 1869), RA, VIC/A 38/60. RA, QVJ 14 Apr. 1869.

The Queen's comment shows that Costa displayed the sober characteristics that appealed to Victorian England. His private life had more in common with the temperance-Protestants of the Sacred Harmonic Society than with the louche world of the Opera. His respectable middle-class status, living in one of Thomas Cubitt's new stucco houses in Eccleston Square, helped him to avoid the stigma of being merely a professional musician. His portraits, like those of Spontini, Spohr and especially Mendelssohn, show a prosperous gentleman rather than a conductor (Figure 2.4). Image was an important part of the process of labelling and interpreting social position in a society that was going through unprecedented expansion and change. It was particularly so for foreign musicians, who did not have the social or educational passports to an assured place in London's class structure and whose profession was widely seen as incompatible with that of a gentleman. Even in his many caricatures, Costa is depicted as dignified and authoritative rather than effeminate and actorly (like Jullien) or cacophonous (as with Berlioz, Liszt and Wagner) (see Figure 2.5 on p. 22).[50]

His reputation as a champion of the rank-and-file English musician helped him to avoid the suspicion that frequently attached to foreigners for favouring their fellow countrymen. As early as 1839, the *MW* gave Costa credit for the fact that 'there is scarcely one foreign artist in the band that could safely be replaced by native talent'.[51] His boast in the 1860s that 73 of his 87 players were English signified a major change in the racial composition of the opera orchestra within a generation.[52] He was seen as one of a small group of foreigners 'whom we regard more as compatriots than as strangers' and gained credit for staying in England 'rather than retiring to lead a *dolce far niente* life in the more genial atmosphere of his native city, Naples'.[53] He showed his cultural loyalty by becoming the leading conductor and composer of the quintessential English medium of the oratorio. Under his regime, the main musical platforms – Covent Garden, the Philharmonic, the Sacred Harmonic Society and the Handel Festival – were seen by many Englishmen as proof that they no longer inhabited a 'Land Without Music'.

It is hard to imagine what more Costa could have done – with his town house, his knighthood and his close association with Court, Church, Lodge and the Handel–Mendelssohn industry – to identify with his adopted country. He adopted every available symbol and was an avid collector of honours. By comparison with other foreign singers and musicians based in London, he appears positively John Bullish. Indeed, Haweis described him as 'a weighty square-built man with powerful arms and something of the real John Bull about the neck and shoulder'.[54]

---

50 Mathieson, 'Embodying Music', 116–25.

51 *MW* (19 May 1839), 23.

52 Costa to Clay (20 May 1862), RAM 2005.1629. *Athenaeum* (10 Feb. 1866), 212.

53 *MW* (22 May 1858), 328. John Ella, *Musical Sketches Abroad and at Home*, ed. John Belcher (London: W. Reeves, 1878). 246.

54 *Pall Mall Gazette* (2 May 1884).

2.4a

Figure 2.4a and b Typical portraits showing Costa with top hat and no musical accessories

But his conspicuous efforts to anglicize himself may have concealed a sense of insecurity. Moreover, he was not wholly successful in making the transition from Neapolitan musician to English gentleman. The fact that he did not marry an Englishwoman, like his brother Raphael or Charles Hallé, probably made it harder to penetrate the inner sanctums of Englishness. Like Benedict and Manns – also musical knights from abroad – Costa could move only part of the way to full integration. Even after 50 years of successful assimilation, he never shared in those unspoken aspects of historic memory, humour, and 'character' that, in the last resort, were thought to mark a true English gentleman. His position remained

2.4b

ambivalent: Gruneisen, having congratulated him on becoming 'Mr Costa', reverted in the same article to calling him 'Signor'.[55]

Costa's career offers few clues as to why he went to such lengths to escape from his Spanish–Neapolitan–Sephardic–Catholic origins into a not wholly convincing English identity. As mentioned above, he may simply have been anxious not to return to Naples, with its political instability, poor job prospects and possible family tensions. Perhaps in addition he simply lacked the imagination and self-confidence to exploit the liminal status of an itinerant musician and break the rules, like Liszt, Chopin and Berlioz. But a more persuasive explanation is that, by the late 1830s, he was well on the way to accumulating power and the trappings of success. Crucial to that success was his personality.

Costa's first four years in England exposed him to a potent mix of painful experiences: the hurt of exile and of family separation; ridicule of his weak tenor

[55] *Morning Post* (16 Mar. 1846).

Figure 2.5 'Our lightning conductor': Costa caricature (*Punch*, 3 Jun. 1882) (courtesy of Westminster City Libraries)

voice and awkward stage manner; humiliation and veiled insults to his masculinity from his first orchestra; the stress of having to produce operas with disaffected players, feckless soloists and chaotic management; the savage criticisms in the press; the dampening of his hopes of early success as a composer; and the struggle to make his way in an alien society. Such experiences would naturally engender in a young immigrant a profound sense of loneliness, vulnerability and even doubt about his identity.

Against this background, it is plausible that several of the central features of Costa's personality were developed as a defensive mechanism against these multiple threats. His bid to be accepted as an English Anglican Freemason can be seen as a search for protection against the prejudices that would otherwise have worked against him as a foreigner, a southern Italian Catholic and perhaps also as a Jew. His correctness over relationships and his frequent recourse to the press to counter false reports suggest a man anxious not to leave any space for criticism. His system of control gave him an instrument for imposing order on his disorderly milieu. His gruff and enclosed manner shielded him against ridicule and humiliation, while preserving a degree of privacy in the midst of his hectic public schedule. There is a remarkable parallel with the description of von Bülow by his friend Walter Damrosch: 'He had a heart most tender and sensitive, but life had dealt this idealist so many hard shocks that he encased his heart in a shell with which to protect it from further onslaughts.'[56]

Costa's protective carapace enabled him to reduce his vulnerability and minimize the disadvantages of his liminal position. It gave him a remarkable imperturbability – what the singer Charles Santley identified as 'impassivity': 'it was impossible to read his thoughts; the only visible sign of approbation or the contrary which he ever vouchsafed was a peculiar twist at the back of his neck'.[57] His unflustered composure served him well when things went awry in performance. He used it in later life to turn to his own benefit his early set-backs – spreading the story of his disastrous debut at Birmingham and proudly showing visitors the miniature razors with which he had been mocked by his first orchestra.[58]

His defensive shell also helped him to impose his will on others. He was able to insist on his demands, however embarrassing this would have been to more clubbable conductors like Balfe and Arditi. His fearsome reputation predisposed musicians, managers, critics and even composers not to cross him. This was well illustrated by the story of Masini, an Italian tenor who skipped rehearsals for *Faust* and airily suggested that Costa should call at his hotel to hear what tempi he preferred. On learning from the Italian Legation of Costa's status and reputation, Masini fled in the night back to Italy.[59] At the height of his authority in the 1850s, Costa's support was seen by visiting musicians as a precondition for success in London. Even Berlioz approached Costa tactfully over the performance of *Benvenuto Cellini* at Covent Garden and of his works at the Philharmonic.[60] Wagner recognized that 'the great Costa' was 'the real leader of music in London' – to the extent of breaking his strict rule by paying a courtesy call on him on arrival.[61]

Other early professional conductors on the Continent – Guhr, Habeneck, Chélard, Musard – felt a similar need to develop an autocratic image. Like them, Costa exploited the metaphor of the military commander, which became one of the clichés of musical journalism (Chapter 5). But unlike them, he was working

56 Walter Damrosch, *My Musical Life* (New York: Charles Scribner's Sons, 1923), 78.

57 Charles Santley, *Student and Singer:The Reminiscences of Charles Santley* (London: Edward Arnold, 1892), 163.

58 Frederick Cowen, *My Art and My Friends* (London: Edward Arnold,1913), 48.

59 Mapleson, *Memoirs*, 129–30.

60 Berlioz to Hogarth (23 Feb. 1853) and Berlioz to Costa (20 Apr. 1853 and 7 Jul. 1853), Hector Berlioz, *CG* 1567, 1588, 1612.

61 Richard Wagner, *My Life*, trans. anon. (London: Constable, 1963), 621.

across three very different domains – the opera, the concert hall and the mammoth festivals. This may explain why he went further than any of his contemporaries in his accumulation of contractual power – and why he defended his authority so uncompromisingly and resigned whenever he failed to get his way.

Costa's other prominent traits fit well with the explanation offered above. Maintaining such defence mechanisms required a high degree of self-discipline. Davison traced his power over the musicians to this: 'a man of strength, order and discipline … a man born to command … He could command himself and he could command others.' The *Daily Telegraph* critic Joseph Bennett also ascribed his authority to his self-discipline: 'He himself set an example of strict discipline … he never relaxed in the discharge of his own duties.'[62] The conductor Alberto Randegger recalled a notice above his desk at Eccleston Square: 'If you come on business do your business and go about your business.'[63] His obsession with punctuality was the subject of many anecdotes, summed up by Mapleson's amusing pen-picture:

> At no theatre where Sir Michael Costa conducted did it begin a minute late. The model orchestral chief arrived with a chronometer in each of his waistcoat pockets; and when, after consulting his timepieces, he saw that the moment for beginning had arrived, he raised his baton, and the performance began. He did not even take the trouble to see that the musicians were all in their places. He knew that, with the discipline he maintained, they must be there.[64]

Developing and sustaining his system also called for exceptional drive and application. Until the illness and fatigue of his last years, Costa's long career was marked by an energy impressive even by Victorian standards. He was 'the ubiquitous Costa' (Percy Scholes) and 'the able, energetic, indefatigable Costa' (Henry Davison).[65] In the early 1850s, he carried a workload unique in English music. In 1851, he directed eight Philharmonic concerts, over 30 oratorio performances, several private and opera concerts, as well as 20 different operas over 66 nights – about 110 nights in all – compared with 59 concerts in George Smart's *annus mirabilis* of 1825.[66] Most of this was crammed into London's short music season: in the second week of April 1850, he conducted a Philharmonic

---

62 *MW* (23 May 1846). *Musical Times* (1 Oct. 1897), 664–6. Bennett, *Forty Years of Music: 1865–1905* (London: Methuen, 1908), 51.

63 *Musical Times* (1 Oct. 1899), 657.

64 Mapleson, *Memoirs*, 131.

65 Percy Scholes, *The Mirror of Music 1844–1944* (London: Novello, 1947), 162. Henry Davison, *From Mendelssohn to Wagner, Being the memoirs of J.W. Davison, Forty Years Music Critic of 'The Times'* (London: Wm Reeves, 1912), 108.

66 John Carnelley, 'Sir George Smart and the Evolution of British Musical Culture 1800–1840' (PhD diss., Goldsmiths College, University of London, 2008), 151–67.

concert on the Monday, *Lucrezia Borgia* on the Tuesday, *Norma* and two acts of *Masaniello* on the Thursday and *Elijah* at the SHS on the Friday.

Many noticed that Costa's forceful personality had its negative side. Gye's *Diary* shows that he could be brusque and domineering. Mapleson confirms this picture, describing him as 'a despot' whom even the formidable Gye feared. Grove referred to his harsh voice.[67] Even his favourite, Adelina Patti, complained of his 'overbearing conduct'.[68] The conductor Frederick Cowen recalled 'a loud angry voice, his eyelids twitching nervously … an abrupt and far from prepossessing manner, which made us all very frightened of him'.[69] Haweis identified in him 'a certain cold dignity, to some repellant' and 'a quickness of temper which occasionally made him enemies'.[70] By the discreet standards of Victorian writing, these portraits are surprisingly blunt. They help to explain why Costa's professional relationships often ended in acrimony. Commenting on the end of Costa's 10-year partnership with Mapleson, Arditi observed that 'he was also becoming a little tired of Sir Michael, whose invaluable services were somewhat obscured by his autocratic ways …'.[71] Even his friend William Spark described how, during his six years at the Leeds Festival, 'his exhibitions of sharp temper, quick speech and over-ruling manner led him to be regarded with fear and jealousy by many who did not understand his real character'.[72]

Gye's diaries frequently remark on Costa's extreme pride and sensitivity. Mapleson detected a Neapolitan tendency towards vendetta, commenting that Costa was 'not only peculiarly sensitive but also remarkably vindictive'.[73] The *Musical Times* obituary regretted his 'inability to forget or forgive'.[74] The most obvious example of this was his feud with the equally spiky Sterndale Bennett. Costa was widely criticized for refusing to conduct his music at the Philharmonic and especially at the 1862 Exhibition concert, where Bennett's *Ode* represented Great Britain.[75] He rejected peace overtures when Bennett's oratorio *The Woman of Samaria* was performed at the Birmingham Festival in 1866, refused to sign the petition for Bennett to be buried in Westminster Abbey and even declined to conduct the SHS performance of the Dead March from *Saul* in Bennett's memory.[76] These episodes reinforced the caricature of Costa as obdurate and, by implication, un-English.

---

67 Grove in *Pall Mall Gazette* (1 May 1884).

68 Gye, 24 May 1872.

69 Cowen, *My Art and My Friends*, 47.

70 *Pall Mall Gazette* (2 May 1884).

71 Luigi Arditi, *My Reminiscences* (London: Skeffington, 1897), 234.

72 Spark, *Musical Memories*, 2–3.

73 Mapleson, *Memoirs*, 306.

74 *Musical Times* (1 Jun. 1884), 321–3.

75 *ILN* (3 May 1862), 461.

76 For the 1862 episode see Costa to *Times* (26 Apr. 1862). On the Birmingham Festival peace overture, see Bennett, *Life of Bennett*, 367.

For those who knew him well, there was a kindly and above all fair disposition behind his intimidating manner. The singer Charles Santley wrote that, despite his 'somewhat cold and distant' manner and 'curtness in his remarks and gestures', his reputation as a tyrant was unmerited.[77] The conductor Frederick Cowen described him as 'very just' and 'not unkindly'. There are plenty of testimonies from orchestral players to his generosity and to the loyalty that this inspired. Stanford, who had much to say against Costa's influence on mid-Victorian music, saw him as 'very kindly … under a cloak of apparent reserve'.[78] Even Lumley, who suffered when Costa led 53 players and 45 choristers from Her Majesty's to Covent Garden in 1846, admitted that they followed him 'just as a band of *condottieri* might in the middle ages have followed an admired captain who had taken service under a new sovereign'.[79] Such loyalty was not driven solely by fear and self-interest. Towards the end of his career, 14 players followed him in 1871 from Covent Garden to join Mapleson's company, where their financial prospects were worse. These testimonies suggest that, behind his forbidding exterior, Costa inspired remarkable respect and devotion.

The caricature of Costa as an uncompromising martinet needs also to be balanced against evidence that he was capable of flexibility and pragmatism. He showed considerable tact when easing out incompetent or elderly players. When radically changing the lay-out at the Philharmonic, he nonetheless allowed the venerable principal bass and cello players to retain their traditional places in front of the conductor. He settled a dispute over whether Blagrove or Sainton should be principal violin by alternating them.[80] He backed away from outright war with the Philharmonic in 1860 over Monday night operas; and he ceded ground to Gye in some of their confrontations. There is a touching story of Costa refusing to release the Opera players for a concert by Sterndale Bennett, but relenting on being told that his brother Raphael might be invited to sing there.[81]

Costa's liminal position in England may account for some of his other characteristics. Anxious to be accepted in an alien world and to avoid ridicule and criticism, Costa was famously conscientious. In a business still coming to terms with the need for professional standards, he was a notorious workaholic. The *Athenaeum* remarked that Costa 'always took special care that proper preparation had been secured before the nights of performance'.[82] According to Mapleson:

---

[77] Santley, *Student and Singer,* 147.

[78] Charles Villiers Stanford, *Interludes Records and Reflections* (London: John Murray, 1921), 35.

[79] Benjamin Lumley, *Reminiscences of the Opera* (London: Hurst and Blackett, 1864), 158. Possibly ghosted by Harriet Grote, the dedicatee. Jennifer Hall-Witt, 'The refashioning of fashionable society: Opera-going and sociability in Britain 1821–61' (PhD diss., Yale University, 1996), 427–31.

[80] Robert Elkin, *Annals of the Royal Philharmonic* (London: Rider and Co., 1946), 45.

[81] Bennett, *Life of Bennett*, 299.

[82] *Athenaeum* (9 Aug. 1879), 187.

> Nothing would satisfy him but to go on rehearsing a work until everything, and especially until the ensemble pieces, were perfect. Then he would have one final rehearsal in order to assure himself that this perfection was maintained.[83]

The picture that emerges is of a man consciously using an austere, authoritarian facade to hide a sensitive and introverted personality. Such a complex make-up inevitably contained a high degree of paradox. The martinet who disciplined a musician for arriving with muddy shoes was also the man who, visiting a sick chorister, quietly slipped five sovereigns into his pill-box with the hint that 'this will do you good'.[84] The stern conductor was also the man who allowed his players to surprise the soprano Castelli by playing a *pianissimo* passage in *Il barbiere di Siviglia* very loudly.[85] The austere disciplinarian of few words – and 'not usually profuse in his compliments' – was also described as an affable gourmet who 'delighted in a bit of gossip or mild scandal' and 'always animated and cheerful, full of racy anecdotes'.[86] The brusque man who appears in Gye's Diary was also the courtier who extemporised elegant compliments about Prince Albert's newly printed *Te Deum*.[87]

A similar paradox marks his attitude to money. He professed a gentlemanly disdain for money. He tried to refund what he thought was an overpayment following a concert at Kensington Palace.[88] There are numerous examples of him performing for nothing at charity and national concerts and helping to finance holidays for musicians.[89] During the Ottoman Sultan's state visit to Covent Garden in 1867, when Gye accepted a gold and diamond broach, Costa (who had composed an ode for the occasion) refused a gift of £200, saying that he did not compose for money.[90] And yet he was exigent about the financial terms of his own contracts; and minor debts were at the heart of his rupture with Gye in the mid-1860s and with Mapleson a decade later.

Most accounts depict his social manner as stiff and humourless. His work ethic had its ludicrous side, as when he told an oboist who arrived late at a rehearsal because he had been attending his wife's confinement not to let it happen again.[91] Believing that he should have correct relations with the press, he punctiliously

83 Mapleson, *Memoirs,* 131.

84 Haweis, *Pall Mall Gazette* (2 May 1884).

85 Diary of John Ella, The John Ella Collection, Faculty of Music Library, The Bodleian Library, Oxford, Mss 163, 2 Jun. 1836.

86 Costa 'not a talkative man' on musical subjects and 'gossip' in Santley, *Student and Singer*, 175; 'not given to compliments' in Walter Macfarren, *Memories: an Autobiography* (London: Walter Scott, 1905), 153; 'racy anecdotes' in Spark, *Musical Memories*, 12.

87 QVJ 2 Dec. 1843.

88 RA, Vic add J 1586 and 1587 of 20 and 24 May 1835. The Palace insisted on paying Costa the full rate of 15 guineas.

89 Ella, *Musical Sketches*, 246. *Times* (14 May 1862). *Morning Post* (6 Sep. 1836).

90 Gye, 20 Jul. 1867.

91 Wilhelm Kuhe, *My Musical Recollections* (London: Richard Bentley, 1896), 61.

invited Davison and his wife to an annual formal dinner and ponderously thanked Joseph Bennett for a sarcastic review in which he had clearly missed the concealed message. But close friends described him as gregarious. 'Always the gentleman, observant of social usage.'[92] For Herman Klein, he was a 'charming well-bred man'.[93] There are stories of Costa joining Lablache and Rubini in a spoof audition of an Italian chef who had pretensions to being a good singer; conspiring with the band to expose John Ella's weak *coup d'archet* after he had compared his colleagues unfavourably with the attack of the Paris Opera;[94] and laughing heartily when hearing a fellow Mason singing the popular song 'Jolly Nose' with a stentorian upper C.[95] He refused a player permission to attend a brother's wedding on the ground that absences were allowed only for funerals – only to relent because 'it may prove to be the same thing'.[96] But the fact that these humorous moments are quoted suggest that they were infrequent.

Such paradoxes help to explain why he was read in contradictory ways by different contemporaries. To a degree unusual even on the faction-ridden London music scene, he had a polarizing effect, attracting enmity from some and devotion from others. Costa's outer shell of reserve made it difficult for many to perceive the man inside. Gye's diary, which describes 21 years of intense collaboration, reveals very little human rapport between them or insight into Costa's nature.

Costa's inner personality remains elusive. But the evidence suggests that a traumatic start in England, perhaps linked with family tensions in Naples, encouraged him to develop a taciturn authoritarian manner and to hide his inner nature behind the trappings of a masonic English gentleman. Thanks to an immense effort of will and application, he ensured that his 'London' persona largely overlaid his Southern Italian persona. There remains, however, a sense that he never wholly escaped from the liminal position of his Spanish–Jewish–Neapolitan origins and that the co-existence of these two identities perplexed many contemporaries.

His public persona and most of his reforms were in place by the mid-1840s. His biography thereafter consists largely of the working out of that powerful combination of system and personality in his conducting career. It was a career that occupied him to the exclusion of almost anything else. If he had married – or become a musical entrepreneur or a socialite – he might have had to adapt further to the London scene. As it was, having successfully established his own rules of the game during his first decade in London, he had no reason to alter a formula which both protected his ego and enabled him to resist intrusion into his sphere of authority. This may help to explain his resistance to innovation, in repertory or musical methods. It helps also to account for the inflexibility which was a marked feature of his later career.

92 *Musical Times* (1 Jun. 1884), 321–3.

93 Klein, *Musicians and Mummers*, 300.

94 F.J. Crowest, *Musician's Wit, Humour and Anecdote* (London: Scott, 1902), 258.

95 Randegger *Musical Times* (1 Oct. 1899), 657. Spark, *Musical Memories*, 5.

96 Klein, *Musicians and Mummers,* 133.

Costa's unusual and commanding personality has been emphasized because his hallmark as a conductor – his total authority over his musicians – rested in part on what the *Musical Times* called his 'secret of command'.[97] His imperturbability and determination to have his own way were a necessary condition for bringing order and discipline to the anarchical world of music in England. But they were not a sufficient condition. For an immigrant, from a city with a weak tradition of orchestral performance, it was also essential to develop a system of musical management. This is analysed in Chapter 4. But first it is necessary to consider the many and varied arrangements which prevailed on the Continent and in England in 1830, when Costa began his career in London.

[97] *Musical Times* (1 Jun. 1884), 321–3.

Chapter 3

Conducting Prior to 1830

In the transitional period between 1800 and about 1850, there was no dominant model for the direction of musical performance, but rather a variety of practices involving three principal roles: leader (*chef d'orchestre* or *Concertmeister*), Musical Director (*maitre de musique* or *Kapellmeister*) and *maestro al cembalo* (accompanist or *répétiteur*). Their functions varied according to the type of music being played. For church music, according to Koch's *Lexikon* (1802), the *Kapellmeister* should beat time throughout and give the singers their cue. For opera, Koch specified that the *Kapellmeister* should direct the singers and chorus and play the figured bass on his clavier, but should leave the instrumentalists to the care of the *Concertmeister* if the latter existed.[1] In performances of instrumental music, the lead more often rested with the principal string player. In very broad terms, orchestral players tended to follow the lead string player; opera singers looked to the *maestro al cembalo* or Musical Director for cues, but often set their own tempi, as did concert soloists; and choruses depended on visible (and sometimes audible) time-beating.

Methods of direction also varied according to the personalities involved, the competence of the musicians and how new or challenging the music was. A composer like Haydn or Spohr could exercise tighter control than men like Henry Bishop or George Smart, who were part-time 'conductors' with other more important roles. The much-rehearsed *Concerts Spirituels* orchestra, almost all trained rigorously at the Paris Conservatoire, needed less direction than a scratch benefit orchestra in London. For a difficult work like Beethoven's Symphony no. 9, the players and singers needed the full attention of both the lead violin and the *Kapellmeister*.

Much also depended on local practice and tradition. This was especially true in Italy and Germany, where practice varied from city to city. At La Scala in Milan and the San Carlo in Naples, the orchestra was normally led by the first violin, who imposed order when necessary by stamping his foot or striking his desk or a candle-stick with his bow. Some Italian houses had a prompter, who could cue the singers and chorus, or a *maestro al cembalo,* who directed rehearsals but, for actual performances, simply sat at a piano 'and turns score he

1 Koch, *Musikalisches Lexikon* (Offenbach am Main: 1802), Einleitung, para. 9, fn. II.

shares with cello and bass leaders'.[2] As late as 1846, the *MW* reported that 'they have no conductors in Italy'.[3]

From Germany, there are reports of some form of baton-conducting in Hamburg (1794) and Berlin (1800).[4] The first baton-conductor in Vienna appears to have been Ignaz Franz von Mosel in 1812 – significantly at a large-scale revival of Handel's *Timotheus* (*Alexander's Feast*). Conducting with a stick or scroll of paper was demonstrated by three major composers: Weber (in 1812 in Berlin and consistently from taking up his post at Dresden in 1817), Spohr (at Frankfurt around 1815–17), and Spontini (at Berlin from 1820). But, during a tour of German music centres in 1825, George Smart noticed that some performances were led by the violin-player (Cologne), some by a violinist waving his bow but rarely playing (Stuttgart, Godesburg, Kassel Opera), some by the fortepiano (Berlin, Hanover, Munich), some by a director wielding intermittently a scroll or baton (Darmstadt, Leipzig, Kassel concert), and others by a pianist who beat time with a roll (Dresden, Vienna).[5]

In France practice mainly reflected the dominance of the Conservatoire-trained violinists.[6] At the Paris *Concerts Spirituels*, the audible (and much-criticized) *batteur de mesure* gradually lost ground to the leading violin. There was a similar though more circuitous trend at the Paris Opera. The Musical Director between 1781 and 1810, Jean-Baptiste Rey, dismissed the first violin who challenged his authority.[7] A painting of 1806 shows the *maitre de musique* standing and conducting with a baton.[8] In 1816, Spontini foiled an effort to put the leader in charge.[9] François Habeneck appears to have used a baton initially at the Opera as late as 1828, when the Belgian writer François-Joseph Fétis contrasted the coldness of his baton-conducting there with the warmth of his violin-conducting at the Conservatoire's *Société des Concerts*.[10] But later in the same year, Habeneck was controlling the Opera orchestra with his bow.[11] A similar regime applied at the

---

2 Louis Spohr, *Autobiography* (London: Longmans, 1865), vol. I, 258. *Allgemeine Musikalische Zeitung*, 43, 102. See also Rimini Opera Regulations quoted in Spitzer/Zaslaw, 392.

3 *MW* (18 Apr. 1846).

4 Adam Carse, *The Orchestra from Beethoven to Berlioz* (Cambridge: Heffer, 1948), 297.

5 Smart, *Journals*, passim.

6 For good descriptions of the evolution of French practice see David Charlton, 'A maître d'orchestre … conducts: New and old evidence on French Practice', *Early Music*, vol. 21 (1993), 341–53; and Southon.

7 Au Redacteur, *Courrier des Spectacles,* issue 1213 (30 Jun. 1800), 2. Charlton, 'A maître d'orchestre conducts'.

8 Painting by Joseph de Berchoux (Paris, 1806) in *NG 2*, vol. 6, 265, under 'conductor'.

9 F.H.J. Castil-Blaze, *De l'Opéra en France* (Paris: Janet et Cotelle, 1820), 445.

10 Fétis, *Revue Musicale* (1828), vol. 3, 146–7.

11 Performance of 20 Aug. 1828, following decision by Superintendant La Rochefoucauld, letter of 24 Jul. 1828, Archives Nationales, AJ/13/120. This account is based on Southon, 444–50, and A.A.E. Elwart, *Histoire de la Société des Concerts du*

Théâtre-Italien, the *Opéra Comique* and most provincial theatres.[12] In the early 1830s, a 'Committee of Professors' recommended 'either the motion of a bow or a baton in the hands of the conductor' but stressed that he should not play an instrument and should intervene only when a change of time or expression was necessary. This was the system later practised by Habeneck, who towards the end of his career rarely played his violin.[13] Even in the late 1870s, the violin-conductor Develdez prescribed the bow as 'l'instrument naturel du chef d'orchestre' and this remained the rule at the *Société des Concerts* until about 1887.[14]

Adam Carse, in his first attempt to trace the parentage of the conductor, placed too much emphasis on the French model. He concluded that 'It was the violinist-director who in the end was destined to develop into the baton-conductor', by converting his bow into a baton and borrowing the gestures of the *batteurs de mesure*.[15] But practice in Paris was untypical. The paternity of the modern conductor was different in other European music centres. In Italy there is a distant claim to *maternity* in the sixteenth-century *maestra* at San Vito Ferrara, who beat time silently 'with a long, slender and well-polished wand'.[16]

In Germany and Britain, the ancestral genes of the conductor owed more to the Musical Director or his junior alter ego the *maestro al cembalo* than to the leader. At the Philharmonic, the Musical Director 'at the pianoforte' was renamed 'conductor' in 1820, while the leader was retained as a separate (and ultimately subordinate) position (Chapter 6).[17] Significantly, it was the *maestro* whose title was gradually taken over by conductors. By the 1840s, when Costa was in full control as conductor, he was frequently referred to as the *Maestro*.[18] By then, the label *maestro,* defined by Busby in 1806 as 'the musician who has the direction and management of the performance', had lost its technical meaning and was redefined in Busby's 1840 reissue simply as 'a master'.

The wide variety of practices was reflected in a 1806 manual on music-directing which advised that 'fusion of the individual members to the reproduction of a single feeling is the work of the *leader, concertmaster, musical director*

Conservatoire Impérial de Musique, avec dessins, musique, plans, portraits, etc. (Paris: Castel, 1860), 325–6.

12 Castil-Blaise, *L'Opéra en France*, I, 444, cited in Carse, *Beethoven to Berlioz*, 311.

13 An engraving by P.S. Germain and an aquerelle of 1843 shows him with bow, but no violin. Southon, 430–35. Also *MW* (26 Mar. 1840), 195.

14 E.M.E. Deldevez, *L'Art du chef d'orchestre* (Paris: Firmin, 1878), 76.

15 Carse, *The Orchestra in the XVIIIth century*, 100–107.

16 Ercole Bottrigari, *Il Desiderio* (1576): 58. Quoted by Denis Stevens 'Why Conductors?', in Joan Peyser, ed., *The Orchestra: Origins and Transformations* (New York: Watson-Guptill, 2004), 228.

17 George Hogarth, *Philharmonic Society of London from its Foundation, 1813, to its 50th Year* (London: Bradbury and Evans, 1862), 26–7.

18 *MW* (23 Feb. 1838), 130; *Morning Post* (28 Jul. 1843); *Morning Chronicle* (16 Sep. 1846).

or conductor'.[19] It is important to bear in mind this patchwork of practices when considering the remarkable transition to conducting between 1820 and 1850. Some music scholars, in their quest to find an ancestor for the all-powerful conductor of later years, have tended to over-define the roles of 'leader', 'Musical Director' and '*maestro al cembalo*'. Applying a later notion of specialization, they have also exaggerated the competitive tension caused when more than one figure directed a performance. In practice, there was often no need for intrusive control in the small baroque and early classical orchestra. An anonymous German source noted in 1799 that:

> Where an orchestra is arranged so that its members can all see and hear one another, where it is staffed with virtuosos, where the composer has included performance indications in the parts, and where there are sufficient rehearsals, then no further direction is necessary: the piece plays itself like a clock that has been wound up.[20]

C.P.E. Bach pointed out that, even when these ideal conditions were not met, 'disorder cannot easily spread' provided that the leader stood next to the keyboard.[21] There was often a reasonable degree of cooperation between the piano and violin-leader. J.S. Bach, Gluck, Haydn and Mozart directed in both ways. Mozart resumed his place at the clavier to re-invigorate a performance in 1782 of *Die Entführung* in Vienna when the orchestra became lethargic. At the first performance of his Paris Symphony at the *Concerts Spirituels*, he planned if necessary to 'snatch the fiddle from La Houssaye, the first violin, and conduct myself'.[22] In both cases, Mozart was clearly not directing throughout and was using an instrument rather than a baton. Many performances benefitted from dual control, not only in the opera house but also at major choral events like the 1784 Handel Commemoration in Westminster Abbey, which was led by the organist Bates (for the choral parts) and the violinist Wilhelm Cramer (in the instrumental sections).[23]

What follows is thus an over-schematic account of the three functions that coexisted untidily when Costa began work as *maestro al cembalo* at the King's Theatre in London in 1829.

---

19 I.F.K. Arnold, *Der angehende Muskidirektor* (Erfurt: Henningschen Buchhandlung, 1806), 8.

20 Deutsche 'Biedermann', *Wahrheiten die Musik betreffend* (Truths about music) (Frankfurt: Eichenbergsche Erben, 1779), 42.

21 J.S. Quantz, *Versuch einer Anweisung die Flote traversiere ze spielen*, trans. E.R. Reilly (London: Faber & Faber, 1966), 211–12.

22 On Gluck see K. von Dittersdorf, *Autobiography*, trans. D. Coleridge (London: Bentley and Son,1896), 111 (keyboard in opera) and 46 (violin in concert). Mozart to Leopold (19 Oct. 1782 and 3 Jul. 1778), Wolfgang Mozart, *The Letters of Mozart to his Family*, trans. E. Anderson (London: Macmillan, 1985), 558.

23 Charles Burney, *An Account of the Musical Performance in Westminster Abbey* (Dublin: 1785), 11/2.

The Theory: Leader, *Maestro al Cembalo* and Musical Director

The leader, usually the first violinist but occasionally a cellist or bass-player, was defined by Busby's *Dictionary* (1806) as 'a performer who in a concert takes the principal violin, receives the time and style of the several movements from the conductor and communicates them to the rest of the band'.[24] It was the leader who guided the dynamics and tempi during the performance, through his playing, his body movements and, if necessary, by beating time with his bow. In the concert hall he was often placed prominently, either on a high chair or standing on a plinth.

The functions of the *maestro al cembalo* were defined as 'the *direction and management* of the performance'.[25] Unless a visiting composer was supervising his own works, the *maestro* often carried the main responsibility for what were known as 'pianoforte rehearsals'. At the performance itself, he sat at the keyboard, playing his part of the basso continuo (if the score required this) and if necessary intervened to correct the performance. His role tended to be more prominent at the opera, where he provided the secco recitative for the singers and often composed or at least re-arranged scores for the instruments that were locally available. The lowly status of the *maestro* was implicit in his salary at the Italian Opera in 1829 of a mere £1 a night, compared with £4 paid to the double-bass Dragonetti.[26]

At many opera houses and some concerts there was also a Musical Director, whose functions overlapped with those of the *maestro* and leader. The 1776 edition of Busby's *Dictionary* stated that he 'arranges, orders and directs the necessary *preparations* for a concert; and also *superintends and conducts the performance*' (my italics). But this did not normally involve conducting in the modern sense. John Ebers, who managed the King's Theatre in the 1820s, confirms that the Musical Director:

> assists the manager in the selection of the performances; and, when fixed upon, he distributes the parts to the singers, and directs the *general routine of representation*, the effecting of which, in the minuter details, devolves on the stage manager, *and the conductor of the music* (my italics).[27]

It is apparent that Ebers did not see the Musical Director as a 'conductor'. Indeed during Ebers' time at the King's Theatre, the post of Musical Director was filled by an odd assortment of people: William Ayrton (later editor of *The Harmonicon*), Petracchi (a 'conductor' from La Scala), the castrato Velluti, the composers Coccia and Rossini and the harpist Nicholas Bochsa. Rossini was said to 'preside' at the

---

24 Busby, *Dictionary*, 1806 edition, under 'leader'.

25 Busby, *Dictionary*, 1806 edition, under 'maestro'.

26 *Harmonicon*, vol. 7, no. 3 (Mar. 1829), 70. Fiona M. Palmer, *Dragonetti in England (1794–1846): The Career of a Double Bass Virtuoso* (Oxford: Clarendon Press, 1997), 113.

27 Busby, *Dictionary* (1786) under 'conductor'. John Ebers, *Seven Years at the King's Theatre* (London: 1828), 361.

pianoforte but his job was mainly to rearrange and adapt imported works for performance in London. Bochsa not only ran the ballet and composed pastiches, but also 'presided' at the pianoforte as 'conductor' of the opera concerts.[28]

Several factors favoured direction from the keyboard rather than another instrument. The keyboard player was often the composer and/or the *Kapellmeister*; he was usually the only person with a full score; he did not have the violin-leader's heavy instrumental duties; he was a key part of the continuo group that provided the rhythmic pulse to the orchestra; and he could coach and accompany the singers, playing the bass line with his left hand and supplying cues (or filling in missing parts) with his right. C.P.E. Bach believed that 'the keyboard, entrusted by our fathers with full command', should be 'the reference point for the beat'.[29] The keyboard-player had several options to intervene – by playing his instrument, striking the desk, waving a baton or using the bass or cello leaders who often flanked him and shared his score.[30] Most German manuals of the late eighteenth century favoured direction from the keyboard.[31] Rousseau's *Dictionary* placed him at the top of a hierarchy in which the singers followed the *basso continuo* and the *batteur de mesure*, the first violin followed the voices and led the players, while the keyboard-player was 'le veritable et premier guide de tout'.[32]

But many forms of music (ballet, concerti, the later symphonies of Haydn and Mozart) did not require backing by the keyboard. Moreover, the keyboard and continuo group (which had largely determined the lay-out of baroque orchestras) was disappearing from some German theatre orchestras and composers were increasingly using other instruments to provide the rhythmic pulse.[33] Even where the keyboard was retained, the *maestro al cembalo's* ability to influence performance was weakened as the harpsichord gave way to the fortepiano, which was less able to penetrate the orchestral sound (itself becoming louder). There were objections that the piano introduced an alien tone-colour in orchestral pieces and reverberated after the other instruments had stopped playing.[34] Unlike the violin, it could not be re-tuned in mid-performance. As the *maestro al cembalo* or Musical Director gradually ceased to be a household employee of the patron of the orchestra, he was less often the person who composed or arranged the music for performance. He did not share the orchestra's esprit de corps. 'With his isolated

---

28 *Times* (4 and 28 May 1829).

29 C.P.E. Bach, *Versuch über die wahre Art das Clavier zu spielen*, trans. William J. Mitchell (Berlin: 1753–62, repr. 1969), 34–5 and 5–6.

30 For Dragonetti's role in steering the orchestra, see *MW* (2 May 1837), 131.

31 'Biedermann' (1779), Forkel (1783), Rochlitz (1799) and Koch (1802). Cited in Spitzer/Zaslaw, 392.

32 J.-J. Rousseau, *Dictionnaire de Musique* (Paris: Duchesne, 1768), 198 under 'ensemble'.

33 Rellstab, quoted in Drescher, 'J.F. Reichardt als Leiter der Berliner Hofkapelle', *Basler Jahrbuch fur historische Musikpraxis,* 17 (1993), 147.

34 *Berliner Allgemeine Musik Zeitung*, n. 6 (1829), 286.

instrument [he] can gain little respect from the rest of the musicians. He will always be a stranger to them.'[35] This was the more so if he lacked the prestige of being himself a competent instrumentalist, as Berlioz was to experience.

As a very broad generalization, at the turn of the nineteenth century the role of the Musical Director or *maestro* was *strategic* – to prepare at the rehearsal stage and to keep a general eye on the performance, working from the full score. The leader exercised *tactical* control of the dynamics and ensemble playing, transmitting the tempo and any other broad guidance from the Musical Director. In the opera house, there was a different division of function, with the Musical Director or *maestro* concentrating on the voices and the continuo, while the leader kept the instrumentalists together. In practice, the role of Musical Director during performances was becoming more honorary, as when Haydn 'presided' at the keyboard (facing the audience) at his London concerts in 1791–93, while the first violin Salomon (facing the players and thus better able to steer them) directed the performance.[36] Describing the set-up in Leipzig in 1831, Wagner wrote that the Gewandhaus concerts 'were not conducted at all … Regularly every winter, with nobody to wave a disturbing baton above him, [the leader] Matthai led smooth precise performances of the principal works of the classical repertory … .'[37] The increasing importance of the violin-leader was reflected in manuals on his duties, which could include selecting the orchestra, tuning, seating arrangements, even cuing the singers and rescuing performance when they went wrong. One authority demanded that the players should follow their leader 'even when he makes a mistake'.[38]

The leader had the advantage that he was at the head of the largest contingent, the string section, whose instruments (already better developed technically) provided the core of the ensemble. He usually had the prestige of being a competent player, whose pre-eminence was recognized by the other musicians. His violin was recommended as being more penetrative than the keyboard.[39] Although the keyboard-player could supply chords and rhythm, the violinist was better placed to guide the phrasing and dynamics, which were increasingly expressed through instrumental parts rather than the *basso continuo*.

An additional advantage for the leader was that he was usually more visible to the other musicians than the keyboard-player, especially in concerts, where he often stood.[40] He was also more centrally placed than the early baton-conductors, who

---

35 Arnold, *Der angehende Musikdirektor*, 139.

36 W.T. Parke, *Musical Memoirs* (London: 1830), vol. 1, 143.

37 Wagner, *On Conducting* (*Über das Dirigieren*, 1870), in *Three Wagner Essays*, trans. Robert L. Jacobs (London: Eulenberg Books, 1979), 55.

38 F. Galeazzi, *Elementi teorico-pratici di musica* (Rome: Cracas, 1791–96), vol. 1, 211.

39 Quantz, *Versuch einer Anweisung die Flote traversiere ze spielen*, 183.

40 Daniel Koury, *Orchestral Performance Practices in the Nineteenth Century: Size, Proportions and Seating* (Michigan: University of Rochester Press, 2010), 37.

tended to stand to one side and to conduct sideways to the audience and orchestra.[41] Observing both Spohr and Liszt in Bonn in 1845, Smart criticized the fact that they faced the primo side and had to turn round to see the singers and the secondo side.[42] Sideways conducting, also seen at the Paris Conservatoire, represented an effort to avoid the twin complaints against early conductors: that they turned their back on the audience (like Spontini); and that they distracted the audience's attention (like Daniel Türk, who used a baton so energetically that he smashed a chandelier).[43] Intrusive conducting was tolerable when a composer directed his own work, but not when someone else got in the way without contributing to the sounds of the performance. Any form of conspicuous direction could cause offense: the convulsive gestures of some violin-leaders made one German observer consider sending for a doctor.[44]

Leading by the example of a fellow instrumentalist was seen as more respectful to the other players who, in a small orchestra, did not need to be regimented by a third party. The anonymous German Biedermann recommended a baton only for conducting student-players.[45] Schumann complained that baton-conducting undermined the players' creativity.[46] Many musicians preferred that time should be beaten only sporadically. Eduard Devrient complained about 'the continued beating throughout a movement that must necessarily become mechanical … the conductor ought to beat time only when the difficulty of certain passages, or unsteadiness of the performers, rendered it necessary'.[47]

As the leading orchestras became autonomous institutions rather than court employees, they were increasingly identified with their violin leaders, who personified their collegial ethos: Cannabich in Mannheim, Salomon in London, La Houssaye and especially Habeneck in Paris. Habeneck demonstrated that a skilled violin-conductor, with adequate rehearsal time, could produce outstanding performances. Berlioz reported that Habeneck and his successors conducted from the violin part, which implied that violin-leaders were at a disadvantage because he 'cannot detect half of the mistakes that are made'.[48] But Nicolas Southon, relying on a surviving part for Beethoven's Symphony no. 3, argues persuasively that

---

[41] J.A. Bowen, ed., *The Cambridge Companion to Conducting* (Cambridge: Cambridge University Press, 2003),104–5. *New Grove 1*, under 'conductor', 389–90.

[42] Smart, *Journals*, 302 and 310.

[43] *Harmonicon*, vol. 8, no. 1 (Jan. 1830), 8. Charles Hallé, *The Autobiography of Charles Hallé*, ed. Michael Kennedy (London: Paul Elek Books, 1972), 116.

[44] 'Biedermann', *Wahrheiten*, 42.

[45] 'Biedermann', *Wahrheiten*, 42.

[46] Robert Schumann, *Music and Musicians*, trans. F.R. Ritter (London: 1891), vol. 1, 37.

[47] Eduard Devrient, *My Recollections of Felix Mendelssohn-Bartholdy*, trans. N. Macfarren (London: 1869), 60.

[48] Hector Berlioz, *The Memoirs of Hector Berlioz,* trans. and ed. David Cairns (London: Gollancz, 1969), 406, n. 1.

Habeneck marked on his violin score the main entries of the other instruments.[49] A similar system seems to have been in operation at the San Carlo in Naples, where a German witness noted in 1829 that 'there is no score. The leading violinist conducts from a part written on two staves.'[50]

Divided control between leader and Musical Director was often compatible with excellent performances, especially by small orchestras. But competition was latent and sometimes, especially at orchestral and choral concerts, highly visible. Wagner recalled the confusion when Christian Pohlenz took over from the leader to direct the choral fourth movement of Beethoven's Symphony no. 9 at Leipzig in 1831.[51] The London critics became, in the 1830s, vociferous in their complaints about the chaos that sometimes resulted from divided direction in concerts (see below).

But paradoxically the problem was most acute in the opera house, where orchestra, soloists, chorus and dancers needed to be coordinated in their different spaces. At the Brussels opera in 1825, Smart reported that the conductor and leader 'did not seem to be very close friends'.[52] In London opera houses, the lead violin often had difficulty in seeing all his players, who were separated from each by the pianoforte blocking the narrow pit. An early nineteenth-century engraving of Covent Garden shows the keyboard-player seated prominently in the centre of the pit, with the players divided on either side and presumably taking the lead from him (Figure 3.1). The Paris Opera went through agonies in deciding where to place the conductor and leader and whether the conductor should beat time continuously. After seeing a bad performance in 1821 at the *Théâtre-Italien*, where the violin-leader (Grasset) beat the time only after two egregious mistakes, Spohr concluded that 'a theatre orchestra, be it ever so good, should be directed by continuous time-beating, because the outer extremities of the orchestra are too far apart' to be managed by the motions of the body or violin of the leader.[53] Significantly, Habeneck began to conduct with his bow (and from a position where he could be seen by all the players) late in 1828, when the Opera was putting on complex works, such as Rossini's *Le Comte Ory* and Spontini's *La Vestale*.[54]

On top of these growing tensions, there were other powerful factors that made it increasingly necessary to achieve more effective central control.

The size of the orchestra was increasing. Haydn had managed with about 23 players at Eszterhaza, though his Salomon concert series in London in the 1790s called for between 40 and 60 players. By 1830 the larger symphonic works

---

49 Southon, 460–64. See also Castil-Blaze's claim to have invented a similar system, *L'Académie Impériale de Musique* (Paris: Castil-Blaze, 1855), 327–38.

50 Hauptmann, *Briefe von Moritz Hauptmann an Franz Hauser* (Leipzig: 1871), vol. I, 67.

51 Wagner, *My Life*, 69.

52 Smart, *Journals*, 66.

53 Spohr, *Autobiography*, vol. 2, 118–19.

54 20 Aug. 1828, Decision by Superintendant La Rochefoucauld (letter of 24 Jul. 1828, Archives Nationales, AJ/13/120). Cited by Southon.

Figure 3.1 Engraving of Covent Garden around 1800, showing the players separated by the centrally placed keyboard-player (detail) (courtesy of the Royal Opera House)

of Beethoven, Spohr and Mendelssohn demanded a wider range of wind and brass instruments – themselves becoming more powerful – and proportionately more string players to balance them. A standard orchestra of 2 flutes, oboes, clarinets, bassoons, 4 horns, 2 trumpets, 3 trombones and kettle drum needed at least 50 strings to balance them (24 violins, 8 violas, 10 cellos and 8 basses). Beethoven's Symphony no. 9, composed mainly in 1823, called for an orchestra of 60. Reflecting this trend, the bible of orchestral structure, Koch's *Lexikon*, raised its specification from 34 players in 1802 to about 58 in 1865.[55] Berlioz wanted an orchestra of 119 and fantasized that his imaginary town of Euphonia would have a super-band of 465 players. Expansion of the orchestra made it harder for either the violin-leader or the keyboard-player to control performances. Describing the position at the Philharmonic in 1820, Spohr commented on 'the impossibility … of an orchestra of 50 or 60 ever obtaining an ensemble'.[56]

It became increasingly difficult for the leader to satisfy the demands of composers for balanced and flexible ensemble, while at the same time playing the often intricate semi-solo parts written for himself. The violinist Ferdinand David, deputizing for Mendelssohn at Leipzig, found it 'embarrassing to have to conduct and lead at the same time. The more modern pieces … demand conducting

[55] H.C. Koch, *Musikalisches Lexikon*.

[56] Quoted in E. Speyer, *Wilhelm Speyer der Liederkomponist* (Munich: 1925), 51.

throughout and by one who is himself not required to play.'[57] *The Harmonicon*, reporting from the Paris Opera, observed that:

> the leader of a numerous musical army will encounter great difficulties if ... he must attend to the singers, to his own particular troops, to the score and at the same time draw those pure sounds from an instrument which ought alone to claim all his attention ... a general should direct his army, and rarely fight himself.[58]

A further drawback of violin-leading was that, since the first violin's part dealt with the higher registers, its prominence often distracted from the harmonics of the score, which were increasingly written for other sections of the orchestra.[59] When a German critic complimented Cannabich on playing 'with such warmth and so powerfully that he is heard above the whole orchestra', he was pointing to one of the leader's defects.[60]

Technical developments were changing the structure and character of the orchestra. The strings acquired better bows. The woodwind and brass became more powerful, with keys and slides that made them fully chromatic. The *basso continuo* and harpsichord were gradually replaced by a wider range of percussion. Other new instruments appeared: bass clarinet (first used in *Les Huguenots* in 1836), valve trumpets and horns (first scored in *La Juive* in 1835), as well as piccolo, English horn, serpentone, ophicleide and (from the 1840s) tuba. Sections of the orchestra were increasingly subdivided to achieve a wider palette of sound.[61] These changes undermined the dominance of the string section and the basso continuo (including the keyboard) which had provided instrumental leadership. Fétis remarked that no musical domain had gone through greater changes than the make-up of orchestras: a combination of new instruments, higher technical skills, and the quest for novelty had led to what he described as the revolutionary *éclat* of 'the Rossinian orchestra'.[62]

From about 1780, composers were writing works that called for greater instrumental skill – beyond the third position in the violin, the first in the viola and outside the clef in the lower strings. Amateurs and 'many-handed' musicians, who could play several instruments, were giving way to professionals who specialized in one. These rank-and-file professionals (*ripieni*) became a separate category of musician, with their own demanding skills that distinguished them from the mix of soloists, teachers and amateurs who had reinforced many eighteenth-century

---

57 J. Eckardt, *Ferdinand David und die Familie Mendelssohn-Bartholdy* (Leipzig:1888),149.

58 *Harmonicon*, vol. III, no. 48 (Jun. 1825), 103.

59 'Biedermann', *Wahrheiten*, 42.

60 *Musikalische Almanach* of 1772, cited in Carse, *Orchestra in the XVIIIth Century*, 98.

61 Alan Houtchens, 'Romantic Composers Respond to Challenge and Demand', in Peyser, ed., *The Orchestra*, 178.

62 Francois-Joseph Fétis, *Curiosités Historiques* (Paris: Janet et Cotelle, 1830), 272.

orchestras. What John Spitzer calls an 'ideology of orchestral performance practice' was emerging in manuals that emphasized the distinction between solo playing and orchestral performance, with the *concertini* soloists communicating their own feelings and the *ripieni* being asked to provide a collective sound.[63] There was a move away from ornamentation and towards uniform bowing, which had previously been unusual enough for Fétis to single it out as a special feature of the *Concerts Spirituels*.[64]

The spread of this new ideology was fostered by the easier movement of players, singers, directors and scores after the Napoleonic Wars. It was increasingly assumed that orchestras everywhere were basically similar, playing to approximately the same pitch and using a more elaborate standard notation. With the correct notation and practice:

> a composer in Naples can send his score to Moscow or to London or to some other distant place and may be confident that, wherever the same rules and musical forms are recognized and implemented, his composition will sound the same and have the same effect.[65]

Whereas the composer-conductor's performance of his own work was by definition authoritative, fidelity became an issue as composers increasingly had to delegate the performance to others. They sought to remedy this by adding more precise dynamic and tempo markings into their scores – even, in the case of Rossini, writing out the ornaments. This raised the status of the published score, but it also boosted the demand for a new type of music professional: one who could deliver authoritative performances of other peoples' compositions. As a result, the Musical Director gained in status, since it was through him rather than through leaders that composers tended to transmit their instructions (as Beethoven, for example, did through Moscheles and Smart).

Finally, what John H. Plumb has called 'the commercialisation of leisure' encouraged the application to music of the processes of specialization that were a marked feature of the early nineteenth-century, notably in England.[66] It is anachronistic to speak of a 'music industry' as early as 1830, but the performance of music was undergoing more rapid change than at any period before or since. The many tasks of musical production were becoming more professionalized – recruitment of players, booking of soloists, publishing of scores, management of the box office, negotiation of leases and contracts, advertising of performances, designing and building of sets. An expanding audience called for a wider range

63 Spitzer/Zaslaw, 393.

64 Spitzer/Zaslaw, 373. Francois-Joseph Fétis, *Music Explained to the World* (Paris: 1844), 250.

65 Arnold, *Der angehende Musikdireftor*, 35.

66 J.H. Plumb, *The Commercialisation of Leisure in Eighteenth Century England* (Reading: University of Reading, 1973), 19.

of musical events, which in turn required more concert venues, with acoustics to match larger orchestras. Whereas Haydn's *Creation* required only 20 players at Eszterhaza, 50 were needed at the Vienna Festival Hall, 100 at the *Burgtheater* and nearly 150 at the *Théâtre des Arts* in Paris.[67]

These pressures encouraged a new focus of attention on the orchestra and how it was directed. But there was remarkably little theoretical discussion of this issue in the early decades of the century.[68] Indeed conducting theory seems to have followed practice. Berlioz did not deal with conducting in the 1843 edition of his *Traité.* He added a supplement on 'The Orchestral Conductor: Theory of his Art' only in 1855, by which time his own baton-conducting was well established. Habeneck wrote 'methods' for the violin but nothing specifically on directing. The first significant work on the theory of orchestral performance was by Fétis (1827–28), who at that time favoured violin-leading. Ten years later, Fétis shifted his position significantly and came out in favour of conducting – with a bias towards the baton rather than the bow:

> If [the first violin] directs with the violin, he will have less effect on the orchestra than if he uses a baton – unless he decides to use his bow as a baton, in which case the violin becomes useless in his hands. Moreover, the bow is less suitable than the baton in showing tempo with precision, because his frail stick tends to vibrate, which undermines the energy of the gesture. The baton has the advantages of marking the arm movements better and of assisting in demonstrating the character of the performance.[69]

The influential treatise on orchestration (1839) by the musicologist Jean-Georges Kastner also recommended a wooden baton as the most precise means of directing an orchestra, though he noted that in practice most orchestras (in France) were directed by violinists using a bow.[70]

Despite the pressures to codify conducting, it remained in the period 1820–50 an embryonic function rather than a precise professional role. It was not a skill which could be mastered by private practice or attending courses. Insofar as there was a role-model, it was the military band-master, who featured prominently in the early manuals and on whom the early entrepreneur-conductors like Musard and Jullien based their technique. Conducting was not taught in conservatories until 1873 (in Paris), long after it had been established and defined on the rostrum. The French conductor-violinist Edouard Deldevez was the first to suggest that

---

67 Spitzer/Zaslaw, 369.

68 Southon, 348.

69 Francois-Joseph Fétis, 'De l'execution musicale', *Revue Musicale*, 1827–28 vol. 2 (Aug. 1827), 583; Fétis, *Manuel des compositeurs, directeurs de musique, chefs d'orchestre et de musique militaire* (Paris: Schlesinger, 1837), 124–5.

70 J-G. Kastner, *Cours d'Instrumentation* (Paris: Meissonnier et Heugel, 1839), 28.

conducting was a teachable skill.[71] Prior to that, it was seen as a role for which, in Barbirolli's apt words, 'a conductor is born and not made'.[72] On Habeneck's death, *Le Figaro* stated that he had been born a *chef d'orchestra*.[73] When William Cusins was appointed to conduct the Philharmonic in 1866, previous experience was not thought necessary.[74]

Practice in England

As on the Continent, the main feature of the period of transition between 1820 and 1850 in England was the coexistence of several different models for direction, depending on genre, context and personality. London had bigger audiences than elsewhere and offered a more diversified range of musical products. With the Exeter Hall (1831 – 3,000 seats), the Crystal Palace (1854 – 29,000 seats), the St James's Hall (1865 – 2,000 seats) and the Albert Hall (1871 – 8,000 seats), London was becoming better provided with venues than any other capital. The relative weakness of royal and church patronage in England gave added importance to the public subscription concert, which was arguably 'an English invention'.[75] Berlioz observed that 'There is no town in the world where so much music is consumed as London.' During his eighth visit to London in 1844, Mendelssohn said that he had heard more music in two months than in two years elsewhere.

But London, isolated culturally by the Napoleonic Wars, moved slowly to catch up with the orchestral changes on the Continent. Although it had more standing theatre orchestras than any other city in the late eighteenth century, none had more than fifty players, whereas there were seven orchestras of this size in France, six in Germany and five in Italy.[76] England was also slow to rationalize its arrangements for musical direction. The conservatism of the English musical scene was reinforced by the absence of any prominent indigenous composers or conductors who could lead the cause of reform.

This favoured the violin-leader, who in practice was still normally the central figure in performances. At the King's Theatre, the veteran leader Spagnoletti acted as intermediary between the orchestra and the Musical Director, William Ayrton.[77]

---

[71] Deldevez, *L'art du chef d'orchestre*, 29.

[72] Barbirolli, 'The Art of conducting', *Penguin Music Magazine*, vol. 2 (1947), 70.

[73] *Figaro* (24 Jan. 1875).

[74] Cyril Ehrlich, *First Philharmonic, A History of the Royal Philharmonic Society* (Oxford: Clarendon Press, 1995), 111.

[75] Simon McVeigh, 'The professional concert and rival subscription series in London, 1783–1793', *Royal Musical Association Research Chronicle,* no. 22 (1989),1–135. Peter Holman 'The British Isles: Private and Public Music' in *Companion to Baroque Music* (New York: 1990), 266.

[76] Spitzer/Zaslaw, 317–19.

[77] Spagnoletti to Ayrton (1821), Rachel Cowgill and Gabriella Dideriksen, 'Opera orchestras in Georgian and early Victorian London', in Niels Martin Jensen and Franco

When the manager of the King's Theatre issued new regulations for the opera orchestra in 1829, one of the objections was that they took from the leader his traditional task of selecting 'the band over which he is to preside and for which the leader is responsible'.[78] The prospectus for 1829 listed the leader but did not mention a Musical Director or maestro.[79] The leader's influence was especially strong at the Philharmonic, where he determined where each player should sit.[80]

The role of the Musical Director was further weakened as his composing duties waned. In 1828, the impresario John Ebers pronounced that 'a composer of operas is an unnecessary part of the establishment'.[81] Moscheles (himself a part-time Musical Director) observed that the man at the piano 'sits there and turns the leaves of the score, but after all he cannot, *without his marshal's staff the baton*, lead on his musical army. The leader does this and the conductor remains a nullity.' (my italics)[82] Indeed divided direction worked, after a fashion, principally because performances were in practice controlled by the leader. Spagnoletti's dominance as leader was reinforced by the presence at his side of the legendary bass–cello partnership of Domenico Dragonetti and Robert Lindley, who helped to transmit his tempi to the rest of the band. Dragonetti was frequently seen to 'pull a whole orchestra back with one accent when they wavered'.[83]

Attempts to define the respective functions of the leader and Musical Director were unproductive. The *MW* commented in 1839 that 'The exact boundary distinguishing the provinces of "leader" and "conductor" [remains] as little defined as the disputed territory in America …'.[84] The critic George Hogarth later drew a plausible distinction between the task of the leader (to give a firm lead and 'attend to all the other performers who were to look to him for the time of the movements and to be *governed by his beat*') and the keyboard player (to 'watch the performance and to be ready to *correct any mistake*') (my italics). But Hogarth observed that the leader could not both execute his own part properly and beat time for the whole band; while the person at the pianoforte, though useful at rehearsal, 'could scarcely exercise any influence over the "going" of the performance without coming into collision with the leader'.[85] Hogarth's description of the confusion at

Piperno (eds) *The Opera orchestra in 18th and 19th century Europe* (Berlin: BWV, 2008), Appendix iii.

78 *Harmonicon*, vol. 6, no. 2 (Feb. 1828), 48.

79 *QMMR*, vol. 1, no. II (1818), 257.

80 BL RPS MSS K.6.d.3.

81 Ebers, *Seven Years at the King's Theatre*, 363.

82 Charlotte Moscheles, *Life of Moscheles* (London: Hurst and Blakett, 1873), vol. 1, 76.

83 Henry Phillips, *Musical and Personal Recollections during Half a Century* (London: CJ Skeet, 1864), vol. 1,130.

84 *MW* (11 Apr. 1839), 231.

85 Hogarth, *Philharmonic Society*, 8–9.

the Philharmonic applied equally to the Societa Armonica, the Ancient Concert and the SHS.[86]

Behind the confusion, the role of conductor was slowly emerging from the retreating shadow of the Musical Director. But the label remained ambiguous.[87] In 1830 the oboist William Thomas Parke stated that, whereas the leader had in the past also been seen as the conductor, the latter had *recently* become a separate figure. He commented that, although this practice 'at length became so familiar that no apparent jealousy exists between them', the conductor's pretension to superiority 'gave considerable uneasiness to the leader'.[88] For Parke, the new conductors, clearly the descendants of the Musical Directors, were a threat to the leaders.

It is not surprising that the increasing use of the label 'conductor' initially added to the existing confusion about how music should be performed. On his arrival in London, Ignaz Moscheles asked Clementi: 'What do they mean by the term Conductor?'[89] Moscheles described a Philharmonic performance in 1821 as being 'under the direction' of Kiesewetter (the violinist-leader) rather than Smart (the 'conductor').[90] During his first visit to the Philharmonic in 1829, Mendelssohn referred to the violinist Spagnoletti as the 'conductor', noting that Smart (billed as 'conductor') merely sat at the piano and turned the pages.[91] In 1843, the *ILN* listed as the Philharmonic's 'conductors' Tom Cooke (a violin-leader), Henry Bishop (a composer-arranger), Moscheles (a pianist) and Smart (an old-style Musical Director).[92] At the Italian Opera, Coccia was listed in 1825 as 'composer and conductor' and in 1826 as presiding 'at the piano-forte … as *Maestro*'.[93]A letter to *The Harmonicon* in 1831 queried the value of this interloper:

> Why, if one of those stuffed figures which the wardrobe of the King's Theatre could supply were to be placed in the conductor's chair, the business would go on just as well as now. There is a great deal of *humbug*, Mr Editor, in conducting, but nowhere is it arrived at so high a pitch as at the Philharmonic concerts.[94]

---

86 On Societa Armonica, *MW* (14 Jun. 1838), 112. Other examples in Carse, *Beethoven to Berlioz,* 330. On Ancient Concert, *MW* (10 Mar. 1837), 187 and *ILN*, (24 Jun. 1843), 439.

87 Hogarth, *Philharmonic Society*, 26–7.

88 Parke, *Memoirs,* vol. 2, 151.

89 Moscheles, *Life,* vol. 1, 76.

90 Moscheles, *Life*, vol. 1, 56.

91 Sebastian Hensel, *The Mendelssohn Family (1729–1847): Letters and Journals*, trans. C. Klingemann (London: 1882), vol. 1, 180. Myles Birkett Foster, *History of the Royal Philharmonic Society of London:1813–1912* (London: John Lane, 1912),6. The Mendelssohn quote is in Larry Todd, *Mendelssohn: A Life in Music* (Oxford: 2003), 206.

92 *ILN* (24 Jun. 1843), 439.

93 *Harmonicon*, vol. 6, no. 3 (Mar. 1825), 47 and vol. 7, no. 11 (Nov. 1826), 250.

94 *Harmonicon*, vol. 9, no. 2 (Feb. 1831), 35.

Pressure to rationalize the arrangements for directing musical performances in England came from three sources: foreign criticism, the musical press and a growing awareness that more effective models of musical direction did exist.

Visiting musicians frequently drew attention to the defective standards of the London music scene. It is reasonable to assume that, when Spohr was in London in 1820, he voiced the conclusions which he later drew from his visit:

> The way of conducting here, both in the opera house and at concerts, is the most topsy-turvy one imaginable. They have two conductors, but neither really functions. The 'Conductor', as he is styled on the bills, sits at the piano and plays from the full score, but gives neither the beat nor the tempo. This is supposed to be done by the 'leader' or first violin; but, as he has only the first violin part in front of him, he can't be of any help to the orchestra, so he contents himself with emphasizing his own part and letting the orchestra keep with him as best it can.[95]

One of the most influential voices was that of Fétis, whose criticisms of English orchestral practice were printed in six long articles in *The Harmonicon* in 1829 (Chapter 4). Mendelssohn, though more diplomatic in public, was equally critical in private, writing to a friend in 1829: 'Everything spiritual is lacking, everything is rough and clumsy; no liveliness but just speed, no respect for the work of art, in short no conductor'.[96] Even in 1844, when he conducted five Philharmonic concerts, Mendelssohn himself had to share the honours with the leader, Thomas Cooke, whose precise and steady leadership was thought by the *ILN* to contribute more than half of the success of the concert.[97]

English journalists and music-lovers were unhappily aware that, as Fétis commented: 'The opinion of the writers on the continent … places the English at the lowest level of the scale of musical facilities.'[98] The much-resented slur that England was a Land Without Music reinforced the argument that the way music was organized in London failed to do justice to the works of Beethoven, Spohr, Meyerbeer and Mendelssohn. Chorley commented that Bishop and Loder's mismanagement of a Philharmonic concert in 1840, in the presence of Liszt and the violinist Molique, 'made our ears tingle and our cheeks burn'.[99] The critic Joseph Bennett recalled the unruly orchestras 'under the Tom Cookes. Henry Bishops, and George Smarts of early Victorian days' with their practical jokers and their derision when Mendelssohn tried to get them to rehearse Schubert's

95 Spohr to Speyer (17 Apr. 1820), E. Speyer, *Wilhelm Speyer*, 51.

96 Mendelssohn to Adolf Bernhardt Marx (9 May 1829), *Felix Mendelssohn, A Life in Letters*, ed. Rudolf Elvers, trans. Craig Tomlinson (New York: Fromm International Publishing, 1986), 67.

97 *ILN* (13 Jul. 1844), 32.

98 Fétis, 'On the State of Music in London', *Harmonicon* new series (1829), 181 et seq.

99 *Athenaeum* (16 May 1840), 403.

Symphony in C.[100] Another potent claim for reform, in the commercialized ethos of English music-making, was that baton-conducting required less rehearsal. The *Morning Post* applauded Chélard's 'perfect execution of *Der Freischütz* at the King's Theatre in 1832 with only three rehearsals'.[101]

The music journals, which proliferated from the 1820s, became for the first time an important advocate of change. The *Athenaeum* ridiculed 'the triple authority of beating time' at the Opera.[102] The *MW* announced that: 'The spectacle of a conductor and leader combating for the direction of the band can no longer be tolerated'.[103] It complained that:

> In every English *orchestra,* we find a leader and a conductor, one of which is manifestly useless. The wisdom of our ancestors has posted one man on a joint-stool to direct an orchestra, if he can, and another a little higher up to overturn all his arrangements, if he likes, and thus bequeathed to us an intolerable absurdity. Down goes the conductor's baton, ditto the heel of the leader's boot – perhaps simultaneously, perhaps not as the case may be.[104]

William Knyvett, who 'conducted' the Ancient Concert from 1832–39, was pointedly advised that the roles of organist and conductor were incompatible.[105] Bishop was chided for doing his utmost to prevent the leader (Loder) from 'sometimes escaping into the right tempo'.[106] It was press ridicule as much as his own inadequacy that led Bishop to give up conducting the Philharmonic in 1845 (Chapter 7).

Visitors to the Continent sent back prescriptions for curing these maladies. A report by *The Harmonicon* from Berlin highlighted the advantages of Spontini's single control, compared with the London system of 'two distinct beats ... one being clapped by the hands of the conductor and the other being stamped, sometimes furiously, with the foot of the first violinist or leader'.[107] The *Athenaeum* stressed the theme that 'the sight of the magic little wand, in efficient hands, controls a band more quietly and effectively than all the beating, stamping and ejaculations of "Mein Gott ..."'.[108] The *Atlas* critic Edward Holmes reported from Germany in 1828 that a baton conductor:

---

100 *Musical Times* (1 Sep. 1897), 598.

101 *Morning Post* (1832), quoted in *Musical Times*, vol. 37, No. 640 (1 Jun. 1896), 372–5.

102 *Athenaeum* (18 Feb. 1832), 116.

103 *MW* (21 Jun. 1838), 133.

104 *MW* (26 Mar. 1840), 186.

105 *MW* (20 May 1836), 159 and (10 Mar. 1837), 187.

106 *Athenaeum* (5 Apr. 1845), 338.

107 *Harmonicon*, vol. 8, no. 1 (Jan. 1830), 5.

108 *Athenaeum* (11 Feb. 1832), 101.

> placed on an elevation in the front of the orchestra, gives the cue to all, very properly setting aside the offices of leader, chorus director etc., which in England frequently causes the band and singers to be wandering in different directions.[109]

But the remedy went far beyond adoption of the baton, to which some contemporaries (and later writers like Adam Carse) gave undue attention.[110] The message from the Continent was that the key lay in how the baton was actually used and in wider issues of organization and especially discipline. 'In Germany, France, etc. … the discipline of bands is considered of more importance than in England.'[111] Not surprisingly, it was from the Continent that the first exemplars of conducting in the modern sense of the word arrived in London.

The Composer-conductors

The lack of reliable scores in the early nineteenth century meant that performances often depended on composers conducting their own work, as had been the norm with the traditional *Kapellmeister*. Composers' contracts often specified that they should, in the words of the Philharmonic's invitation to Beethoven in 1815, 'superintend the production' of a work before handing over to the leader or the *maestro al cembalo*. A typical example was Pleyel's London visit in 1791, where he was expected to write 12 pieces and 'direct them at the pianoforte'.[112] Rossini was engaged at the King's Theatre in 1824 to preside at the keyboard for the first three nights of his opera *Zelmira*.[113]

In the early nineteenth century, a new type of composer-conductor emerged – authoritative figures, like Spontini in Berlin, Weber in Dresden and Spohr on a wider circuit. Together with the next generation (Mendelssohn, Berlioz, Wagner, Schumann and Liszt), they enjoyed special prestige on the international circuit. Although they secured their appointments primarily on the strength of their compositions, they were, with a few exceptions (notably Beethoven and Schumann), highly competent conductors, especially of their own works. Many had a clear orchestral reform agenda, as in Wagner's 1848 Memorandum to the Dresden authorities *Concerning the Royal Orchestra*.[114]

A major reason for their prestige as conductors was that they embodied the creative intelligence behind their compositions and, with reliable complete scores

109 Edward Holmes, *A Ramble Among the Musicians of Germany* (London: 1828), 38.

110 For example, Carse, *Orchestra in the XVIIIth Century*, 90.

111 *Morning Post* (27 May 1829).

112 Parke, *Memoirs*, vol. 1, 151.

113 Parke, *Memoirs*, vol. 2, 195.

114 Edward Devrient, *Aus seinen Tagebüchern*, ed. Kabel (Weimar: 1848), vol. 1, 422. Cited in Joachim Köhler, *Richard Wagner, The Last of the Titans* (New Haven, CT: Yale University Press, 2004), 214.

often unavailable, could give authoritative performances of them. The *Spectator* noted, after Mendelssohn's 1844 series at the Philharmonic, the special benefit of having a conductor 'who occupies the post as a distinguished composer'.[115] The status of composer-conductors was apparent in the high salary (£200) that Spohr received from the Philharmonic in 1820. They demanded both moral authority (to ensure that their scores would not be tampered with) and executive authority (to achieve the dynamics that their increasingly complicated scores required). Significantly, two of the greatest composer-conductors, Berlioz and Wagner, were influential theoreticians of conducting; the English translation of Berlioz's *Grand Traité* was in its third edition by 1858.[116]

In London, in the absence of a competent English role model, the benefits of central control were demonstrated initially by visiting composer-conductors. Spohr claimed in his *Autobiography* that he definitively established baton-conducting at the Philharmonic in April 1820:

> At the morning rehearsal … I took my stand with a score at a separate music-desk in front of the orchestra, drew my directing baton from my coat pocket and gave the signal to begin. Quite alarmed at such a novel procedure, some of the Directors would have protested against it; but, when I besought them to grant me at least one trial, they became pacified … the triumph of the baton as a time-giver was decisive and no one was seen again seated at the pianoforte during the performance of symphonies and overtures.[117]

This account, written 45 years after the event, has been convincingly dismissed.[118] Although Spohr used the baton at the rehearsal, he wrote at the time that he 'conducted in the old-established way from the score in the evening, when it is *de rigeur* for the conductor to be at the piano'.[119] At his benefit concert two months later, he led as violinist, with George Smart at the pianoforte.[120] But Spohr, a non-pianist, does seem at times to have stood on a rostrum, facing the orchestra 'in a very novel and superior manner', asserting his authority over the advertised 'conductor' (Thomas Attwood) in a way described as 'unwelcome to many' and unnecessary for experienced players.[121] Spohr did not, as he claimed, revolutionize English orchestral habits; but he contributed eloquently to the mood for change and, by his own example, provided a glimpse of the future.

---

[115] *Spectator* (18 May 1844).

[116] Berlioz, *Grand Traité d'Instrumentation et d'Orchestration Modernes* (Paris: Schonenberger, 1843) and Wagner, *Über das Dirigieren*.

[117] Spohr, *Autobiography*, vol. 2, 81–2.

[118] Arthur Jacobs, 'Spohr and the Baton', *Music and Letters*, vol. 31 (1950), 307–17.

[119] Spohr to Speyer (17 Apr. 1820).

[120] *Times* (18 Jun. 1820).

[121] *Morning Chronicle* (4 May 1820). *Allgemeine Musik Zeitung* (1820), 744.

Figure 3.2 Caricature of Carl Maria von Weber (courtesy of Royal College of Music)

The other influential early exponent was Weber (Figure 3.2), who appears like Spohr to have directed in several different ways. In London in 1826 he was described as conducting the Philharmonic 'in the old manner, standing in front and giving the time with a roll of paper' and as 'facing the audience with a baton in his hand, with which he gave the time to the orchestra'.[122] At a concert in the Argyll Rooms, he was seen 'marking the time with his usual animation' in the Overture to *Euryanthe*.[123] But when Moscheles performed his own 'Recollections of Ireland' on the piano at the same concert, Weber merely signalled the start, leaving it to the leader to steer the orchestral performance.[124]

The librettist of *Oberon*, James Planché, recorded that, during a rehearsal in 1826, Weber stood in the pit (the stalls), leaning on the back of the orchestra (today's pit), and had to leap over the partition to intervene and correct an error. On another occasion, Weber 'snatched the baton from the conductor' in

[122] Francois-Joseph Fétis, 'Music in London', *QMMR*, vol. 8, no. 30, 145. *Harmonicon*, vol. 4, no. 40 (Apr. 1826), 40.

[123] *Morning Post* (10 Apr. 1826).

[124] Ignaz Moscheles, *Recent Music and Musicians as Described in the Diaries and Correspondence,* ed. his wife, trans. A.D. Coleridge (New York: Da Capo, 1970), 82–3.

order to make a point.[125] The *Morning Post* reported that, for the premiere, he 'entered the orchestra *with the other instrumental performers* and took his seat at the piano' (my italics).[126] This accords with the Covent Garden playbill announcing that he would 'preside' – in other words, sit at the pianoforte in the orchestra.[127] Weber offered a model that was still in transition. At times he simply beat the tempo for a few bars before leaving the field to the orchestra.[128] But his direction sometimes achieved impressive results: Cox recalled him 'throwing his whole heart and soul into the work, imparting a stimulus to principals, band and chorus such as they had never experienced before'.[129]

Weber influenced conducting in England not only through his own example, but via his impact on the young Mendelssohn, who became the most potent role model in England for symphonic and choral music, though not for opera.[130] Like Weber, he was not an intrusive conductor – 'his movements were short and decided and generally hardly visible'.[131] He stood half-facing the audience and sometimes ceased beating when the performance was going satisfactorily.[132] He initially 'conducted' from the piano or the viola desk, though he may have used a baton at concerts in his family home in his late teens; he certainly did so at the the performance of J.S. Bach's *St Matthew Passion* in 1829.[133] By the time he took over the Leipzig Gewandhaus in 1835, he was ready to end its traditional division of power between leader and *Kapellmeister*. He was helped by the timely demise of the leader Matthai, who had led all except choral performances since 1817. With his friend Ferdinand David as first violin, Mendelssohn was able to introduce a 'new and desirable plan', which established baton-conducting there.[134]

Despite his prestige as a composer and conductor, Mendelssohn's career demonstrated the sort of obstacles which confronted anyone who tried to exercise

---

125 J. R. Planché, *Recollections and Reflections* (London: Sampson and Low, 1901), 56 and 81.

126 *Morning Post* (13 Apr. 1826).

127 Playbill printed in John Warrack, *Carl Maria von Weber* (London: Hamish Hamilton, 1868), 330.

128 *Harmonicon*, vol. 4, no. 40 (Apr. 1826), 85. Confirmed by Schumann in Alfred Dörffel, *Geschichte der Gewandhausconcerte zu Leipzig* (Leipzig: 1884), 85 and Berlioz, *Memoirs*, 306.

129 John Edmund Cox, *Musical Recollections of the Last Half-Century*, (London: Lensley Bros,1872), vol. I, 132.

130 Julius Schubring *Reminiscences of Felix Mendelssohn-Bartholdy*, cited by Todd, *Mendelssohn*, 228–9.

131 Ferdinand Hiller, *Mendelssohn, Letters and Recollections,* trans. M.E. von Glehn (London: 1874), 156–8.

132 Devrient, *Recollections*, 58–61. Julius Benedict, *Sketch of the Life and Works of the Late Felix Mendelssohn-Bartholdy* (London: Murray, 1850), 24–6.

133 Schubring, *Reminiscences*, 373 ff. Devrient, *Recollections*, 58–61 (though Devrient implies that he began using a baton when much younger, 6–7).

134 *Allegemeine Musikalische Zeitung* (14 Oct. 1835).

tight control over musicians. At the Dusseldorf opera house in 1833–35, where his title was 'chief superintendent of the musical performances', his insistence on controlling the players' contracts, salaries and seating in the orchestra led to a bitter dispute with the musicians and the theatre director Carl Lebrecht Immermann.[135] His attempts to discipline the sometimes drunken chorus led to him shouting at them 'like Boots at an inn'.[136] Even in a more limited role in Berlin in the 1840s, Mendelssohn struggled with insubordinate players until they 'took me for Spontini'.[137]

He had similar travails In London.[138] He used a baton when conducting his Symphony no. 1 at his first Philharmonic concert in 1829, when he was 'led to the pianoforte like a young lady' by the leader, François Cramer. But the other ten items in the programme were rehearsed and 'conducted' by J.B. Cramer and the concert as a whole was led by François Cramer.[139] During his 1832 visit, Mendelssohn was anxious not to offend the 'conductor' or the leader. John Ella claimed that he, together with Costa and Meyerbeer, persuaded him to conduct the performance using a baton, only to be met by 'the frowns of the fiddlers whose authority Mendelssohn's baton so completely usurped'.[140] He seems to have been still sharing the direction with the leader at his 1833 concert, since Weichsel signalled the start of the final work while Mendelssohn was still offstage.[141] But Mendelssohn's nine visits to London left a profound legacy; he demonstrated in particular the value of good conductorship and, after his five concerts at the Philharmonic in 1844, 'the propriety of making the appointment permanent'.[142] His early death in 1847 was a critical factor in the career of Costa, since it enabled him to fill the vacuum left by Mendelssohn at the Philharmonic and indirectly at the SHS and Birmingham Festival.

Although some composers conducted with distinction into the next century, the dominance of the composer-conductors was short-lived. Conducting required, as Kastner and Berlioz pointed out, specific skills which many composers lacked.[143] It also demanded time and energy. Mendelssohn found that the duties of conductor

135 Felix Mendelssohn, *Letters of Felix Mendelssohn-Bartholdy, 1833–47*, ed. Joseph Rietz (Boston: Oliver Ditson and Co., 1869), 18–19.

136 Mendelssohn, *Letters 1833–47*, 28.

137 Mendelssohn to Schleinitz 29 Oct. 1841, Eckhardt, *Ferdinand David,* 156.

138 *Musical Examiner* (10 Aug. 1844).

139 Mendelssohn to Fanny (26 May 1829), Hensel, *The Mendelssohn Family*, vol. 1, 184. *Morning Post* (27 May 1829).

140 Ella, *Supplement to Musical Union Record* (11 Jun. 1867), quoted in *Musical Times*, vol. 37, No. 640 (1 Jun. 1896), 372–5.

141 *Atlas* (19 May 1833), 325.

142 *Spectator*, no. 17 (1844), 466.

143 G. Kastner, *Manuel générale de musique militaire* (Paris: Firmin-Didot, 1848) cited by Southon, 358. Berlioz, *Memoirs,* 406.

conflicted with his 'principal aim' of composing.[144] Even assiduous travellers like Berlioz and Liszt were increasingly taken up with the composition of more elaborate works and their busy writing careers. To ensure that their works were performed as they wished in the growing number of musical centres in Europe, they wrote more precise instructions into their scores and mainly contented themselves with ensuring that initial performances set a standard for later ones. In the longer term, their legacy was to strengthen the case for a new type of conductor, who specialized in performances of *other peoples'* works.

The Entrepreneur-conductors

The other influential model during the period of transition was what John Spitzer has termed the entrepreneur-conductor, typified by Johann Strauss in Vienna, Philippe Musard in Paris, Benjamin Bilse in Berlin and Jullien in London.[145] Their programmes appealed to a wider audience by offering accessible music and glamour at low prices. But they were competent musicians and their standards and programme content were often high. 'Napoleon' Musard was a former Conservatoire prize-winner and his Paris concerts from 1833 to 1840 deployed 90 players, many from the Conservatoire.

The new fashion for promenade concerts hit London in 1838. The *MW* announced that:

> the success of Musard's concerts in Paris and the increasing taste for music in England has induced Mr Pilati to undertake the establishment of a series of instrumental concerts for the performance of overtures, quadrilles, waltzes and gallops, so arranged as to offer a promenade between the acts.[146]

Pilati included in his 60-strong band several leading players from Costa's Italian Opera orchestra. As the fashion caught on, the next year saw at least seven prom-style concerts.[147] In 1840, a series at the Crown and Anchor featured the violinist Jullien, who was to become the archetypical entrepreneur-conductor in England.

Jullien put on popular-classical programmes by up to 80 players for a shilling (5 pence in today's money) or half a crown (12.5 pence), at a time when the Philharmonic was also providing mixed programmes (without the polkas and gavottes) with a smaller band for half a guinea. He brought showmanship as well as enterprise, combining features of the earlier Vauxhall/Ranelagh pleasure

144 Mendelssohn to Klingemann (Mar. 1841), Karl Klingemann, *Felix Mendelssohn Bartholdy: Briefwechsel mit Legationstrat Karl Klingemann in London* (Essen: 1909), 258.

145 John Spitzer, 'The entrepreneur conductors and their orchestras', *Nineteenth-Century Music Review*, vol. 5, no. 1 (2008), 3–24.

146 *MW* (2 Feb. 1838), 74 and (5 Mar. 1838), 764.

147 Details in Weber, *Great Transformation of Musical Taste.*

gardens with the growing taste for a mixed diet of arias, solos, topical quadrilles and symphonic works. As an entrepreneur, he ran his players as employees in a commercial venture, marketing musical performances as a product. He was erratic and over-ambitious, veering between profitability and the bailiffs, but showed remarkable resilience over 21 seasons. He was denounced as a charlatan by many in the musical establishment, for his posturing and extravagant self-promotion. His audiences were criticized as undiscriminating and occasionally rowdy: there was a good deal of eating, drinking and even dancing. But Jullien employed many of the best players from the Opera and briefly hired Berlioz to conduct in 1848. He gradually added more serious content to his programmes, though these efforts were met with 'loud (and sometimes riotous) disapproval'.[148] By the time he died in 1860, bankrupt in a French lunatic asylum, he had persuaded his 'vast promiscuous assemblage' to listen in 'profound silence and earnest attention' to programmes devoted to Mozart, Beethoven and Mendelssohn.[149]

Jullien's qualities as a conductor were his energy, power of communication (to the audience as well as the band) and ability to combine the popular with the serious. The author Edmund Yates exaggerated when he commented that 'as a musician he was perhaps the greatest benefactor this country ever had'.[150] But Davison credited him as 'a refiner of public taste' and Chorley conceded that he had 'a genuine enthusiasm ... for what was good'.[151] Jullien's career illustrated the widening gap between classical and popular music. But he also pioneered the way for the more sober and serious concert programmes of Costa and later August Manns at the Crystal Palace.

The other legacy of the entrepreneur-conductors was that they helped to establish the conductor as the authoritative centrepiece of the orchestra and as a box office draw in his own right. They advanced the notion (which Costa later developed) of the conductor as manager. They also projected the image (which the later virtuoso-conductors took further) of the conductor as performer. But Jullien, unlike Costa, was not a structural reformer in the same sense as Costa. Although he used the baton from about 1840, he continued to conduct from the middle of the orchestra, mainly facing the audience, with his players (especially double basses) dispersed randomly around him on a steeply raked stage (Figure 3.3).[152]

This arrangement enabled showmen like Jullien and Musard to 'interpret' the music to the audience by their facial expressions and body movements. But it interfered with the conductor's more important task of communicating by eye or

148 *ILN* (21 Nov. 1861), 530.

149 *ILN* (27 Jan. 1855), 88.

150 Edmund Yates, *His Recollections and Experiences* (London: Bentley, 1884), 182.

151 Henry Chorley, *Thirty Years of Musical Recollections*, ed. Ernest Newman (London: Alfred A. Knopf, 1926), 320.

152 Thomas Ryan, *Recollections of an Old Musician* (New York: E.P. Dutton, 1899), 69–70.

Figure 3.3 Jullien conducting (in the midst of his orchestra) at the English Opera House (*ILN,* 23 Dec. 1843, 413) (courtesy of Westminster City Libraries)

face with the musicians. It also served to discredit Jullien as an indigenous role model for the new conductor in England (Figure 3.4.).[153]

The Beginnings of Reform in England

By 1840, various models of musical control had been demonstrated in London by Spohr (1820), Weber (1826), Mendelssohn (1829–47), Chélard (1832), Hummel (1833), Strauss (1838) and Musard (1840). Between them, they had shown that new techniques of direction could draw effective performances from London orchestras. But there was no authoritative London-based conductor capable of using these techniques to achieve what Habeneck was doing in Paris, Mendelssohn in Leipzig or Lindpainter in Dresden. Some elements of continental practice were applied by the early London-based 'conductors'. One important early experimenter was George Smart. As early as 1823 a critic described how he 'occasionally flourishes a white roll over the heads of the celebrated performers …'.[154] Smart adopted the baton at the Philharmonic from 1833, as did Henry Bishop, who is

[153] See also *ILN* (23 Nov. 1850) for Jullien concert at Drury Lane.

[154] *QMMR*, vol. 5 (1823), 367.

Figure 3.4 *Punch* cartoon, showing Jullien conducting a Prom concert (courtesy of Westminster City Libraries)

also recorded as doing so at Drury Lane in 1838.[155] Smart also used a baton at the Handel Commemoration in Westminster Abbey in 1834, where he sat at a piano-desk with his back to the audience (Figure 3.5). Smart was criticized by the conservative music-lover Mount Edgcumbe for 'this foreign adoption', which meant that 'the conductor is everything' and 'the leader … instead of being the most conspicuous person, was not visible'.[156]

Smart was perhaps the most competent of the English conductors from the era of divided direction and his standing was boosted when he secured an Irish knighthood in dubious circumstances in Dublin. But it is an exaggeration to assert that Smart 'more than anyone in Britain … established the authority of [the conductor]'.[157] As Nicholas Temperley remarks, he was not a conductor as the

---

155 *Athenaeum* reviews of Mar. 1833, quoted in *Musical Times* (1 Jun. 1896), 372–5. *MW* (4 Oct. 1838), 69.

156 Robert Mount Edgcumbe, *Musical Reminiscences* (London: John Andrews, 1834), 232.

157 Percy Young, *Beethoven: a Victorian tribute* (London: Denis Dobson, 1976), ix. See also Carnelley, 'George Smart', 2 and 20.

Figure 3.5 Smart conducting at the Westminster Abbey Handel Commemoration, 1834 (detail) (*The Mirror,* 5 Jul. 1834)

term is now understood.[158] He was frequently criticized for exercising insufficient control and for being upstaged by the leader. At Victoria's chaotic coronation in 1838 he tried to conduct and play the organ, to which the *MW* objected: 'Sir George can do no such thing.'[159]

All of the other early London 'conductors' were distracted by other more important roles as arrangers and instrumentalists. Bishop, knighted as a composer, was 'the tamest of tame conductors'.[160] Cipriani Potter, too, was a composer rather than a conductor. Charles Lucas and Tom Cooke were string players. The pianist Moscheles received good reviews for giving the first respectable performance of Beethoven's Symphony no. 9 in 1841 but was dismissed by the *ILN* as 'infirm of purpose ... fidgety ... a cypher' who 'never anticipates' so that 'performers did as they liked'.[161] The *MW* later ridiculed as 'semi-conductors' the earlier generation of Smart, Bishop, Potter, Neate, Moscheles – with their 'differences of opinion *and still greater varieties of method* ... doing all that clever men and a bad system could possibly accomplish to banish every prospect of unity of

---

158 Temperley, *New Grove 2*, 23, 533–4.

159 *MW* (1838), 74. At the subsequent musical festival Smart conducted with the baton and Turle played the organ.

160 Robert Bowley *The Sacred Harmonic Society: A Thirty-five Year Retrospect* (London: private printing, 1867), 4.

161 *Times* (4 May 1841). *ILN* (9 Aug. 1845), 90.

effect and solid improvement in the orchestra' (my italics).[162] In 1838 the same journal contrasted these with Johann Strauss, who galvanized the players from the centre of the orchestra.[163] The critic of the *Morning Post* was probably thinking of these men when he mocked conductors who merely followed the 'swing' of the orchestra instead of creating it.[164]

For this reason, it is misleading to assert, as Carse does, that baton-conducting 'became the rule' at the Philharmonic from 1833.[165] The first Philharmonic conductors, having spent their careers within the structure of divided control, took up the baton too late to develop an effective baton technique. In 1842 Sterndale Bennett was mocked for conducting the Philharmonic 'in German time, while his subjects executed in English tempo'.[166] 'How often', the *MW* asked, 'do we witness a Conductor whose exertions are fully occupied in a continued struggle to catch the time which the band, or singers, have fallen into?'[167] Indeed, the introduction of the baton in incapable hands probably aggravated the problem of divided control by making the competition between conductor and leader more conspicuous. As late as 1844 the soloist at one Philharmonic concert was reported to be:

> fettered by the discordant beatings of no less than three different individuals, viz – Sir George Smart, who wielded the baton – Mr Loder, the leader for the evening – and Mr T Cooke, *not* the leader for the evening. These gentlemen were all beating different times, and the consequence was that the band was bewildered.[168]

The early London 'conductors' did not enjoy the prestige of the composer-conductors. They also lacked other pre-requisites of professional conducting. They did not have the contractual power to select and discipline the musicians. They did not enjoy continuity with the orchestras they conducted. Placed at the piano in the middle of the orchestra, facing the audience, they did not have the physical authority which Costa and later Manns and Hallé established. As Joseph Bennet observed, 'the typical conductor of their day was a poor creature with no real qualification for leadership'.[169]

Many musicians and critics had diagnosed not only the problems (divided leadership, lack of continuity, inept baton technique, bad lay-out, poor rehearsal practice) but also the remedy. Chorley prescribed the solution as 'undeviating

162 *MW* (30 Jun. 1855), 415–6 and (20 Mar. 1852), 177.
163 *MW* (14 Jun. 1838), 109.
164 *Morning Post* (Mar. 1846).
165 Carse, *Beethoven to Berlioz*, 325.
166 *Athenaeum* (21 May 1842), 460.
167 *MW* (12 Apr. 1838), 241–2.
168 *MW* (25 Apr. 1844), 141.
169 Joseph Bennett, *Musical Times* (1 Oct. 1897), 664.

discipline exercised by one master mind and one master hand'.[170] The *MW* repeatedly argued that 'Orchestral performance … will never reach perfection in England until the office of leader … be definitely abolished and the conductor invested with unshackled authority.'[171] Busby's *Dictionary*, which had not mentioned the conductor in its 1806 edition, described him in 1840 as 'one who *arranges and superintends a public or private performance*' – whereas the leader was now redefined simply as 'he who plays the first or principal violin in a concert' (my italics).

What mattered more than the technical mechanics of direction was the overall competence and ascendency of those who aspired to control the expanding resources of the orchestra. The new professional conductors were distinguished not by their wielding of the baton but by their ability to dominate musical institutions which had previously been governed by aristocratic patrons or, in the case of the Philharmonic, run in a collegiate manner by the players. In a review of recent history in 1855, the *MW* identified what had been missing in England as 'a Cromwell … to take the reins of power' – someone with the personality and authority to combine these new ideas into a system for controlling every aspect of performance.[172] Bennett, with the benefit of hindsight, made the same analysis:

> Slow and uncertain was the evolution of the English conductor proper … A strong man was needed to set matters right – to enforce discipline, to secure at least an outward show of respect for art, and generally to transform chaos into an ordered realm. He came in the person of Michael Costa.[173]

---

170 *Athenaeum* (5 Jun. 1841), 446.
171 *MW* (26 Mar. 1840), 186.
172 *MW* (30 Jun. 1855), 415–16.
173 *Musical Times* (1 Sep. 1897), 598.

Chapter 4
Costa's System

Chapter 3 examined how, when Costa arrived in London late in 1829, arrangements for controlling the orchestra were in flux. Lax habits persisted, in the audience as well as the orchestra. An illustration of Covent Garden before the 1856 fire shows members of the audience walking around and chatting during the performance (Figure 4.1). This chapter describes the system that Costa imposed during his first 20 years in London. Its essence was the combination of many measures – not only the use of the baton, but contracts and pay-scales, rehearsal practice, orchestral lay-out, acoustics and coordination of performances. Together these elements amounted to a new system operated by a new breed of professional conductor-manager, of which Costa was the London prototype.

Whereas reform in Paris was pioneered in the concert hall, in London it occurred first at the opera. One explanation lay in the growing need to combine under one director all the complex variables of operatic performance – orchestra, singers, chorus and staging. Sir Charles Mackerras expressed surprise that even Mozart's operas could be performed during his lifetime 'without a proper conductor

Figure 4.1 Covent Garden before 1856, showing Costa with his back to the orchestra and half-attentive audience (detail) (*ILN*, 6 Dec. 1856, 562) (courtesy of Westminster City Libraries)

directing the whole proceedings'.[1] Central control was even more necessary in larger-scale works like *Der Freischütz*, *Guillaume Tell* and especially the operas of Meyerbeer and Halévy, with their ambitious theatrical effects. The fact that London opera houses, unlike those in Paris, enjoyed no financial subsidies meant that British managers had a powerful incentive to organize the production process more efficiently in order to limit their escalating costs. The drive for efficiency – especially to reduce delays and programme changes – intensified as the smaller venues began to offer more competition, following the official deregulation of the theatres in 1843.

But a key explanation lies in Costa himself: a man whose early years at the opera were marked by financial instability, maladministration and bitter power struggles and left him obsessed with the need for efficiency, order and authority. In retrospect his tight control over the musical side of the opera (and later the concert hall) seemed pre-ordained, given his dominant personality and his unique 47-year tenure as Musical Director at one or other of the two main opera houses under embattled and distracted managers. But his first four years at the King's Theatre offered virtually no evidence of the reforms that were to come.

The State of the Italian Opera

Following his traumatic start at the Birmingham Festival in 1829, Costa's painful baptism continued at the Italian Opera. In the junior post of *maestro al cembalo*, he found himself subordinated to two powerful personalities. The violinist Paolo Spagnoletti had been with the orchestra since 1814 and was its unchallenged leader. The 'Director of the Opera and Stage Manager' was Nicholas Bochsa, a Frenchman on the run from scandals in Paris, who had worked his way up from ballet-master to being in charge of 'the whole of the opera'.[2] Spagnoletti and Bochsa dominated the manager, François Laporte, who was struggling with a 20 per cent deficit and litigation worthy of Dickens's *Bleak House*.[3] Laporte was 'deficient in the art of enforcing discipline and of maintaining order' and 'subject … to periods of despondency and depression'.[4] He appears as 'Doldrum the Manager' in the Ingoldsby ballad 'A Row in an Omnibus (Box)' about the riots in 1840 which forced him to re-engage the baritone Tamburini. He went bankrupt during 1834 and briefly managed his theatre from prison.[5]

---

1 Charles Mackerras, 'Opera conducting', in Bowen, ed., *Cambridge Companion to Conducting*, 65.

2 Prospectus in *Times* (28 Jan. and 18 Mar. 1829).

3 Chorley, *Musical Recollections*, 121.

4 Lumley, *Reminiscences*, 7–9.

5 Hall Witt, *Fashionable Acts: Opera and Elite Culture in London 1780–1880* (New Hampshire: University Press of New England, 2007), 159. The *Times* put his losses at £19,000 (1 Sep. 1836).

The situation that Costa inherited is well summed up in new cost-cutting Regulations published by Bochsa and Laporte in 1829 and in the grievances published by 16 leading players who then resigned.[6] Under the Regulations, the orchestra was engaged for 50 nights a season instead of 60, receiving only half-rates for additional performances and nothing for rehearsals and benefits. The musicians were also banned from sending deputies in their place and from playing elsewhere (except at the Ancient Concerts and Philharmonic).[7] This stricter regime was similar to the one that Costa would later impose. But Bochsa and Laporte, savaged by the musical press who took the side of the underpaid players, failed to secure its acceptance.[8]

In Costa's first year as *maestro al cembalo*, the King's Theatre orchestra, which had rarely been mentioned in reviews, became a focus of criticism. It was described as 'vastly inferior to what it had been' and as a 'broken up orchestra', performing in a way which would produce 'an outcry in a barn'.[9] 'We never before heard so many blunders and so much bad playing as in this theatre'. In *Don Giovanni*, 'The band was, as it has always been this season, a chaos. The few superior players in it do more harm than good – they expose the faults of the majority'.[10] The *Times* wrote that a production of *La cenerentola* was 'hardly well enough for a company of strolling players', a 'stigma' on the management and an 'utter affront' to the audience.[11] In 1831, Costa's second year, the orchestra was still 'reduced in numbers, deficient in rehearsals'. The company exhibited 'scenes of confusion … unparalleled in the annals of the King's Theatre'.[12] Laporte, relying on a handful of stars, was justly accused of being 'indifferent how the subordinate parts were filled, whether in opera, ballet or band'.[13]

These three features – a financial-legal imbroglio, truculent underpaid musicians and administrative ineptitude – marked Costa's formative years at the King's Theatre. At the same time, his attempts to project himself as a composer were unsuccessful. He was blamed for making the only 'blot' in an otherwise excellent Philharmonic concert: a 'wretched' Fantasia for horn distinguished only

---

6 The Regulations are in Cowgill and Dideriksen, 'Opera orchestras', vol. 1, Annex C. 'An Explanation of the Differences existing between the Manager of the Italian Opera and the non-conforming Members of the late Orchestra' is in *Harmonicon*, vol. 7, no. 2 (Feb. 1829), 35 and summarized in the *Times* (24 and 26 Jan. 1829).

7 For fuller details see Cowgill and Dideriksen, 'Opera orchestras', vol. 1, 277.

8 For the plight of the lesser musicians, see passim A.V. Beedell, *The Decline of the English Musician 1788–1888* (Oxford: Clarendon Press, 1992); Deborah Rohr, *The Careers of British Musicians 1750–1850:A Profession of Artisans* (Cambridge: Cambridge University Press, 2001); and Cyril Ehrlich, *The Music Profession in Britain since the Eighteenth Century* (Oxford: Clarendon Press, 1995).

9 Parke, *Memoirs*, vol. 2, 270. *Harmonicon*, vol. 7, no. 4 (Apr. 1829), 97.

10 *Harmonicon*, vol. 7, no. 3 (Mar. 1829), 70 and vol. 6 (Jun. 1829), 145.

11 *Times* (22 Feb. 1830).

12 *Harmonicon*, vol. 9, no. 1 (Jan. 1831), 1.

13 *Athenaeum* (23 Feb. 1833), 124. Also *Morning Chronicle* (27 Feb. 1832).

by its difficulty of execution. 'We don't know who Costa is and we hope nobody will tell us'.[14] His first ballet score, *Kenilworth*, was dismissed as undistinguished.[15]

There is little documentary evidence about Costa's transition from his lowly position as *maestro al cembalo* to the post of Musical Director. The orchestra and chorus, treated as 'subordinate' elements of the opera, were rarely mentioned in contemporary accounts unless they were conspicuously awful. The lengthy memoirs of Alfred Bunn, who managed Covent Garden for eight years, barely acknowledge the existence of the orchestra and do not refer to the *maestro* or Musical Director. Significantly, the King's Theatre prospectus for 1830 did not name the occupant of either post, though it listed the leader, poet, prompter, chorus master and 'scenist'. But early in 1831 Costa appeared as '*Director of the Music and at the pianoforte*'.[16] Three months later, Bochsa's position was so precarious that he had to auction his furniture and instruments. In the same month, Costa was billed as 'conductor' (presumably in the old style, at the pianoforte) of Paganini's celebrity series of concerts at the King's Theatre concert room, though he attracted attention only for supporting Paganini as he fainted before a barrage of applause that 'completely drowned the full orchestra'.[17] By 1834 Costa had progressed to '*Director of the Music and Composer*'.[18] But it was not until 1836 that he acquired the title he was to enjoy for most of his career: '*Director of the Music, Composer and Conductor*' (my italics).[19]

A major opportunity for Costa to consolidate his position arose when Laporte impetuously went off to manage Covent Garden in 1832, leaving the King's Theatre in the hands of a 28-year-old dilettante called Monck Mason. The year 1832 was inauspicious, with riots over the Reform Bill, an outbreak of cholera and an unmusical new court following the recent accession of William IV. Moreover the King's Theatre was not equal to Mason's ambitious repertoire, which included six premieres and a seminal season of German opera (Chapter 4).[20] Mason's productions were panned by the critics. A disastrous *Il barbiere di Siviglia* was hissed. Vaccai's *Giulietta e Romeo*, 'directed' by the composer, was 'shamefully turned out'.[21] Mason's intended premiere of Meyerbeer's *Robert le diable* was pre-empted by three pirate performances at lesser theatres; it started an hour late, dragged on until 1.40 in the morning and its lead soprano, Cinti-Damoreau,

---

14 *Athenaeum* (30 Apr. 1831), 284.

15 *Times* (7 Mar. 1831).

16 *Morning Chronicle* (26 Jan. 1831).

17 *Times* (6 Apr. and 5 Aug. 1831).

18 *Morning Chronicle* (25 Jan. 1834).

19 *Morning Post* (23 Feb. 1836).

20 Donizetti's *L'esule di Roma* and *Olivio e Pasquale*, Vaccai's *Giulietta e Romeo*, Paccini's *Gli Arabi nelle Gallie*, Bellini's *La straniera* and (in French) Meyerbeer's *Robert le diable*.

21 *Athenaeum* (14 Apr. 1832), 244.

quit over a pay dispute three days later.[22] Meyerbeer told his wife that 'Mason's sloppy management tries my patience to its limits 20 times a day'.[23] The season degenerated into a series of last-minute cancellations and substitutions. A letter in the *Times*, complaining of unfulfilled promises, carried an Editor's note that he had received 20 similar letters of complaint.[24] By October, Mason was in the Court of Bankruptcy and Laporte limped back from a failed season at Covent Garden.[25]

Henry Chorley, looking back 30 years later, dated the renaissance of the opera to 1832, 'the year when (happy event for England) the Italian orchestra was placed under the direction of Signor Costa …'.[26] But Chorley overlooked how savagely his predecessor at the *Athenaeum* had criticized the King's Theatre musicians in the period 1832–34. In Spontini's *La vestale*, 'The inaccuracies of the singers in the concerted passages would have disgraced Sadler's Wells; and the accompaniment of the horns and trombones in the Invocation and the chorus singing were bad enough to deserve special mention'.[27] In Rossini's *Pietro l'eremita* (*Mosè in Egitto* shorn of biblical references), 'so imperfect a performance reflects a disgrace on Il Maestro, whoever he may be'.[28] Costa's personal position was still fragile. He was not mentioned on the playbills, even when his own ballet scores were being performed. A notice for *Der Freischütz* and Costa's ballet *Une heure à Naples* named the 'Maitre de Chapelle' (Chélard), 'Chorus trainer' (Roeckel), 'Leader of the Band' (Spagnoletti) and the Stage Managers (Broad and Derossi) but not Costa.[29] Meyerbeer's *Robert le diable* was entrusted not to him but to a visiting French conductor, Tulou.[30] The *Athenaeum* advised Mason to bring Habeneck from Paris or Carl Guhr from Frankfurt 'to give us an idea of a conductor's duties'.[31] Even Costa's friend Cox recalled that 1832 was 'one of the greatest operatic fiascos that was ever made in this country'.[32]

During the 1833 season, the singing and playing of the Italian Opera continued to attract harsh criticism. In Rossini's *Tancredi*, the chorus badly needed 'a proper drill-sergeant' and the band sounded 'dreadfully weak'. A performance of *Norma*,

22 *Athenaeum* (23 Jun. 1832), 404.

23 Meyerbeer-wife (4 May 1832), Heinz and Gudrun Becker, eds, *Giacomo Meyerbeer, A Life in Letters*, trans. Mark Violette (London: Helm, 1983), 50.

24 *Times* (2 Jun. 1832).

25 Kristan Tetens, 'Continental Opera in the London of William IV: Thomas Monck Mason and the King's Theatre, Haymarket, 1832', unpublished paper delivered at the Fifth Conference on Music in Nineteenth-Century Britain at the University of Nottingham (2005).

26 Chorley, *Musical Recollections*, 34.

27 *Athenaeum* (31 Mar. 1832), 212.

28 *Athenaeum* (18 Feb. 1832), 116.

29 Playbill at the National Museum of the Performing Arts, London. Also *Morning Post* (9 Mar. 1832).

30 *Athenaeum* (16 Jun. 1832), 388.

31 *Athenaeum* (17 Mar. 1832), 180.

32 Cox, *Musical Recollections*, vol. 1, 233 and 271.

with Giuditta Pasta, was 'little better than a rehearsal with the chorus and band'.[33] Programming remained chaotic, starting at any time from 7 pm to 8.30 pm. The chorus refused to appear in *Le nozze di Figaro* because they had not been paid. In April, some of the Italian stars did not arrive from Paris in time to perform Rossini's *L'Italiana in Algeri*, so the German troupe was hurriedly put on in *Fidelio*, which Hummel conducted 'with spirit and precision'.[34] There was uproar when Bellini's *Il pirata* was replaced by *Fidelio*, allegedly because of influenza.

The damning criticisms from the period 1832–34 suggest that Costa was struggling to manage an unruly orchestra without the authority and techniques that enabled visiting composer-conductors to deliver more precise and polished performance. But behind the scenes, important changes were beginning to take place. The most significant – Costa's assertion of undivided control over the musicians – is not well-chronicled. The build-up of a conductor's authority is a covert process, involving many intangible factors, minor skirmishes and invisible acts of personal assertion. Costa's authority at the opera no doubt grew with each small success in asserting his will and disciplining incompetents. The most visible sign of change – though not the most important – was the introduction of the baton.

The Baton and Undivided Control

Several writers left the impression that Costa began to conduct with a baton from a rostrum in 1832. Chorley stated that 'Signor Costa took up the baton' in 1832. The composer George Macfarren wrote that Costa conducted from a rostrum in 1832 within a day of seeing Chélard occupy a 'conductor's desk raised above the rest of the orchestra' and that the pianoforte forthwith ceased to be used 'except to prompt the singers'.[35] But they were writing 30 and 40 years after the event, which they had almost certainly not witnessed.

Costa seems to have had no reform agenda in 1832. He had no direct contact with progressive music centres on the Continent, where reforms were being introduced. He did not visit Paris until the winter of 1835–36, when his opera *Malek Adhel* was premiered there. His experience at the San Carlo in Naples will have shown him an excellent orchestra (according to Berlioz in 1831) under a correct and spirited violinist (as recalled by Spohr from 1817). But several visitors complained about the leader's noisy beating on what Mendelssohn reported to be a tin candle-stick.[36] The San Carlo was clearly functioning under the pre-reform system, with the violin-leader in charge of performances. Its lay-out seems, however, to have been

---

33 *Athenaeum* (25 May 1833), 332, and (29 Jun. 1833), 420.

34 *Athenaeum* (30 Mar. 1833), 204 and (13 Apr. 1833), 235.

35 *Musical Times* (1 Dec. 1872), 668.

36 Spohr, *Autobiography*, vol. 2, 13. Berlioz, *Memoirs*, 196. Felix Mendelssohn, *Letters of Felix Mendelssohn-Bartholdy from Italy and Switzerland*, trans. G. Wallace (New York: Leypoldt and Holt, 1866), 151.

comparatively modern, with first and second violins divided and all players visible to both the *capo d'orchestra* and the leader (who was centrally positioned with his back to audience in order to command the players).[37]

As *maestro al cembalo* at the King's Theatre, Costa fitted in with the London practice, sitting at the fortepiano, while the leading role rested with the redoubtable Spagnoletti. The old system of divided control was clearly still in force at the start of the 1832 season, when the *Athenaeum* criticized 'the Gran Maestro Signor Costa' for competing with the 'prompter', who had 'entire control over the choristers', and 'the leader with his long bow moving in the air like the telegraph at the Admiralty', while the bass-player Dragonetti laboured to prop up the tottering fabric.[38] In the same season, the *Athenaeum* remarked that 'the numberless blunders committed drove the conductor to the piano in the hope of taming down [the players'] wild irregularities'.[39]

A sustained rise in standards was not noticed until about 1835. Costa's reforms are thus best seen as a gradual process over the previous three years. During this period, he had the chance to observe at the King's Theatre the conducting of three visiting composer-conductors – Nicola Vaccai, Vincenzo Bellini and especially Hippolyte Chélard. Together with Mendelssohn at the Philharmonic, they demonstrated new approaches which Costa gradually absorbed in three related areas: the baton and the technique for using it; the more prominent placing of the conductor; and the power relationship between conductor and leader.

The baton evolved originally from the requirements of military bands and later from the need to give an audible beat to the opera chorus and ballet. Initially it was a large upright stick, as is still used in some military bands on the march. In musical performance, it shrank by 1800 to a small stick or roll of paper, which could be move horizontally as well as vertically.[40] It is not clear whether Bellini used a baton when he put on *Norma* at the King's Theatre in 1833, though a correspondent described the performance as taking place with 'the orchestra and chorus under Bellini's direction'.[41] But Vaccai appears to beaten time actively in 1832, when he conducted his *Giulietta é Romeo* and 'nothing but the strenuous and maestro-like conducting of the composer in the orchestra could have kept the performers together'.[42] Something like a baton may have been used sporadically at the King's Theatre by Costa's predecessor Bochsa, who was criticized in 1829 for using 'a mopstick' to 'break time'. But this appears to have been an exception:

---

37 Spitzer/Zaslaw, 352–3. Koury, *Orchestral Performance Practices,* 35.

38 *Athenaeum* (18 Feb. 1832), 116.

39 *Athenaeum* (3 Mar. 1832), 148.

40 Raymond Leppard, 'Music and the conductor', *Journal of the Royal Society of Arts*, vol. 121, no. 5207 (Oct. 1973), 707–16.

41 Giuseppe Pasta to Rachele Negri, M.F. Giulini, *Giuditta Pasta e suoi tempi* (Milan: 1935), 166.

42 *Athenaeum* (14 Apr. 1832), 244.

later in the same year, a critic was still hoping ‘to see the baton ere long at the Italian Opera; it matters not whether it be a violin-bow or a roll of parchment’.[43]

When he became Musical Director in 1832, Costa was not using a baton, though the campaign to do so was clearly gathering momentum. The *Athenaeum* expressed regret that ‘out of friendship for his friend Spagnoletti, Mr Mason has *denied himself the honour of introducing the system of leading with the baton*’ (my italics).[44] During the 1832 season, however, a powerful model was demonstrated at the King’s by Hippolyte Chélard, who conducted a German troupe which performed in parallel with Mason’s company. The *Morning Post* reported that ‘Herr Chélard, a distinguished musician and disciplinarian, conducted the band with a baton, on the principle so often advocated in our notices of the Philharmonic concerts.’ The *Spectator* reported, that ‘The conductor with his baton, instead of sitting at the pianoforte, stood on a conspicuous elevation, seeing and being seen by every person in the orchestra’.[45] These comments strongly suggest that Chélard’s conducting was, for London, novel in combining the baton with a conspicuous position in the orchestra.

Chélard’s short visit was later described as ‘the solitary success’ of the opera season.[46] The contrast with normal practice at the King’s Theatre was widely remarked. In Chélard’s own *Macbeth*, he coaxed the King’s Theatre band with his *baton de mesure* to play ‘with spirit and precision’, that ‘surpassed all previous performances’.[47] Reviewing Mason’s production of Pacini’s *Gli Arabi nelle Gallie*, the *Athenaeum* wrote that:

> The imperfect performance of the concerted music, the blundering accompaniments, the hurrying of the finales, the utter disregard of *chiaroscuro* were woefully conspicuous to a person who had witnessed the previous night’s performance [under Chélard] of *Der Freischütz*.

It recommended Mason to hire Chélard, ‘for his skilful maestro-like conducting’.[48] The *Morning Post* ran a long review of Chélard’s and Mendelssohn’s conducting to underline their superiority.[49] But although Chélard offered a convincing remedy for London’s orchestral ills, one-off visitors could not change London practice.

Costa almost certainly knew Vaccai, Bellini and Chélard from their time in Naples, where the latter two had studied under Zingarelli in the 1820s. He must also have seen their performances at the King’s Theatre. He shared a concert

---

43 *Harmonicon*, vol. 7, no. 3 (Mar. 1829), 70. *Morning Post* (27 May 1829).

44 *Athenaeum* (11 Feb. 1832), 101.

45 *Morning Post* (1832) and *Spectator* (1832), quoted in *Musical Times*, vol. 37, no. 640 (1 Jun. 1896), 372–5.

46 Chorley, *Musical Recollections*, 37.

47 *Times* (5 Jul. 1832). *Athenaeum* (7 Jul. 1832), 444.

48 *Athenaeum* (19 and 12 May 1832), 325 and 310.

49 *Morning Post* (27 May 1832).

with Chélard in June 1832 at the theatre's Concert Room, where they were billed as 'Conductors' and 'Directors of the music'.[50] The limited available evidence suggests that Costa decided to follow Chélard's example sometime in 1833. It is clear from the reports quoted above that he was not using a baton during Chélard's visit in 1832. Towards the end of the 1833 season, however, the *Examiner* accused him of 'rapping his book as offensively as ever' so that 'We almost expect to see the notes leaping from the page *under his baton*' (my italics).[51] The *Morning Post* commended Costa in May 1834 for adopting the baton, implying that this had happened only recently.[52] This squares with the retrospective claim of Costa's friend Gruneisen that he began to use the baton from 1833 'following the example of Chélard, who, *in the preceding season*, had directed the performances with the stick' (my italics).[53]

Although there was a rush to adopt some form of baton control in London in the period 1833–34, competition between conductor and leader remained rife. Use of the baton at the Philharmonic in 1833 did not enable Smart and Bishop (and the other early 'conductors') to impose their will on the well-established leaders there (Chapter 7). In May 1834, Costa was still sharing power at the opera with the leader: the *Morning Post* detected an improvement in the orchestra due to 'Spagnoletti's moral influence over his coadjutors'.[54] But four months later, Costa's position was strengthened when Spagnoletti died and was replaced by a more malleable leader in Nicolas Mori. Costa himself seems to have dated his control of the orchestra to 1834. In a letter of 1862, he wrote: 'My orchestra is composed by 87 professors ... Only three of them arrived after 1848, all the others have been under my command [unclear] since the year 1834!!!'[55]

These changes were remarked on by two observers. In 1835, the writer Thomas Love Peacock reviewed Lord Mount Edgcumbe's *Musical Reminiscences* (1834), which had criticized George Smart for his conspicuous behaviour with a baton at the Handel commemoration of that year.[56] Taking the same theme, Peacock condemned 'the *novel* introduction of a conductor into the orchestra, not playing himself but beating time with a noisy baton'. He added 'Assuredly *our Italian conductor* verifies the remark of Dr Burney: "Rousseau says that the more time is beaten the less it is kept".' Peacock went on to protest against the conductor (who must be Costa since he was the only Italian opera conductor in London in the mid-1830s):

---

50 They are referred to as 'Conductors' in a King's Theatre playbill of 14 Jun. 1832 in the late Tony Gasson's Collection; and as 'Directors' in *Times* (8 Jun. 1832).

51 *Examiner* (28 Jul. 1833).

52 *Morning Post* (22 May 1834).

53 Gruneisen, *The Opera and the Press*, 16–17.

54 *Morning Post* (22 May 1834).

55 Costa to Clay (20 May 1862), RAM 2005.1629. Costa's claim that only three new players joined his band after 1848 is highly questionable.

56 Mount Edgcumbe, *Musical Reminiscences*, 229–35.

> keeping up, in the very centre of observation, a gesticulation and a *tapage* that make him at once the most conspicuous and most noisy personage in the assembly, distracting attention from the sights and sounds that ought exclusively to occupy it.[57]

In the same year, the *Times* critic, probably Thomas Alsager, complained that Costa was becoming too conspicuous:

> In his capacity of 'Conductor', Signor Costa no longer sits at the pianoforte, but holds a long roll of paper, with which he seems to think he ought to make himself as conspicuous as he can in marking time. Signor Costa may be assured that, as most of the members of this orchestra were already eminent in the profession before he was born, they can very well manage to get through their part in the *Gazza ladra* and other operas they have been performing for years past, without any interference whatever of his. We are surprised that the leader suffers such an encroachment *on his attributes* to continue.[58]

Raymond Leppard wrongly assumed that Costa (like Spontini) held the baton in the middle, 'which must be very hard to follow'.[59] All illustrations of Costa conducting show him holding a baton of varying thickness but normal length in the modern way. But like other early baton-conductors, he appears to have begun with a rather crude technique and with mixed results. In 1834, he was berated for 'belabouring his book with his baton as a thresher belabours his wheatsheaf, and keeping up an uninterrupted and most merciless tapage'.[60] The *Examiner* complained in 1833 of him 'threshing time' with 'his obstreperous metronome', so that 'the voices seem to be going by machinery'.[61] It later drew an analogy with a marionette:

> It is rather amusing to see his incessant motion of head, hands and arms; it does not appear like beating time, there is no regularity in it, but it attracts notice as do the movements of the figures, which throw out legs and arms when the string is pulled.[62]

The *Morning Post* commented ruefully 'we should not like to be near Signor Costa while he was vainly striving to have the time kept'.[63] In 1838, an otherwise appreciative article in the *MW* nonetheless described his mode of conducting as

---

57 Thomas Love Peacock, 'Mangled Operas', 235–50.

58 *Times* (13 Mar. 1835).

59 Raymond Leppard, 'Music and the conductor', 714.

60 *Examiner* (15 Jun. 1834).

61 *Examiner* (28 Jul. 1833).

62 *Examiner*, (22 Apr. 1838).

63 *Morning Post* (23 Mar. 1835).

'trop prononcée'.[64] But as the rest of Costa's system became gradually embedded, he was able to develop a control technique that enabled him to mark the time divisions more economically (Chapter 5).

Excessive gesticulation was a fault shared with many early conductors. Berlioz and Mendelssohn both satirized Habeneck for stamping and battering the prompt box and conductor's stand.[65] Berlioz himself was censured by Spontini in 1843 for too much gesture.[66] Balfe was widely criticized for stamping: Chorley begged him to 'prevail upon his foot and his baton to perform *piano*. On Saturday the two out-thumped the great drum.'[67] Another early fault was a tendency to noise. Chélard was advised in July 1832 to adopt 'some less cacophonous and misleading signal than hissing'.[68] Costa too was reported to hum and sing when performers missed their cues.[69]

Overall, Costa's conducting technique seems to have emerged over several years. He adopted the baton in 1833, demoting the leader on Spagnoletti's death in mid-1834. But he did not develop a restrained baton technique until the second half of the 1830s and moved to a more prominent position in the orchestra only around 1834 (see below). The notion of a slow process of consolidation would fit in with the thesis that Costa, as a new boy on unfamiliar ground and surrounded by powerful established personalities, was still feeling his way. Charles Nicholson, principal flautist at the Philharmonic and the opera, writing in 1836, lends support to the conclusion that Costa's system began to come together in the mid-1830s:

> A very great improvement has taken place *within the last few years* in the orchestras of this country, which may be mainly attributed to the introduction of Conductors, whose province it is to mark the time with a baton or stick (my italics) … .[70]

Further corroboration comes from the fact that it was only around 1835 that the orchestra began to receive better reviews.[71] At the opening of the 1835 season, 'The overture to *Semiramide* went magnificently and never before did we hear the strength, brilliancy and precision of the band to better effect'.[72] By 1839, the *MW* pronounced the orchestra 'more numerous, more efficient in all its subordinate

64 *MW* (14 Jun. 1838), 111.

65 'A Victim of the Tack', *Soirées de l'Orchestre,* ed. Léon Guichard (Paris: Gründ, 1968),

66 Dixième Soirée. Spontini to Berlioz (20 Nov. 1843), *CG*, 866, vol. 3, 138. Berlioz, *Memoirs*, 413–14. Mendelssohn to Lea (6 Apr. 1825), in *A Life in Letters*, ed. Elvers, trans. Tomlinson, 36.

67 *Athenaeum* (31 Mar. 1849), 339.

68 *Examiner* (15 Jul. 1832); *Times* (7 May 1833).

69 *Morning Post* (1 Jun. 1843 and 29 Apr. 1874).

70 Charles Nicholson, *School for the Flute* (London: 1836), 18.

71 *Morning Post* (23 Mar. and 15 May 1835) and *Morning Chronicle* (25 Aug. 1835).

72 *Morning Post* (23 Mar. 1835).

departments' than any other in London.[73] By then, Costa had firmly established his dominant position, both physically within the orchestra and morally in relation to the leader. But this was only one of the measures by which Costa brought the orchestra under effective central control. The crucial element was how he actually used the baton (Chapter 5) and the other ingredients of his system – the management of the musicians' contracts, rehearsal practice, lay-out and coordination of performance.

Management of the Musicians

Before Costa's time, responsibility for managing the musicians at the opera was mainly the job of the leader, who carried the performance, and the manager, who carried most of the financial risk. In city-based concert societies, management was increasingly in the hands of committees representing the collectivity of the players. Mendelssohn discovered this when he tried unsuccessfully to take control at Dusseldorf in 1833–35 and even, to some extent, at the Leipzig Gewandhaus. Both at the opera and later at the Philharmonic, Costa's management of the musicians challenged these entrenched interests. His creed was summed up in his letter of resignation to Gye, where he insisted that the conductor must have 'the free selection and uncontrolled direction' of both players and chorus.[74]

By 1836 John Ella remarked with surprise that Costa was now the 'responsible agent' for the opera band, who were 'not in contact often with the manager'.[75] A letter of 1838 from Laporte shows that Costa was not only in charge of the music, but was making the payments to players, drawing up the playbill, and passing on instructions to Laporte's fixer, Lumley.[76] He was also sharing with Laporte responsibility for auditioning the chorus.[77] Costa justified his direct management of the musicians on grounds of efficiency. But sensitive issues of status and power were also involved, which went to the core of Costa's personality and his uncertain position in English society. Four key areas of management were at stake: numbers, pay, standards and discipline.

Numbers

In 1832, the King's Theatre orchestra had only 50 players, compared with Berlin (94), Paris (80) and Milan (68).[78] During that year, when the profligate Monck Mason was manager, Costa was able to increase the orchestra to 56 players. He gradually built his forces up to 76 players and a chorus of 69. This entailed a

73 *MW* (19 May 1839), 23.
74 ROHC, Costa to Gye corr. (27 Jan. 1869).
75 Ella Diary, 29 Feb. 1836.
76 Laporte to Costa, 28 Mar. 1838, RAM.
77 *Morning Post* (5 Feb. 1838 and 2 Mar. 1838).
78 *Athenaeum* (11 Feb. 1832),100.

significant increase in the orchestra's share of the theatre's expenditure – from 7.67 per cent (1821) to 9.73 per cent (1833) and 16.94 per cent (1834).[79] By 1843, the band cost twice as much as under Laporte.[80]

Costa's success at the King's Theatre provided the base from which he further expanded the orchestra and chorus at Covent Garden. The numbers quoted should be treated cautiously, since they probably indicate the maximum complement required for the Meyerbeer productions. In practice, the actual size of the orchestra was often smaller. Even with this caveat, it is clear that Costa made effective use of his 'privilege of making engagements ad libitum in the musical department'.[81] Cowgill and Dideriksen estimate the size of the Covent Garden orchestra at 80 (1847), 84 (1848) and 86 (1863), and the chorus at 90.[82] This broadly fits with the *MW* report that Costa had 169 musicians in 1846.[83] There was a steady tussle between Costa and Gye over the size of the payroll. In 1853 there were rumours of cuts and the *Morning Chronicle* warned that 'The orchestra has always been one of the main props of the Royal Italian Opera and to allow it to degenerate would be the worst policy.'[84] As Gye's finances became more precarious, he tried in 1867 to limit the chorus to 80, begging Costa to give up the increases he had made earlier in the decade.[85] But Costa's only compromise was to agree that, when an opera required bigger resources, he would take on casuals. The tussle over the size of the musical establishment became one of the main reasons for their split in 1869.

Numbers were less of a problem at the Philharmonic in 1846 (where he inherited an orchestra of about 76 players) and the SHS (where three-quarters of the players and most of the singers were amateurs).[86] The 3500 singers and players whom Costa mustered for the triennial Handel Festival were seen as one of its prime attractions (Chapter 7). One significant innovation, in which Costa appears to have been a pioneer, was in the use of female altos, perhaps to make up for the shortage of good male altos. George Smart had noticed, during his 1825 visit with Mendelssohn to the Berlin Singacademie, that two-thirds of the 150 singers were female and that they sang alto as well as soprano parts. But he had added that 'female voices are ever prone to drop – too small for a chorus – [you] require the shrill boys' voices'.[87] The English practice, however, at the Ancient Concert was to use only male altos and Smart did the same at the Handel Commemoration in Westminster Abbey in 1834. Costa's introduction of female altos at the SHS in 1847

79 Cowgill and Dideriksen, 'Opera orchestras', 272.

80 *Morning Post* (18 Apr. 1843).

81 *Morning Chronicle* (26 Dec. 1846).

82 Cowgill and Dideriksen, 'Opera orchestras', 295–6.

83 *MW* (26 Dec. 1846), 676.

84 *Morning Chronicle* (23 Mar. 1853).

85 Gye to Costa (31 Jan. 1867).

86 Gruneisen gives 75 (57 strings, 5 brass, 12 wind, drum), Ella Collection, f81; *ILN* (21 Mar. 1846) gives 77 (same plus ophicleide and harp, which were presumably hired as necessary).

87 Smart, 1825 Journal, f. 47, cited by Carnelley, George Smart, 201.

was a foretaste of their more extensive use at the Handel Festivals (Chapter 7). In common with other British conductors, he did not employ female instrumentalists.

Pay

Once Costa had the numbers he sought, the focus of dispute shifted to their salaries. This was an expense that managers saw as easier to constrain than the other big items – the lease and the soloists. It brought Costa into fierce dispute not only with managers but also, in 1850, with the star singers who made up the oligarchy known as 'the Commonwealth' (Chapter 6). But with Laporte, Lumley and Gye distracted by their financial-legal worries, Costa was able to build up unprecedented powers in this sensitive area. Having witnessed the strains when Laporte tried to squeeze salaries arbitrarily in 1829, he sought to create a clear but by no means generous pay-scale. One of the most vivid images of Costa as manager-conductor is of his attendance at the theatre for the Saturday payment of salaries, where he intervened to fine the laggards and reward the virtuous.[88] On balance the players probably gained financially from Costa's regime, though there was a cost in terms of other engagements which they had to forego as the opera programme was stretched from three to five nights a week. At the Philharmonic, Costa was able to exploit the increase in subscriptions to rationalize the pay regime, which had previously depended on arrangements negotiated individually by the seven directors (Chapter 7).[89]

It became part of the Costa caricature that he controlled all appointments, including the pay and contracts of the leading singers. Speculating on who would sing the lead parts at Covent Garden in 1861, the *Morning Chronicle* commented that 'No doubt Mr Costa has decided some of these questions long since … .'[90] But it is clear from Gye's diary that these decisions rested with the impresario. Dideriksen surmises that Costa did not have any influence in this area after 1849.[91] But Costa had considerable leverage over the soloists through his Italian connections and his control of access to the prestigious royal concerts and festivals. He often acted as the intermediary between Gye and the soloists, who respected him and were afraid to cross his powerful personality.[92] When Gye and Costa clashed over whether *Faust* was ready for performance, Tamberlik and Madame Carvalho both said the opera could be done – 'not, of course, in

---

88 William Kuhe, *Musical Recollections*, 58.

89 A new scale of Philharmonic fees for 1846 is set out in BL 48. 9/2: £20 for principals and £13–£15 for rank-and-file. According to Elkin there was a further increase in 1852. *Annals*, 47.

90 *Morning Chronicle* (18 Mar. 1861).

91 Gabriella Dideriksen, 'Repertory and rivalry: Opera at the second Covent Garden Theatre 1830–56' (PhD diss., University of London, 1997), 214.

92 For example with Lablache and Formes (Gye, 1 Feb. 1854) and Jeanne Castellan (Gye, 19 Jun. 1855).

the presence of Costa'.[93] His indirect influence is apparent in letters instructing Laporte's assistant Lumley to make the final payment owed to Madame Castelli and to refrain from paying Lablache or Tosti without talking to him.[94]

On the choral circuit. Costa deflected the many requests for roles in SHS concerts by explaining that 'the choice and engagement of singers rest entirely with the gentlemen of the Committee of the SHS in which I never interfere'.[95] When Sullivan wanted to select soloists for the Leeds Festival, the secretary assured him that 'Sir Michael Costa never asked to have a voice' in these appointments'.[96]

Standards

Because the size of the orchestra and chorus was limited by genuine economic constraints, Costa needed to be able to replace incompetent players. This was a delicate process since the rank-and-file musicians were underpaid and some had influential protectors. The process of weeding out is understandably not well chronicled. Ella regretted in his diary that one player, Rubbi, had been dismissed; but he added that it was 'lucky for a band to have a conductor respected and relied upon by the manager and to possess the confidence of those under his control, such as is the case now at the Italian Opera'.[97] In 1843, the *Morning Post* credited Costa with replacing the previous arbitrary selection process by one based on 'system and qualification'.[98]

The temporary influx of talented foreign players during the 1848 revolutions enabled him to replace several older players and warn others that they would be dropped if they did not improve.[99] But attracting good players remained difficult after 1850, when many returned to the Continent. Costa head-hunted the trombonist Cioffi from New York; and his principal cellist, August van Biene, claimed to have been recruited after Costa heard him busking in Hanover Square.[100] During the intense competition with Her Majesty's in the period 1847–52, the superior calibre of Costa's musicians gave Covent Garden a telling advantage (Chapter 6).

The standards he achieved at the opera house filtered into Costa's orchestras at the Philharmonic and the festivals, which took their core players from the opera house. But weeding out remained a problem throughout his career. A year after his death, Shaw remarked that 'some of Costa's men have become in the course

93 Gye, 26 Jun. 1863.

94 Costa to Lumley (19 Aug. 1837 and 5 Apr. 1839), the collection of the late Tony Gasson.

95 Costa letter of 10 May 1874. RAM 2005 1638.

96 Spark to Sullivan, (14 Feb. 1880), http://www.leedsfestivalchorus.co.uk/history/conductor-trouble.html.

97 Ella Diary, 29 Feb. 1836.

98 *Morning Post* (18 Apr. 1843).

99 *MW* (22 Jan. 1848), 62.

100 *New York Times* (24 Jan. 1913). *Morning Chronicle* (28 Mar. 1846).

of time rather pressingly eligible for superannuation'.[101] One of Costa's novel measures to raise orchestral standards was to place stronger players alongside weaker ones in order to educate and strengthen the latter. He introduced this first at the opera: the *MW* commented in 1839 that Costa 'had now presided long enough over this band to distinguish the educated from the uneducated musician – to know where he can place implicit reliance and where attention is most required'.[102] Gruneisen described this as a key element in his new lay-out at the Philharmonic, commenting that it was possible only because of Costa's 'personal knowledge of the temperament, execution, and trust-worthiness of the individual members of the band'.[103] Grove claimed that Costa lacked Manns's ability to train up an orchestra. But other observers suggest the opposite: Shaw for example saw Costa (along with Manns) as 'the only chief under whose baton orchestras display good training'.[104]

The opera chorus was slower to come up to scratch. Although Costa took advantage of the 1833 strike to bring in new singers, it was described in 1836 as 'not quite at its worst, but very near it'.[105] The chorus began to attract regular praise only from 1838, when Costa became directly involved in its auditions.[106] By 1847 the *Times* pronounced it to be a more important asset than the ballet.[107] Criticizing some ragged and uncertain choral singing in *Robert le diable* in 1849, the *Morning Post* added the comment: 'a rare case in this theatre'.[108]

Discipline

The indiscipline of English orchestras was a frequent theme in press reports and memoirs of the 1830s. Adolphe Adam commented on the tendency of members of the Covent Garden orchestra to get drunk on pay-day, with the result that Saturday night performances were marked by strange 'couaks' from the oboe and clarinet and snores from the bassoons.[109] The Philharmonic was described as 'intractable', with 'many rebellious subjects … who fancy they are as competent to teach the conductor as he is to instruct them'.[110] Indiscipline of a different sort underlay the poor coordination and ensemble playing that foreigners observed in London. The *MW* quoted a telling comparison by a German observer in 1836: 'In London, you hear distinctly that the music is produced by many; whereas in Paris, it appears

[101] George Bernard Shaw, *Shaw's Music*, ed. Dan H. Lawrence (London: Bodley Head, 1981), vol. 1, 344.

[102] *MW* (19 May 1839), 23.

[103] *Morning Post* (Mar. 1846).

[104] Graves, *George Grove*, 124–5. *Shaw's Music*, vol. 1, 169.

[105] *Athenaeum* (26 Mar. 1836), 227; and (28 May 1836), 386.

[106] *Morning Post* (5 Feb. 1838 and 2 Mar. 1838).

[107] *Times* (26 Mar. 1838).

[108] *Morning Post* (14 May 1849).

[109] Adolfe Adam, *Souvenirs d'un Musicien* (Paris: 1868), 54–7.

[110] *Morning Herald* (1845).

as if the whole were the work of one mind and one hand.'[111] Just before Costa's arrival at the Philharmonic, another writer commented that each player there performs 'too much in solo fashion', whereas 'second-rate performers, under the entire subjection of the conductor, will execute a classical work with better taste and feeling than the first-rate performers who are too proud to be led'.[112] As late as 1852, the same journal asked why the Philharmonic players, as skilled as their equivalents in the Paris Conservatoire, produced poorer ensemble playing: 'Whence then comes the difference? It is discipline – obedience.'[113]

Discipline was the leitmotif of Costa's career. It was the most obvious change noticed in his orchestras and was reflected in the military metaphors most associated with him (Chapter 5). By 1839, the *MW* judged that the opera orchestra was 'in a finer state of discipline than any other band in London'.[114] Success in imposing discipline at the opera made it easier to do the same at the Philharmonic, which shared many of the same players. Costa's conditions for taking on the Philharmonic included a pledge from the directors 'to support me in the strict discipline of the orchestra'.

Costa's ability to impose tight discipline remained personal to him, with the result that orchestras behaved differently when others were on the rostrum (Chapter 5). Some attributed this to Costa's 'moral power' (Davison) or 'moral discipline' (Ella).[115] But it also rested in part on his control over the musicians' contracts, which required them to 'attend punctually and perform at the rehearsals that may be appointed by the Musical Director'.[116] One of the unusual features of Costa's system was that he filled in the details of the musicians' contracts and sent them to the Manager for automatic signature, after which they were stored at his private residence.[117] Gye repeatedly tried to wrest back control over the players. In 1855, he amended some of the chorus engagements but Costa's solicitor brought them back, saying that Costa would not allow them and that Gye must 'sign all the chorus and band engagements in blank for Costa to fill up afterwards!!!' Gye tried to refuse but eventually gave in, on condition that two players should be omitted – a condition that Costa blithely ignored.[118] This set the pattern for fixing musicians' contracts until Costa's resignation in 1869.

The value of the discipline that Costa put on himself and his players was shown in the heavy burden they bore during the busy London season. In May 1851, they rehearsed *Fidelio* at Covent Garden for five hours before tackling a long Philharmonic programme including Mozart's Symphony no. 39 and Beethoven's

---

[111] Friedrich von Raumer in *MW* (15 Apr. 1836), 73–4.

[112] C.F. Flowers in the *Literary Gazette*, quoted in Carse, *Beethoven to Berlioz*, 223.

[113] *MW* (28 Feb. 1852), 135.

[114] *MW* (19 May 1839), 23.

[115] *MW* (21 Mar. 1846), 130–31 and Ella, *Musical Sketches*, 248.

[116] John Ella's Contract of 21 Aug. 1846. Text in Goulden, Appendix A.

[117] ROHC, Gye to Costa corr. (5 Apr. 1869).

[118] Gye, 30 Mar. 1855.

Symphony no. 4.[119] His regime of discipline, which was gradually felt in other London orchestras through their need to hire opera house players, was one of the most striking innovations of the early Victorian period. It was a prerequisite for the superior performance of London orchestras under the major conductors of the next generation – Richter, Campanini, von Bülow. Even Wagner, when criticizing the 'music-brokers' of Costa's generation, acknowledged that they had had 'done some good to our orchestras: much that was crude and ridiculous has been abolished; details of elegant expression have been treated with more care … .'[120]

Lay-out

As orchestras expanded, musicians across Europe wrestled with the questions of whether to group or disperse instruments, whether players should sit or stand, how to place them in relation to singers, and how to balance the strings with the increasingly powerful brass and wind instruments. John Ella wrote in his Diary in 1836 that the strings should be arranged 'on the principle adopted in Paris, violins in front *concentrated*, cellos, idem, violas and double bass spread all over the orchestra'.[121] But Paris too was struggling, with a steep rake and a block of singers occupying the centre of the orchestra (Figure 4.2).

As often is the case, Fétis is an eloquent source on the defects of English musical practice:

> The arrangement of the orchestra at the Philharmonic Concerts in London, seems to be made on purpose to prevent the performers from seeing and hearing one another. The basses are in front, the first violins behind them, the second above them in a kind of gallery, the flutes and oboes about the centre, the bassoons in a gallery corresponding to that of the second violins and altos, the horns on one side and the trumpets on the other; in fact there is no unity, no plan … In the matter of music, the English too often do precisely the reverse of what ought to be done.[122]

He also criticized the almost perpendicular lay-out of the instruments; the placing of the conductor at the piano; and the fact that the leaders, 'facing the public in the midst of the other violins', could not direct the players with their eye but merely indicated the movements before playing 'as simple violinists'.[123] Visibility was a problem when Mendelssohn was introduced to the Philharmonic in 1829: 'the furthest rows had to get up so that I could see them'.[124] The *Athenaeum* commented

[119] *Times* (27 May 1851).
[120] Wagner, *On Conducting*, 52.
[121] Ella Diary, 22 Feb. 1836.
[122] Fétis, *Music Explained*, 241.
[123] Fétis, 'Music in London', 215–6.
[124] Mendelssohn to Fanny (26 May 1829). Cited in Hensel, *The Mendelssohn Family*.

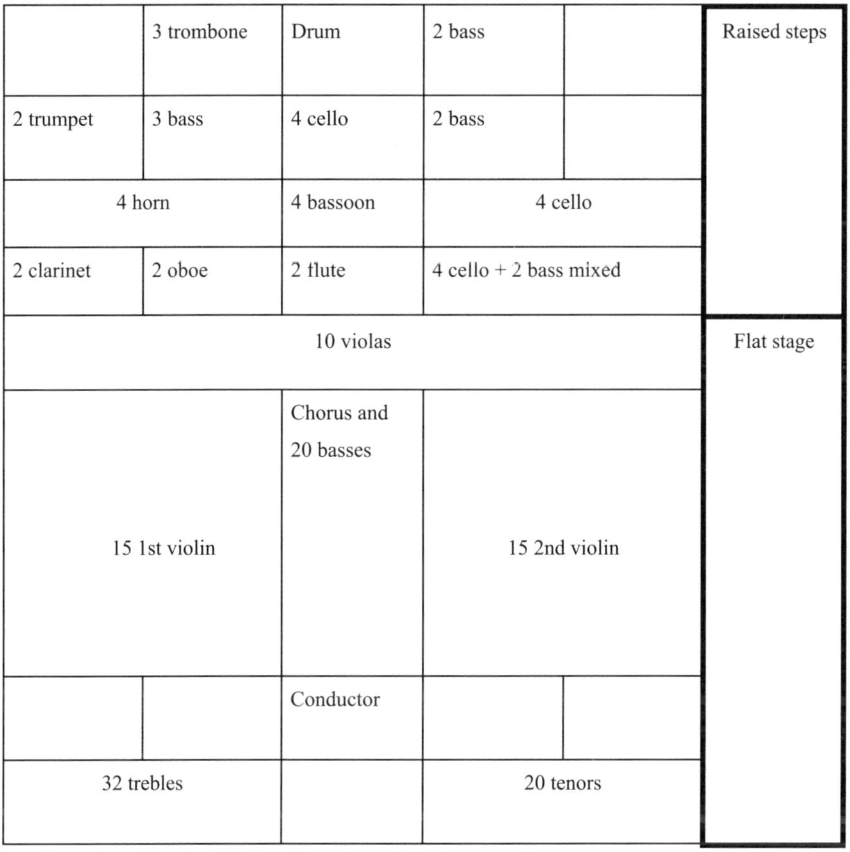

	3 trombone	Drum	2 bass		Raised steps
2 trumpet	3 bass	4 cello	2 bass		
4 horn		4 bassoon	4 cello		
2 clarinet	2 oboe	2 flute	4 cello + 2 bass mixed		
10 violas					Flat stage
15 1st violin		Chorus and 20 basses	15 2nd violin		
		Conductor			
32 trebles			20 tenors		

Figure 4.2 Lay-out of Paris *Société des Concerts*, 1840 (based on *MW*, 26 Mar. 1840)

that it was not surprising that the brass at the extremities of the Philharmonic performed so tamely when 'the leaders play and conductors beat time where they cannot be seen'.[125]

In 1840, after the Philharmonic had moved from the Argyll Rooms to the slightly larger Hanover Square Rooms, the higher strings were grouped on either side of the conductor and in front of the basses (Figure 4.3).[126]

It is clear from the detailed descriptions by Gruneisen and Hogarth of Costa's reforms at the Philharmonic in 1846 that the Philharmonic had previously retained several practices which were gradually being reformed on the Continent. The

---

[125] *Athenaeum* (5 May 1832), 292.

[126] Moscheles, *Life*, vol. 1, 288. *MW* (6 Feb. 1840), 83. It is not clear from the latter where the cellos sat: presumably on either side of the violas.

		organ		
	trombones	drums	cymbals	
	horns		trumpets	
	flutes oboes	clarinets	bassoons	
bass		violas		bass
	principal cello		principal bass	
1st violins	3 violins	pianoforte		2nd violins
	principal violin	conductor		
	singers	singers	singers	

Figure 4.3 The Philharmonic lay-out in 1840 (based on *MW*, 6 Feb. 1840, 83)

conductor, surrounded by the continuo group of leading violin, cello and bass, still faced the audience from the centre of the orchestra, where he could not be seen by the singers.[127] The conductor was often separated from the players by the increasingly redundant fortepiano. Such lay-outs were seen as inefficient and there seem to have been various experiments in the 1840s as the roles of leader, conductor and the basso continuo changed. Two illustrations of the Philharmonic in 1843 show the players variously standing and sitting and the double basses sometimes, but not always, placed prominently to the front (Figures 4.4 and 4.5).

Costa's new lay-out at the Philharmonic in 1846 was noticed immediately – by Queen Victoria among others. The Philharmonic Secretary Hogarth described it as 'a complete revolution'.[128] It is illustrated in different variations by Carse, Nettel,

---

[127] Article by Gruneisen preserved in Ella Collection, f81. Details in Goulden, Appendix C. Hogarth's account is in *ILN* (21 Mar. 1846), 193.

[128] *ILN* (21 May 1846), 193.

Figure 4.4 The Hanover Rooms in 1843 (detail) (*ILN*, 24 Jun. 1843, 439) (courtesy of Westminster City Libraries)

Figure 4.5 Another illustration of the Hanover Rooms in 1843 (detail) (*ILN*, 24 Jun. 1843, 440) (courtesy of Westminster City Libraries)

Ehrlich and (most questionably) Wooldridge.[129] The fullest reconstruction, based on Gruneisen's and Hogarth's detailed accounts, is at Figure 4.6.[130]

Costa's lay-out involved five radical alterations. First, he grouped the violins and violas in an arc round the conductor, followed by the horn and woodwind sections, then the brass, and finally the double-basses round the back. Second, he reduced the steep rake by more than half, so that the brass no longer dominated the other players.[131] Third, he moved the choir from the front flanks to behind the orchestra.[132] Fourth, the fortepiano (a 'ridiculous appendage … the resource of all incompetent conductors') was removed, except when needed for performance.[133] Finally, he himself 'faced his troops instead of fronting the audience', thus ensuring that he was at all times visible to all the members of the orchestra.[134] Unlike Jullien, who made himself the focal point for the audience, Costa aimed to ensure that he was the focus for the players and singers. As a result of Costa's reforms at the Philharmonic, Londoners heard for the first time 'an orchestra that was a single musical instrument instead of a body of individuals'. Nettel later stated that Costa's lay-out provided 'the basis of our modern arrangement of forces'.[135]

Similar reform of the lay-out was required on the oratorio circuit, where the chorus traditionally stood behind the 'conductor', who was himself often obscured by the leader.[136] At the SHS, Costa removed the conductor's box, lowered the front of the orchestra (which largely followed the Philharmonic model) and raised the choir so that all could see him.[137] At his first appearance in charge of the Birmingham Festival in 1849, Costa caused surprise by moving the rostrum back so that he could see all the singers, soloists and players.[138] He retained the principal cello and bass in the centre, with the first and second violins on either side; the violas, woodwind, brass and larger strings were arrayed in ranks behind.[139] At the Handel Festivals, he developed a highly elaborate lay-out in which each performer's place was specified so that his podium was visible to all (see Figure 4.14 on p. 99). This enabled him to exercise sole control of his massive forces, without resorting to the sub-conductors that were common in Paris.

---

129 Carse, *Beethoven to Berlioz*, 479; Nettel, *The Orchestra in England*, 145; Ehrlich, *First Philharmonic*, 74; David Wooldridge, *Conductor's World* (London: Barrie and Rockliff, 1970).

130 Gruneisen's version suggests 4 cellos in row 4, but this augments the cellos and reduces the 2nd violins by 2 and is at variance with all other sources.

131 *Daily News* (13 Mar. 1846).

132 *Daily News* (13 Mar. 1846).

133 *Morning Post* (Mar. 1846).

134 *ILN* (21 May 1846), 193.

135 Nettel, *The Orchestra in England*, 144–5.

136 *Times* (19 Apr. 1847).

137 *Daily News* (2 Nov. 1848).

138 *ILN* (8 Sep. 1849), 170.

139 *ILN* (8 Sep. 1849), 168.

bass	bass	bass	organ	bass	bass	bass
bass	3 cello	2 trumpet	2 drum	3 trombone	3 cello	bass
	4 horn	2 flute	2 clarinet	2 oboe	2 bassoon	
	2 violin	3 viola	2 cello	3 viola	2 2nd violin	
4 1st violin		4 1st violin	4 viola	4 2nd violin		4 2nd violin
	4 1st violin	leading violin, bass and cello Costa			4 2nd violin	

Figure 4.6 Costa's 1846 lay-out. Author's schema based on Gruneisen's and Hogarth's accounts

Costa initially had little scope to improve the lay-out of the orchestra at the King's Theatre where, as Rowlandson's aquatint of 1809 shows (Figure 4.7), the players were congested in two rows, and separated by the continuo group of harpsichord, bass and cello, which was placed half left. He took over some of the parterre in 1838 to accommodate his expanding orchestra and adopted a more prominent position for himself.[140] But as late as 1843 the *ILN* was still contrasting the expansive lay-out of the Philharmonic orchestra with 'the little regiment which Costa musters in such orderly strength in the little pit between the stalls and the stage of Her Majesty's Theatre' (Figure 4.8).[141]

At Covent Garden, too, the pit was initially cramped (Figure 4.9). But in the rebuild after the 1856 fire it was expanded to a depth of 13 feet (Figure 4.10). (Today's pit is over 18 feet.) The *ILN* reported the new lay-out there as a significant innovation. 'The players sit now, not in straight lines as formerly but in curves, the first and second violins and the tenors [violas] being immediately next to the audience … The violincelli and double basses have been brought more forward at each extremity.'[142] The *Times* noticed that the violins were concentrated on each side of the conductor; the violas were divorced from the cellos, who 'now play out of the books of the double-basses'.[143]

140 *MW* (29 Mar. 1838), 220.

141 *ILN* (24 Jun. 1843), 439.

142 *ILN* (11 Mar. 1848), 168.

143 *Times* (10 Mar. 1848).

Figure 4.7 The King's Theatre, aquatint by Rowlandson, 1809 (detail)

Figure 4.8 Her Majesty's Theatre in 1844 showing the cramped pit (*ILN*, 15 Jun. 1844) (courtesy of Westminster City Libraries)

Changes of lay-out also affected the positioning of the conductor. Whereas some, especially in German orchestras, continued to face the audience, Costa from his first concert at the Philharmonic faced the orchestra. The problem of placing the conductor was more perplexing in the opera house. At the Paris Opera, the *chef d'orchestre* stood 'close to the lamps' and had to turn round to see the performers. At the *Théâtre-Italien*, he stood towards one side of the stage, with all the musicians in front of him, but had to turn round to see the soloists and chorus. Costa too had difficulty in catering to the different needs of the orchestra and

Figure 4.9 Covent Garden opening in 1847 (detail) (courtesy of Westminster City Libraries)

Figure 4.10 Architect's drawing showing Covent Garden's enlarged pit in 1858 (detail)

the singers. At Her Majesty's in 1843, he is shown close to the stage, beating time for the singers, with his back to the orchestra (Figure 4.11).

But increasingly he stood in a position more visible to the players, especially when the role of the orchestra was paramount, for example for the overture. An illustration of Covent Garden in 1855 shows Costa facing the orchestra, with

Figure 4.11 Costa conducting at Her Majesty's Theatre,1843 (detail) (*ILN*, 22 Jul. 1843) (courtesy of Westminster City Libraries)

Figure 4.12 State Visit of Victoria and Napoleon III to Covent Garden in 1855, Costa lower right (detail)

his back to the audience, including the Queen and the Emperor Napoleon III (Figure 4.12).

Although the pianoforte ceased to occupy a central position in the orchestra, Costa retained a small keyboard for rehearsal and occasionally to cue or rescue the singers. The *Morning Post* reported that 'Costa has been frequently called upon to accompany on the pianoforte many long scenas, duets, trios etc. on the spur of the moment from memory'.[144] In 1853, he was 'obliged several times to resort to his small pianoforte' to help the soprano Angiolina Bosio.[145] In 1872, a *Vanity Fair* cartoon shows Costa seated at a desk with a keyboard below (Figure 4.13).

One reason for retaining the piano may have been that Costa sometimes used it to accompany recitatives. This task had been wrested from George Smart by the veteran cellist Lindley, who 'wanted to lead in oratorio as he did in the

Figure 4.13 *Vanity Fair* cartoon of Costa, 1872

[144] *Morning Post* (29 Aug. 1836).

[145] *Morning Chronicle* (15 Jul. 1853). Also *Morning Post* (3 May 1852); *Times* (4 Apr. 1851).

Opera house'.[146] Lindley was famous for his recitative accompaniments at the opera and continued in this role under Costa until his retirement in 1851. He also retained his prominent position at the front of the Philharmonic during Costa's reorganization of the lay-out there. But there is evidence from 1837 that opera recitatives were at least sometimes being accompanied not by the bass or cello but by Costa on the pianoforte.[147] The system for accompanying recitatives may have remained flexible, because in 1874 a critic noted that Costa struck a chord for the recitatives in *Le Nozze di Figaro* and expressed the hope that 'ere long means will be contrived to have the recitatives in all such operas as *Le Nozze di Figaro* accompanied upon a pianoforte as in the olden time, instead of with the violincello and double bass as is now the custom'.[148] Two months later the same critic pointed out that Costa's occasional use of his small piano in *Die Zauberflöte* enabled the soloists 'to catch the required sound more readily than they could with the violincello and double bass, at all times a most unsatisfactory method of accompanying recitatives'.[149]

Acoustics and Pitch

One important aspect of Costa's lay-out was his concern to improve the acoustics. He was probably the first conductor in the country to address this problem systematically. In this respect, the removal of the high rake at the Philharmonic was especially important. The *ILN* commented that Costa had 'studied the principles of acoustics and successfully blended the tones of the orchestra'. Gruneisen claimed that one of Costa's main innovations at the Philharmonic was 'the placing of the instruments for their proper blending of tone'. This was designed in part to achieve a better balance between the strings and 'the modern excess of brass and wind instruments'; but a more important aim was 'the classification of the executants' according to their competence and audibility.[150]

At the opening of Covent Garden in 1847, the *ILN* reported that Costa had improved the balance of instruments:

> by adding to the strength of the stringed ones, the braying of the brass has been balanced. We never heard such first violins for brilliancy, and the luscious tones of the tenors and violincelli and the power and crispness of the double-basses were quite as delightful … there was an observance of the nicest graduations of time and of varied colouring altogether unprecedented in an English orchestra.[151]

[146] Smart, quoted by G. Macfarren, *Musical Times* (1 Dec. 1872), 668.

[147] *MW* (5 May 1837), 126.

[148] *Morning Post* (18 May 1874).

[149] *Morning Post* (6 Jul. 1874).

[150] Gruneisen, Ella Collection, f. 22.

[151] *ILN* (10 Apr. 1847), 234.

Reporting the brick-laying ceremony for Mapleson's abortive National Opera House in 1875, the *Era* commented that 'The lines of the auditorium are taken from those of La Scala at Milan, and will be of the elongated horseshoe form, which Sir M. Costa states is the best for acoustic purposes.'[152]

Costa faced more acute problems at the opening of the Albert Hall, where the acoustics were notorious and the biggest organ in the world proved to be out of tune. Henry Cole recalled that Costa was broken-hearted at the first rehearsals. 'Flat, although there were 1200 performers.' He later laid on large-scale concerts to test the changes needed in the acoustics.[153] The Crystal Palace presented even greater acoustical challenges. At the trial run for the new Handel Festivals in 1857, the *ILN* commented that it was 'little better for musical purposes than the middle of an open field'.[154] Costa secured a major improvement by demanding, against the advice of the architect (Paxton), that the nave should be enclosed.[155] By 1865, the acoustics were satisfactory for the grand choruses but, in solo passages,'a man must shout and a woman must scream in order to make themselves heard'.[156] It was not until further experiments in 1868 that 'the music was clearly and distinctly audible, from the thunder of the whole orchestra to the softest tones of every single voice or instrument'.[157] By then the Crystal Palace was 'the grandest as well as the most agreeable music hall in existence'.[158]

The first half of Costa's career witnessed a steady increase in orchestral pitch from about A = 430 vibrations in the 1830s to about 452, a semi-tone higher, two decades later. The strains this increase put on players and singers, together with variations within and between European countries, generated conflicting pressures to agree a standard pitch. Shaw made fun of the battle which raged from the 1860s, in which the military, woodwind players, contraltos, basses, and organ and piano manufacturers defended the new higher pitch, while sopranos, tenors and violinists campaigned for a lower level.[159]

Costa found himself caught in the middle of this tug-of-war. He resolved the discrepancy between Covent Garden, the Philharmonic and the SHS around 1850 by aligning them at 452 vibrations, the pitch of the opera house orchestra, which provided the nucleus for the others. This became the standard for the Crystal Palace and Albert Hall organs, Broadwood's pianos and for Hallé's orchestra, which took several of its leaders from Costa's.[160] But the campaign for a return to a lower pitch gathered pace after 1859, when the French authorities settled 'A' at 435 vibrations,

---

152 *The Era* (12 Sep. 1875).

153 *Times* (13 Apr. 1871).

154 *ILN* (27 Jul. 1857), 640.

155 Gye, 11 and 13 Apr. 1856. *ILN* (28 Jun. 1862), 665.

156 *ILN* (8 Jul. 1865), 18.

157 *ILN* (13 Jun. 1868), 591.

158 *ILN* (20 Jun. 1868), 614.

159 *Shaw's Music,* vol. 1, 277–80 and 194–7.

160 *New Grove 5*, vol. 6, 796.

which was followed by Brussels and some German centres. In the late 1860s the sopranos Adelina Patti and Christine Nilsson threatened that they would no longer sing at the opera house pitch.[161] Despite the difficulties (especially for the clarinets), it appears from a score of *La sonnambula* at the Royal Opera House that Costa lowered 'Ah non credea' half a tone for Patti in 1867.[162] Five years later, the Covent Garden orchestra, now under Vianesi, adopted a lower pitch, which 'at first somewhat impaired the orchestral effects' especially in the woodwind section.[163] Nilsson's willingness to stay with the Mapleson-Costa company suggests that Costa made similar changes to accommodate her there in the 1870s.

Costa encountered similar problems at the SHS, where the sopranos and tenors were struggling with pitches higher than Handel or Beethoven had envisaged. The tenor Simms Reeves boycotted the SHS and began to to sing with Joseph Barnby's Oratorio Society, which had adopted the lower French pitch.[164] The *ILN* appealed to Costa to resolve the Reeves/SHS problem 'for we have no doubt that the committee of the Society, in this as in everything else, would be guided by his opinion'.[165] But resistance remained strong, especially from the many amateur players, who could not afford to change their instruments. A proposal from the Society of Arts in 1869 to fix the pitch at 440 vibrations, between the Paris and London levels, pleased no one. When Prince Albert refused to release Reeves from performing at a royal concert, Costa tried instead to compromise by transposing the music down. But when he did the same for the *Missa Solemnis* in 1870, the *ILN* accused him of heresy and compared him unfavourably with Barnby.[166]

Pitch thus became another subject on which Costa, because he was assumed to be all-powerful, was held responsible for defects in English musical practice. Shaw described him as 'a stickler for high pitch' and blamed him for the pitch of the Albert Hall organ.[167] He implied that Costa had prevented the Philharmonic from adopting the French pitch (though the French decision was taken five years after Costa had left the Philharmonic).[168] Shaw was wrong to describe him as a major obstacle to change in this area: the most that can be said is that he did not give a lead here as he had on other reform issues earlier in his career. Pitch was a problem which afflicted the musical world as a whole and, given the economic and institutional intractabilities, it could not be solved by a conductor's fiat. Musicians seem to have muddled through, transposing opera scores which were pitched too high and learning how to adjust their instruments to different requirements. This

161 Patti in Gye, 30 May 1867. Nilsson in *Graphic* (4 Oct. 1873) and Gye, 31 Jan., and 8 Mar. 1869.

162 Ringel, 243, n. 62.

163 Gye, 14 Feb., 2 Mar. and 13 Apr. 1872. *ILN* (10 Aug. 1872).

164 *Grove 1*, vol. 2, 758. Reeves in *ILN* (28 Nov. 1868, 9 Jan. 1869 and 2 Apr. 1870).

165 *ILN* (19 Dec. 1868), 591.

166 *ILN* (2 Apr. 1870), 355.

167 *Shaw's Music,* vol. 1, 280,

168 *Shaw's Music,* vol. 2, 457.

may have eased the way to a partial resolution at the Philharmonic in 1895. But the issue was not settled definitively (at 440 vibrations) until the International Standards Association's London conference of 1939.

Rehearsals

As orchestras expanded and the repertoire became more complex, there was a greater emphasis on the need for symphonies and operas to receive careful preparation. Fétis in 1837 prescribed one run-through, followed by a rehearsal to correct faults before getting down to the real work of realizing the composer's intentions.[169] Spontini relied on multiple rehearsals or insisted on rehearsals by section, as von Bülow did later at Meiningen, taking separate rehearsals for each of the five string sections.[170] For complicated works, Berlioz recommended separate rehearsals for each of the string sections, the woodwind, the brass, the percussion and even the harps when numerous.[171]

English writers on music tended to exaggerate how much rehearsal time was normally allowed to Spontini in Berlin or to Habeneck in Paris. For example John Ella implied that the prolonged rehearsals for Beethoven's Symphony no. 9 were typical of practice at the *Société des Concerts*.[172] The *Times* claimed that Nicolai had been allowed 13 rehearsals for this work at the Vienna Philharmonic.[173] The manager Alfred Bunn left an amusing picture of the 'slow coach progression' of rehearsals at the Paris Opera, where singers met sporadically to discuss costumes and dining arrangements and only gradually engaged with the music.[174] But even on the Continent, rehearsal time was at a premium and the new profession of conductor struggled to use it more efficiently. There were rarely more than two rehearsals for Philharmonic concerts in Vienna or the *Concerts Spirituels* in Paris.[175] Berlioz reflected this when he wrote that:

> In the majority of European cities nowadays Musical Artisanship is so ill-distributed, performers so ill-paid and the necessity to study so little understood that economy of time should be reckoned among the most imperative requisites of the orchestral conductor's art.[176]

---

169 Fétis, *Manuel des compositeurs*, 122–3.

170 *Weimarer Zeitung* (16 Dec. 1880), cited by Alan Walker, *Hans von Bülow: A Life and Times* (Oxford: Oxford University Press, 2010), The Meiningern Miracle, part 4.

171 Berlioz, Supplement to *Traité*, 257.

172 Ella, *Musical Sketches*, 396–7.

173 *Times* (12 Jun. 1849).

174 Alfred Bunn, *The Stage, both before and behind the curtain* (London: 1840, Richard Bentley), vol. 3, 182–5.

175 I am grateful to Professor Weber for this information.

176 Berlioz, Supplement to *Traité*, 246.

English critics were correct in claiming that the rehearsal regime in London was less generous than on the Continent. The *laissez-faire* economics of the music industry in London did not normally permit multiple rehearsals. This was manageable in the opera world, where London productions often followed hard on the heels of Paris and where, as Chorley observed, 'all the efficient rehearsal and preparation which is done at all is done there and not in London'.[177] But there were frequent complaints that shoddily prepared performances prevented London musicians from understanding new pieces and correcting errors in the often defective scores. The *QMMR* contrasted the serious approach to rehearsal on the Continent with the predicament of the composer in England, who

> must consider himself fortunate if he can have his opera tried over five or six times; with the band scarcely complete on any one occasion. New music is frequently brought before the public after having been merely run through ONCE – and that, perhaps, so closely to the performance, that the author has hardly time to correct any mistakes.[178]

This was equally true of benefit concerts, where promoters sought to attract customers by offering works not in the current repertoire and therefore often under-rehearsed.[179] The *MW* described a typical London rehearsal:

> What haste! What inaccuracy! What a scrambling to get to the end … what a shutting up of fiddle cases; what a pocketing of flutes and clarionets, and a running in all directions! … everyone is in a hurry, but the poor author; who, in this general hurry, discovers the sad presage of the imperfect performance of his music and its probable failure.[180]

The London rehearsal regime clearly lacked the rigour which the composer-conductors and music-writers believed was necessary for the increasingly heavy repertoire. Its lax ethos is clear from the approving comment of John Edmund Cox that George Smart 'never wearied his forces by tedious repetitions at rehearsals, nor provoked them by constant fault-finding'.[181] Four years before Costa took over the Philharmonic, Chorley observed a rehearsal that rattled through the programme 'without one solitary check or control on the part of the conductor'.[182] These constraints often applied even to foreign composer-conductors, who were accustomed to a more generous allowance of rehearsal time on the Continent. Mendelssohn, who had 11 rehearsals for *A Midsummer Night's Dream* in Leipzig,

177 *Athenaeum* (6 Aug. 1836), 555.
178 *QMMR*, vol. 5, no. 20, 433–4.
179 Fétis, 'Music in London', 245. A criticism endorsed by editor.
180 *MW* (16 Feb. 1843), 64.
181 Cox, *Musical Recollections*, vol. 1, 91.
182 *Athenaeum* (9 Apr. 1842), 323.

complained that at the 1837 Birmingham Festival he was forced to cram seven performances into four days, with only one day for rehearsal. 'That is how calves are led to the slaughterhouse.'[183] Wagner was horrified to discover that the Philharmonic's 'economical arrangements' allowed him only one rehearsal.[184] Berlioz joked that London impresarios had 'brought the art of accelerated musical rehearsals to a degree of splendour unknown to other nations. On our side of the British Channel, to learn and stage a five-act opera, ten months are required; on the other side, ten days.'[185] Berlioz had to abandon his plan to perform the *Symphonie Fantastique* at the Philharmonic on being told that a single rehearsal was 'l'usage invariable de la Société'.[186]

The positive corollary of this situation was that London orchestras were famous for their sight-reading and ability to perform with minimal rehearsal. Reviewing a performance of *Lucrezia Borgia* in 1848, the *Times* commented with perverse pride that 'What cost M. Habeneck 18 months of hard labour scarcely cost Mr Costa as many days.'[187] In 1848, when the royal family demanded that *Les Huguenots* be put on at two weeks' notice, compared with 96 rehearsals in Paris, the *Times* boasted that:

> In England we manage these things differently … Mr Costa is not easily to be daunted and, sure of his band and chorus as of himself, he undertook the unexpected task and … accomplished it to admiration.[188]

But the obverse side was that rehearsal constraints were also often quoted to excuse inadequate results. A middling performance of Beethoven's Symphony no. 9 in 1849 led the *ILN* to compliment Costa on what he achieved 'with the materials at his command … and scanty preparation'.[189] The *Times* commented that 'only a conductor like Mr Costa, whose quickness, decision and personal as well as artistic influence over his orchestra are so great, could have managed to effect what was effected last night'.[190]

Because of the parlous finances of the opera and concert business in London, Costa was rarely allowed more than one orchestra rehearsal for a concert or an oratorio. His only option was therefore to ensure that rehearsal time was used more efficiently. He did this in several ways.

---

183 Hiller, *Mendelssohn*, 213. Mendelssohn's Diary, 18 Sep. 1837, quoted by Todd, *Mendelssohn*, 357.

184 Wagner to Hogarth (28 Dec. 1854), Hueffer, *Half a Century*, 45.

185 Berlioz, *Soirées de l'Orchestre*, 107 and Ehrlich, *First Philharmonic*, 81.

186 Letter to Berlioz (9 May 1853), BL Loan 48.6/3.

187 *Times* (25 Aug. 1848).

188 *Times* (21 Jul. 1848).

189 *ILN* (31 Mar. 1849), 339.

190 *Times* (12 Jun. 1849).

First, he applied strict rules of punctuality. Berlioz complained that London players came and went from rehearsals, never giving him a full complement: 'That is how discipline is understood in this country.'[191] One of Costa's conditions for taking on the Philharmonic was that rehearsals should be brought forward an hour to 11.00 am, later advanced further to 10.00 am. He did this to permit the players to rest before the opera, since rehearsals had in the past frequently continued until 5.00 pm.[192] Hallé had similar problems over the timing of rehearsals in Manchester, finally threatening to resign in 1855 unless the Gentlemen's Society agreed to move rehearsals close to the performance.[193] Costa characteristically fined players who turned up late and even closed the doors so that late arrivals were not admitted.[194] His obituary in the *Musical Times* observed that 'the orchestra became a model of punctuality and serious work'.[195] Mapleson, who poked fun at his fixation with clocks, conceded that 'his love of order, punctuality, regularity in everything, stood him in excellent stead'.[196] Poor attendance at rehearsal was a particularly serious problem at the amateur SHS, but Costa secured a change of rules in 1853 permitting the suspension of players who were guilty of 'negligent attendance'.[197] His reputation ensured that, when he took over the Birmingham Festival in 1849, 'Everyone was at his post at the appointed hour, Mr Costa as usual before the rest, and nobody detained an instant longer than was absolutely requisite.'[198]

Second, he applied his rules equally to everyone, regardless of status. Mendelssohn described how in 1846 Grisi, Mario and Lablache 'lounged quietly in with their cool nonchalance' for a rehearsal around 10.00 at night.[199] But there are numerous stories of Costa publicly rebuking stars for missing rehearsals or turning up late.[200] Patti, who later became notorious for refusing to attend rehearsals, submitted to Costa's rules, though she complained that he forced her to sing out at rehearsal and demanded too many rehearsals for revivals.[201] The contrast with Giuditta Pasta's contract of 1826 shows how far Costa had extended control over rehearsals:

191 A.W. Ganz, *Berlioz in London* (London: Quality Press 1950), 37.

192 *Morning Post* (18 Nov. 1845). *MW* (15 Mar. 1851), 161.

193 *MW* (15 Sep. 1855), 603. Hallé Diary 1896, 353 and 355. I am indebted to Robert Beale for this material.

194 *Morning Post* (28 Apr. 1862).

195 *Musical Times* (1 Jun. 1884), 321.

196 Mapleson, *Memoirs,* 131.

197 SHS cuttings at Royal College of Music Centre for Performance History, London.

198 *Times* (5 Sep. 1849).

199 Mendelssohn to Frau Frege, *Letters of Felix Mendelssohn-Bartholdy,* ed. Rietz, 407.

200 Santley, *Student and Singer*, 181. Ella, *Musical Sketches,* 248. Gye, 16 Jun. 1865.

201 Gye, 4 and 9 Jul. 1863. H Sutherland Edwards, *The Prima Donna* (London: Emington and Co., 1888), vol. 2, 85.

> Clause 6. 'In all the operas in which she will take part, Mme Pasta will alone decide on the performers and their roles, the absolute management of rehearsals and staging of the said operas. No one will have the right to interfere with the rehearsals or production of these operas.

Third, he banned visitors from the rehearsal room, a privilege that managers had advertised to attract subscribers.[202] John Ella wrote in 1836 that:

> I have ever considered it bad policy to allow strangers to attend rehearsals. It is impossible to dictate to a singer or performer without wounding his *amour propre* in the presence probably of his pupils as well as friends.[203]

Mendelssohn attracted adverse comment when he interrupted an open Saturday rehearsal at the Philharmonic to correct mistakes in 1844.[204] The following year, it was said that 'the orchestra regards every stop as a personal affront, to be resisted and resented by free-born Britons'.[205] Costa seems to have enforced his 'stringent edict' from 1851, when the *MW* reported that it enabled him to make corrections, which previously 'no conductor could have ventured to enforce, and no orchestra would have endured'.[206] There was a similar trend at the opera, where Costa enjoyed contractual control over rehearsals. When the Prince of Wales was exceptionally allowed to attend a rehearsal, Gye warned him not to mention it to anyone.[207] According to Richard Strauss, Von Bülow had similar trouble excluding the Duke of Meiningen from closed rehearsals.[208]

Fourth, he prepared thoroughly in order to make the fullest use of rehearsal time. This was especially necessary at the big festivals, where singers came from a variety of choirs, accustomed to different tempi and performing styles.[209] Costa tackled this by appointing 'sub-committees to audition each vocal part' and introducing regional rehearsals early in the year, so that singers arrived at the festivals prepared to perform after a single rehearsal.[210] He also prepared himself meticulously. His performing scores for the SHS carry metronome markings for virtually every section, with liberal dynamic markings in blue pencil.[211] August Manns, who succeeded Costa in the Handel Festivals, claimed that Costa relied

202 Mason's prospectus for 1832 in *Times* (5 Sep. 1831).

203 Ella Diary, 29 Jun. 1836.

204 *Morning Post* (14 May 1844). *Athenaeum* (18 May 1844). Bowen, ed., *Cambridge Companion to Conducting*, 107.

205 *Athenaeum* (2 Aug. 1845), 772.

206 *MW* (15 Mar. 1851), 162.

207 Gye, 30 May 1867.

208 Richard Strauss, *Recollections and Reflections,* ed. Willi Schuh, trans. L.J. Lawrence (London: 1953), 125.

209 *Examiner* (24 Jul. 1871).

210 *Times* (30 Aug. 1861).

211 SHS scores at the Foundling Museum, London and RCMA.

too much on 'cues'. But such attention to preparation and cues was a sign of the new professionalism, as practised by Habeneck and Berlioz. Ella commented privately: 'Costa proves a very able *maestro*; takes great pains and saves us much trouble.'[212] The baritone Charles Santley praised him for never wasting a moment of time at rehearsals.[213]

Fifth, he drove his musicians hard in rehearsal. Before 1846, the frequent notices that Philharmonic players should 'remain for the whole of every concert and rehearsal' showed that rehearsals had often been skipped.[214] In his first year with the Philharmonic, the *Times* commented that 'It is the merit of Signor Costa that he has none of the *laissez-aller* in his composition, but at rehearsal *will* have every passage repeated until it goes right there.'[215] But, having exposed errors mercilessly at rehearsal, Costa nursed the orchestra to disguise their errors during performance – unlike Habeneck, who often pointed out mistakes in public.[216]

Finally, and most significantly, he ended the practice under which leading players sent deputies to represent them at rehearsals, happily paying a small fine for non-attendance out of the high fees they obtained elsewhere. The Philharmonic had long given up its rule that players must obtain the directors' permission before sending a deputy. Costa introduced a more stringent regime, threatening to engage 'substitutes at the expense of performers absent' and announcing that anyone absent from rehearsal without permission would forfeit his engagement.[217] Ella was probably exaggerating when he claimed that 'The complete band attended at all future rehearsals … The six or eight rehearsals were gradually reduced to two or three, and finally the choir and band were so thoroughly drilled that the revival of any opera never required more than one patient rehearsal'. But Costa clearly secured a change of ethos at London rehearsals.

Overall, the main virtues of Costa's rehearsal regime were its rigour and intensity. Haweis wrote that 'He could do more in one rehearsal than others did in six … He would have full numbers, implicit attention – but no needless toil … .'[218] Bellini wrote to his friend Florimo after the London premiere of *I Puritani* in 1835. 'They write to me that Costa performed miracles of work because the impresario wanted the chorus to learn the opera in six days time!'[219] The *Morning*

---

212 Ella Diary, 17 Mar. 1836.

213 Santley, *Student and Singer*, 181.

214 Examples of directors' notices about the need for punctuality and full attendance are given in Elkin, *Annals*, 34.

215 *Times* (21 Apr. 1846).

216 Costa exposing mistakes at rehearsal in *Morning Chronicle* (19 May 1857). Habeneck doing so in performance in Fétis. *Manuel des compositeurs*, 126.

217 Ella, *Musical Sketches*, 247–8. Confirmed by Cox, *Musical Recollections*, 180.

218 H.R. Haweis, *Pall Mall Gazette* (2 May 1884).

219 Bellini to Florimo (25 May 1835), BE 556, in Herbert Weinstock, *Vincenzo Bellini* (London: Weidenfeld and Nicolson, 1971), 195–6.

Post claimed implausibly that he put on *Lucia di Lammermoor* a day and a half after the score was received from Paris.[220]

Costa's strict regime became a publicity asset. By 1841, the prospectus for Her Majesty's boasted that members of the opera orchestra were now required to attend all rehearsals. Costa was commended for postponing the opening of the 1848 season when revolution in Paris prevented the soloists from travelling to London: 'Costa would not risk the musical reputation of the theatre with hurried rehearsals.'[221] But the delays that he imposed became an increasing source of friction during the rivalry between Covent Garden and Her Majesty's, when Gye worried that Costa's perfectionism would enable Lumley (and later Mapleson) to pre-empt his new productions (Chapter 6). Mapleson too implied that Costa's diligence went too far.[222] Another downside was his tendency to overwork his forces – a criticism levelled against many perfectionists, including von Bülow, who 'drilled the players so hard that they were almost in a state of mutiny'.[223] Lumley alleged that over-rehearsal of Costa's opera *Don Carlos* left both Mario and Lablache hoarse.[224] At the Birmingham Festival in 1862, Costa's chorus was 'languid from over-much work'.[225] The *Herald* critic wrote of 'severe and frequent' rehearsals for the first SHS performance of Mozart's *Requiem*.[226]

Costa's ability to get reasonable results with limited rehearsal owed much to his long tenure and the high degree of continuity in his orchestras. This meant that his musicians were familiar with his baton technique and understood what effects he wanted to achieve. Ella noted in his diary that 'One of the advantages of a musical establishment being under the permanent direction of one person is … being able to revive operas without the tedium of frequent rehearsal.'[227] Costa was also helped by the increasing focus of the opera repertoire on a small number of works: Covent Garden put on 40 performances of *Les Huguenots* in 1850–53. He could do the same, to some extent, at the SHS, where the main oratorios featured every year and poor initial performances could be redeemed by re-worked repeats (as with Mendelssohn's *St Paul* in 1850).[228] But repetition was not usually an option with the demanding symphonic repertoire of the Philharmonic. Costa's performances there were later compared unfavourably with some of the New Philharmonic concerts by Berlioz, who was allowed 'a sufficient number of

220 *Morning Post* (18 Apr. 1843).

221 *ILN* (11 Mar. 1848), 168.

222 *Mapleson Memoirs*, 131.

223 Alexander Mackenzie, *A Musician's Narrative* (London: 1927), 92.

224 Lumley, *Reminiscences*, 79.

225 Charles Villiers Stanford, *Pages from an Unwritten Diary* (London: Edward Arnold, 1914), 109.

226 *Herald* (10 Feb. 1853).

227 Ella Diary (3 May 1836).

228 *Times* quoted in *Musical Times* vol. 3, no. 69 (1 Feb. 1850), 277.

rehearsals, something almost without precedent in England'.[229] Costa also lacked the advantage enjoyed by Manns, who could treat his mid-week concerts as a dry-run for the more important Saturday platforms.[230]

Infrastructure and Coordination

Operating during the season in several spheres – opera, oratorio and private and public concerts – Costa had to develop ways of ensuring that scarce musicians were available for a variety of venues. This problem was especially acute in London, where numerous events were crammed into the short season. But his control of the resources of the opera house gave him unique power to coordinate rehearsals and performances with those of other bodies that drew on the opera orchestra and soloists. Costa was the only person who could resolve conflicting claims on the players from opera managers, the Philharmonic directors and the festivals. The importance of this role became clear after he left the Philharmonic, which found itself in 1857 putting on a concert on the same day as the Handel Festival. From 1862, the Philharmonic lost about 40 players when Covent Garden insisted that its players should be available to perform on Mondays, the Society's traditional concert night.

But Costa's contribution to the music industry went beyond this basic form of coordination. His direction of the massive Victorian state and festival occasions (Chapter 7) demanded a new approach to galvanizing the unprecedented forces involved. Smart and Bishop had conducted the opening of the 1851 Great Exhibition 'huddled' in the Crystal Palace transept, 'without a proper orchestra' and to 'little or no effect'.[231] When asked to conduct at the re-opening of the Crystal Palace at Sydenham in 1854, Costa characteristically told the organizing committee that it would be 'unwise that any musical performance should be entered into unless upon a very large scale'. He wanted 'an amateur spirit' to prevail, but demanded three military bands and his own Covent Garden orchestra – a total of 1,710 performers.[232] The chorus, three times larger than in 1851, was recruited from 21 provincial choirs. Costa insisted on a 6,000-square-foot stage, with a 42-foot rake so that everyone could see the conductor.

This concert demonstrated Costa's ability to coordinate a large army of musicians. They were channelled by 38 marshals and colour-coded so that they all knew their place. Chorus management on this scale raised tricky questions: How much space to allow to each singer? (21 inches.) How to deal with interlopers from the New Philharmonic who wanted to take part 'as a body'? (Separate entrances,

[229] Berlioz, Addition to *Soirées de l'Orchestre*, no. 21.

[230] I am grateful to Professor Musgrave for this insight, which is corroborated by the *Pall Mall Gazette* (12 Apr. 1875).

[231] Bowley, *The Sacred Harmonic Society*, 33.

[232] Robert Bowley, *Account of the re-opening of the Crystal Palace*, RCM Centre for Performance History. Much of the following detail draws on this valuable source.

guarded by marshals, for audience and singers.) Should ladies be allowed to wear bonnets? (No.) The orchestra of 285 was carefully auditioned and separately rehearsed, with Costa attending those for the brass bands. He made frequent visits to Sydenham 'ascertaining the capability of the place for sound, likewise arranging the plans, the stand or seat of each instrument and allocating the individual spaces'. He decreed which musicians should play in the quieter sections. His team also supervised the printing of the specially arranged scores, the provision of 300 uniform music stands and the transport of musicians and heavy instruments.

The programme was musically conservative – the National Anthem, the Hallelujah Chorus and Old Hundredth – but the audience of over 30,000 was treated to a magnificent state spectacle.[233] There were unsteady moments, especially at the opening of the Hallelujah Chorus, but 'a few beats from Mr Costa … brought them up to the mark'. Victoria wrote that the performance was 'led most beautifully by Mr Costa. I cannot describe the splendid effect of the music, it was beyond all description.' Palmerston told the SHS that it was 'the finest effect which Her Majesty has ever heard'.[234] The 1854 concert marked a turning point in large-scale performances in Britain. It created the template for Costa's handling of the Handel Festivals and other major state events (Chapter 7). The complex map for seating the musicians at the trial run for the 1858 Handel Festival was remarkable enough to warrant printing in the *ILN* (Figure 4.14).

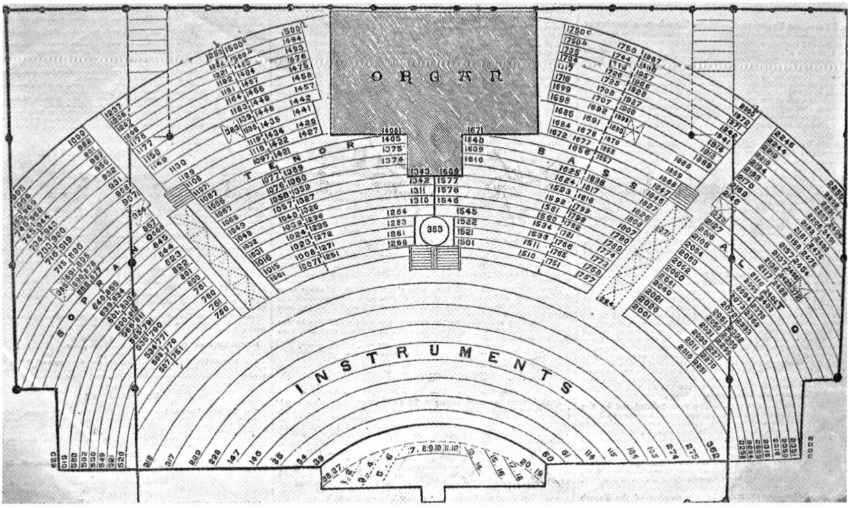

Figure 4.14 Lay-out for the Handel Festival at the Crystal Palace Sydenham (*ILN*, 13 Jun. 1857, 571)

233 *Times* (12 Jun. 1854).

234 Palmerston to SHS (20 Jun. 1854), Bowley, *Sacred Harmonic Society*, 34.

After Costa's death, George Grove implied that 'the secret of Costa's uniform success' lay in his army of helpers, which drained the SHS coffers:

> At the zenith of his career, Sir Michael never moved without such men as Bowley, to prepare the whole scheme of the transaction for him, Sainton, Blagrove, Hill, Lucas, Howell, Pratten, Lazarus, the Harpers, Chipp and others of equal eminence at the principal desks, Peck and Henry Wright to distribute the parts. With the perfect organisation and efficient execution of such lieutenants, failure was impossible.[235]

But, in disparaging Costa, Grove was in part motivated by a wish to boost the reputation of his protégé August Manns, who was Costa's successor at the Handel Festival. Not the least of Costa's qualities was his ability to attend to the details when necessary and thereafter to delegate to a self-reliant support team. The composer Charles Willeby commented that 'He liked a strong staff about him and he liked them to be self-reliant.'[236]

The Conductor-manager

Costa's authority at the opera house extended beyond the orchestra and chorus. His contract described him as 'Superintendent of the *mise-en-scène*'. He put a broad interpretation on the clause in his contract that 'Mr Gye is to cause the Orders of Mr Costa for the Services of the Theatre *in all matters committed as above to his charge* to be respected and obeyed' (my italics). His remit included the appointment of the *maestro al piano*, the chorus master and the copyist. This led many to exaggerate Costa's power. The *Times* critic wrote in 1837 that 'he could command with absolute power not only scenes, dresses and decorations, but could exact from his orchestra and chorus as much drilling as he found necessary for his purpose'.[237] The *MW* claimed that Costa 'ruled not only the orchestra, but also the stage: actors, machinists, scene-shifters and all subordinates came under his surveillance'.[238] But according to Hermann Klein, Costa left stage matters to the stage staff, unlike Carl Rosa, who tried to manage everything.[239] As the music industry became more specialized, Costa found himself increasingly in competition with the new professionals of stage management and their respective boundaries became a major source of conflict during the 1860s (Chapter 6).

The ingredients of Costa's system, together with his extensive contractual powers (Chapter 5), gave him a degree of authority that was unprecedented

---

235 Grove, 'The Secret of Sir Michael Costa's Success', *Pall Mall Gazette* (1 May 1884).

236 Charles Willeby, *Masters of English Music* (London: Osgood, 1893), 17–18.

237 *Times* (19 May 1837).

238 *MW* (12 Feb. 1848), 99.

239 Klein, *Musicians and Mummers*, 99.

in England. He came nearer than anyone in the country to meeting Berlioz's prescription that the director of an orchestra should be a 'conductor-instructor-organiser'.[240] His mixture of power and personality enabled him to impose orchestral reforms that Laporte and Bochsa had failed to implement at the King's Theatre a few years earlier. Building up his authority involved negotiating a fine line between musicians (who were insecure and under-paid) and managers, (who were operating on a financial-legal tightrope and had good reason to fear bankruptcy). He made himself indispensable to both, as was clear from the frequent requests that he should resolve disputes between players and managers.

For the managers, Costa challenged their ability to control their timetables and costs. But the surrender of power to the conductor was implicit in Chorley's acute prescription for proper orchestral direction: 'undeviating discipline exercised by one master mind and one master hand'.[241] Costa brought order to a business which had frequently suffered from the disorderly behaviour of bands and choruses. Managers benefitted from his ability, after 1838, to avoid the musicians' strikes that had frequently damaged their business. He could persuade the musicians to work long and irregular hours for modest pay. Managers were also beholden to him for turning orchestras round in a very short time – a matter of a few weeks at the Philharmonic and the SHS – and for delivering good performances with a minimum of rehearsal. Underlying these benefits was the threat that he would move to a rival house and take the better musicians – and his box office appeal – with him (as he did in 1847 and 1871).

For the musicians, Costa challenged their collegial solidarity, especially at the Philharmonic, and their faltering efforts to defend their interests collectively. His strict discipline was reinforced by his dominant position at the opera (the nucleus of all major orchestras until the late 1850s) and his control of the players' access to private concerts and festivals, on which they depended to supplement their meagre salaries. But his dictatorship was mitigated by the fact that it was on balance a benevolent one, since he was concerned for their welfare. William Kuhe and Joseph Bennett were exaggerating when they credited Costa with transforming a mundane employment into 'a vocation':

> If he could not raise their salaries, he at any rate contrived to raise their artistic worth … Orchestral players … came to be looked upon both by operatic managers and vocalists as artists entitled to a full measure of consideration and respect.[242]

But Stanford, a more critical observer, admitted that 'orchestral players had no warmer champion or friend. He fought their battles tooth and nail and raised their

[240] Berlioz, *Memoirs*, 406.

[241] *Athenaeum* (5 Jun. 1841), 446.

[242] Kuhe, *Musical Recollections*, 58–9. Bennett, *Musical Times* (1 Oct. 1897), 666.

pay and their position in the profession.'[243] The Directors of the Leeds Festival complained that players were able to extort high fees because they knew that Costa had insisted upon their engagement'.[244] The *ILN* commented that 'He was their champion as well as their conductor; and the hard-worked instrumentalist … knew that, while Costa wielded the baton, his earnings were secure from reduction and his valuable time was not occupied unnecessarily.'[245] In this he differed from Habeneck, who was increasingly seen as an agent of the management.[246]

The delicate balance was illustrated in Costa's handling of the central issues of pay and numbers. He employed more players and choristers and at higher pay-rates than the opera managers and the festival directors wanted. But his pay-scales were not unduly generous; several players refused to perform at the Philharmonic even at the increased salaries that he persuaded the directors to offer. Moreover, his regime of discipline ensured that his orchestras delivered good value for money. Costa provided a reliability and continuity that, at least until the 1860s, others could not match.

Most contemporary writers saw in Costa a combination of sympathy and severity, detecting benevolence behind his gruff autocratic manner. The clarinettist Henry Lazarus described him as 'a lion in the orchestra and a lamb out'.[247] The critic Joseph Bennett wrote that 'In battles with managers, he acted as the leader of his men and if, when they offended, there was little chance of escaping reprimand, there was equally small chance of being overlooked if they deserved approbation … .'[248] Stanford remembered Costa as a martinet but 'for all his tyranny, a true friend of the orchestral player … Many were the great kindnesses which he did in secret to a young musician or a struggling artist.'[249] William Spark claimed that Costa paid for 'scores of impecunious, unfortunate members of his band' to take sea-side holidays.[250] John Ella recalled his many acts of generosity to 'the poor invalided chorister' and the 'member of his band in pecuniary difficulties'.[251] The weight of evidence goes well beyond conventional Victorian politesse.

Costa's friends went too far when they claimed that his players 'almost worshipped him' (Kuhe) and that he was 'the most popular *chef d'orchestre* that ever resided in England' (Spark).[252] The evidence points to respect rather than affection. Costa did not inspire the 'warmth and love' that Claudio Abbado

243 Stanford, *Pages from an Unwritten Diary*, 206.
244 Fred R. Spark to Sullivan, (14 Feb. 1880).
245 *ILN* (7 Feb. 1846), 98.
246 Southon, 149.
247 *Pall Mall Gazette* (2 May 1884).
248 198 Bennett, *Forty Years,* 52.
249 Stanford, *Interludes, Records and Reflections*, 35.
250 Spark, *Musical Memories*, 9.
251 Ella, *Musical Sketches*, 246/7.
252 Kuhe, *Musical Recollections*, 57. Spark, *Musical Memories*, 2.

defined as the key ingredient between conductor and players.[253] The *Musical Times* obituary observed that he inspired esteem rather than love, but also 'the fear with which a warmer feeling can hardly exist'.[254] Much was made of the warm reception he received from the players at concerts – for example when the players led ovations for him at the end of his first Philharmonic season.[255] But the remarkable loyalty which he inspired was reinforced by powerful sanctions. There may be some truth in the violinist Tollebecque's claim that those who followed Costa from Her Majesty's to Covent Garden in 1847 did so to protect their work opportunities elsewhere.[256]

An assessment of Costa's overall achievement will be made in Chapter 9. But his claim to attention rests essentially on his ability to meld disparate elements of reform into a single system and to embed it in the opera, the SHS and, less firmly, the Philharmonic. Although most of the ingredients of Costa's system were borrowed from others and were introduced piecemeal, it is right to treat the result as a system because he applied it systematically in all the institutions where he conducted. 'System' was the term used by the *Morning Post* to describe his method of management.[257] His ability to forge such a system chimed well with the trend towards greater professionalism that was affecting every aspect of the emerging music industry. Conducting – like music publishing, journalism and the management of concerts – was becoming a separate branch of an increasingly specialised business. The wider context was thus favourable to change and reform. Costa happened to be the man in that generation who had the authority, the personality and the longevity to systemize reforms in all of the main London orchestras. How far he was able to use his system to become a successful conductor is the subject of Chapter 5.

253 Claudio Abbado interview with BBC Radio 4, 10 Oct. 2011.

254 *Musical Times* (1 Jun. 1884), 321.

255 *ILN* (4 Jul. 1846), 11.

256 Tollebecque to *Times* (4 Jan. 1847). *Morning Chronicle* (5 Jan. 1847).

257 *Morning Post* (18 Apr. 1843).

Chapter 5
Costa as a Conductor

Contractual Authority

With few exceptions, all of the major conductors of the nineteenth century demanded a high degree of authority over their forces. As the first major figure who aspired to become a conductor without strong credentials as a composer (like Weber, Spohr, Mendelssohn and Balfe) or an instrumentalist (like Habeneck, Moscheles and Hallé), Costa was obsessively mindful of his authority. It was his most marked personal characteristic. The *Times* obituary commented that other conductors with similar musical skills could not 'govern in like manner' because they lacked his 'personal ascendancy'.[1] He was described as 'perhaps the severest martinet who ever wielded a baton' (Klein), who 'ruled everyone with a rod, or rather a baton, of iron' (Cowen).[2] All commentators touched on this theme, taking it positively or negatively according to their perspective. A fierce caricature of him in the magazine *Entr'acte* carried the caption: 'He will have his way' (Figure 5.1). Lesser conductors who lacked his 'iron rule', like Julius Benedict, were advised to acquire it.[3]

Costa was exigent about how his authority was defined in his written contracts at the opera house. Charles Santley recalled being reprimanded by him for accepting a part at Covent Garden on the basis of an oral understanding with Gye: 'never do business with the theatre without having all arrangements reduced to writing'.[4] Costa's six surviving contracts encapsulated the balance of power between him and his managers and show how much importance both sides attached to them.[5]

There is no contract from the 1830s, when Costa built up the core of his authority during Laporte's lax regime. But a letter from Laporte in 1838 shows Costa effectively running the company in the manager's absence.[6] One insight into the pressure on Costa to bring order to the house comes from his battle for the right to appoint the librarian/copyist. John Ella's diary recorded in 1836 that a rehearsal of *Beatrice di Tenda* was 'abruptly terminated … owing to the imperfect

---

1 *Times* obituary (30 Apr. 1884).

2 Herman Klein, *Thirty Years of Musical Life in London* (London: Heinemann, 1903), 54. Cowen, *My Art and My Friends*, 47.

3 *Morning Post* (26 Apr. 1859).

4 Santley, *Student and Singer*, 181.

5 Five are in the ROHA; the 1845 contract from Her Majesty's Theatre is from the personal collection of the late Tony Gasson. Texts in Goulden, Appendix A.

6 Costa to Laporte (28 Mar. 1838), RAM 2006.939.

Figure 5.1 Costa caricature (*The Entr'Acte,* 25 Feb. 1882). Andrew Saint, *A History of the Royal Opera House* (London, 1982) (courtesy of the Royal Opera House)

condition of the parts'. In the same year, Ella complained that much rehearsal time was lost while parts were corrected after Laporte replaced the resident copyist by 'persons totally unfit for the employ'.[7] By the time of his first extant contract (1845), 'all the personnel of the opera' were under 'the immediate command (*direction* in French) of Mr Costa'. But he was not satisfied until he forced Gye to write explicitly into his 1867 contract that he had the exclusive right to name the librarian/copyist. When Gye later had a dispute with the librarian, Horton, the latter blithely informed him that 'he considered Costa his master not me!!'[8]

Costa's 1845 contract with Lumley gave him extensive powers. Lumley undertook to 'give the necessary instructions so that Mr Costa's arrangements for

[7] Ella Diary, 17 Mar. and 24 Jun. 1836.

[8] Gye, 3 Mar. 1869.

the functioning of the Opera can be facilitated and respected by all the members of the Italian Opera'. Costa also had control over 'rehearsals in the theatre foyer and the *mise-en-scène*' (my italics).[9] The fact that he was a founder member of the new Covent Garden company, four years before Gye became manager-lessee, enabled him to buttress the authority he had built up under Lumley. Costa's unprecedented range of powers at Covent Garden gave him added status and reduced his vulnerability to the mismanagement which had traumatized his first years at the opera. They included a ban on outsiders attending piano rehearsals (to make better use of scarce rehearsal time), six weeks' notice of all new operas (to reduce the risk of last-minute programme changes) and control over the pay and contracts of the musicians (to underpin Costa's authority over them). Gye's attempts to wrest back some of these powers soured their relations in the 1860s and culminated in their split in 1869.

Status was especially important at the Philharmonic, where Costa had previously been black-balled and where the orchestra tended to follow its long-standing leaders rather than the part-time 'conductors' (Chapter 7). No Philharmonic contract has survived. But, before accepting the post, he insisted on having the authority he already enjoyed at the opera. 'Long experience in the Direction of the Opera has convinced me that, to ensure the perfect performance of any composition, the entire command of the band is necessary.'[10] His main conditions were that the post of leader should be abolished; performers should not be absent from rehearsals without his permission; and the directors should pledge to support him in the strict discipline of the orchestra.

The fact that Costa specified these conditions shows that they were not normal practice at the Philharmonic. This is confirmed by a *MW* report that '*In future* there will be no leader at these concerts … The direction of the orchestra will be vested solely in the conductor, as at the Opera House' (my italics).[11] Chorley saw it as a significant innovation that Costa had the powers that had been denied to Mendelssohn, Moscheles or Sterndale Bennett.[12] The directors tried to resist Costa's conditions and conceded only when he made clear that he would not accept the post otherwise. It appears, however, that they retained control over the Society's programmes and the contracts of 'the artists, vocal and instrumental', leaving Costa with the power to dismiss 'for misconduct or incompetence'.[13]

He was better placed to dictate terms at the SHS, where his Opera orchestra provided the nucleus of a largely amateur body. He made his habitual demand for 'supreme authority' and asked for assurance that:

---

9 Contract in French from the collection of the late Tony Gasson.

10 Costa to Hogarth (11 and 13 Aug. 1845), BL Loan 48. 13/7.

11 *MW* (7 May 1846), 112.

12 *Athenaeum* (3 Jan. 1846), 18.

13 *Morning Chronicle* (5 Jan. 1847).

> the amateur members of the orchestra would place themselves as unreservedly under the sway of his baton and would attend rehearsals as diligently as the professional members, over whom he was accustomed to exercise the strictest control.[14]

Total control at the festivals was of course essential, given the need to galvanize large numbers of amateurs from many different choirs (Chapter 7). By then his prestige and reputation was sufficient to over-awe the 3,500 musicians involved.

One important facet of Costa's battle for authority was his status on the playbills. This was a neuralgic issue, since the conductor's contribution to musical performances was not yet fully recognized. Opera and concert bills in the 1830s listed even junior performers ('Master Cooper, pupil of Spagnoletti'), and often identified the leader, designer, and occasionally even the stage manager and chorus master without mentioning the conductor. Costa was not included on the playbill, even when conducting his own works. For example, the playbill for *Der Freyschutz* (sic) on 9 May 1832 mentioned neither the conductor (Chélard) nor the composer and conductor of the ballet that followed (Costa). At benefit concerts and at Covent Garden from 1847, by contrast, he was usually listed as composer and conductor.

Many of the early conductors were martinets, but the extent of Costa's powers was unusual. He held his positions for unprecedentedly long periods and, for the first two decades, faced virtually no competition. It may have helped him that he could claim to be an operatic composer, in a country where Fétis claimed 'we find only arrangers'.[15] But, most importantly, his powers were underpinned by his daunting personality. After his departure, managers made sure that no conductor exercised the power that he enjoyed over the players' salaries and contracts.

Although the mechanical aspects of conducting considered in Chapter 4 continued to evolve for the rest of the century, the basic model was largely in place by the 1850s. That is not the case with the more artistic elements – style, beat, tempo and especially interpretation. It is difficult to make a fair assessment of the first generation of professional conductors, whose approach was seen as outdated in the self-consciously modern mood of the 1870s. This is especially true of Costa, whose style of conducting remained unchanged for the last three decades of his career while fashions changed radically. The effect of this on his reputation is examined in Chapter 8.

---

14 F.G. Edwards, *Musical Haunts of London* (London: Curwen, 1895), 25. Cox, *Musical Recollections*, vol. 2, 60.

15 Fétis, 'M. Fétis on the state of music in London', *Harmonicon* (1829), 276.

Style

Most of the composer-conductors of the early nineteenth century had an unostentatious style. Spohr conducted 'without the slightest contortion of countenance'; Weber was usually 'quiet and undemonstrative'; and Mendelssohn's 'movements were short and decided and generally hardly visible'.[16] The early English 'conductors' – Bishop, Smart, Benedict, Surman, – were tentative and unassertive. Eduard Hanslick described Sterndale Bennett as 'a slack and unenergetic conductor' and William Cusins as conducting 'very piously ... like an English clergyman'. Arthur Sullivan's conducting at the Leeds Festival (1884–98), was portrayed as 'quiet and unobtrusive in the orchestra. No gymnastic exercises, no stamping of the feet, no loudly expressed directions.'[17] Eduard Hanslick described him as 'altogether a drowsy fellow ... presiding in the comfortable recesses of a commodious armchair, his left arm lazily extended on the arm-rest, his right giving the beat in a mechanical way, his eyes fastened on the score'.[18] Shaw too commented on his lack of vigour and earnestness: 'one cannot help thinking that he would get a firmer grip sometimes if he took his gloves off'.[19] Of the next generation, Hallé and Manns were more effective but they too were not extravert. Hallé's style was described as 'precise and dignified (no acrobatics)'; and 'decisive, and ... free from exaggeration'.[20]

An exception to this relaxed gentlemanly style was given by the entrepreneur-conductors. An American reviewer described how Jullien 'not only rides the whirlwind and controls the storm, but ... furnishes the tempest, the thunder, and the lightning'.[21] Musard also went to extreme lengths to make himself the centre of the performance. He was described as magnetizing his audience, while his eyes flashed lightening and his gestures incarnated the music.[22]

Costa occupied a middle position between these two approaches. He was energetic and alert, but histrionics would have been contrary to his personality. Reticent by nature, he conducted undemonstratively. His manner was summed up by Henry Davison as 'the embodiment of calm collected will, without the least show and ostentation'.[23] Bennett remarked on his 'calm dignity'. The *MW* wrote that, in reducing English orchestras to order and discipline, 'he did not bluster.

[16] E.L. Gerber, *Lexikon der Tonkünstler* (Leipzig: 1790–92) and *Wiener Allgemeine Muzik Zeitung* (1822), 174, both cited in Carse, *Beethoven to Berlioz*, 341. Devrient, *Recollections*, vol. 2, 59.

[17] http://www.leedsfestivalchorus.co.uk/history/conductor-trouble.html.

[18] 'Dr Hanslick on Music in England' *Musical Times* (1 Sep. 1886), 518–20.

[19] *Shaw's Music*, vol. 1, 237.

[20] Algernon Forsyth, cited by Beale, *Charles Hallé, a Musical Life* (Aldershot: Ashgate, 2007), 39.

[21] *Courier and Enquirer* (30 Aug. 1853), quoted in Vera Brodsky Lawrence, *Strong on Music, Vol. 2: Reverberations* (Chicago: University of Chicago Press, 1995), 363.

[22] Pougin, cited by Southon, 66.

[23] Davison, *From Mendelssohn to Wagner*, 108. Bennett, *Forty Years*, 109.

A few quiet words and the matter in hand was settled without appeal'.[24] For the *Times* obituary, his hallmark was his quiet decisiveness: 'Calm, cool and full of resource, he evaded danger and got on the safe side of it before many conductors would have made up their mind what to do.'[25] The *Graphic* traced the secret of Costa's power to 'the calmness which is most calm at the moment of danger'.[26] This reassured his players: 'no one felt so free as when under Costa's baton, for he protected everyone, securing to each a fair field of display'.[27] Many commented on the contrast with Wagner, whose beat at the Philharmonic confused the players and who was virtually paralysed by 'Albert Hall stage fright' in 1873.[28]

The *Times* also commented on his presence of mind and dexterity, which enabled him to rescue performances by bringing the players or singers back together after a false entry.[29] The *ILN* noticed that, in Mendelssohn's *St Paul*, when some of the SHS chorus mistook the beat during the chorus 'This is Jehovah's temple':

> it was astonishing with what presence of mind and promptitude the conductor pulled through the difficulty and restored order … This result proves how much depends on the moral and intellectual influence of the musician who wields the baton.[30]

His decisiveness was praised by Stanford who, when struggling to rehearse a movement in triple time which ended with a long accelerando, was rescued by a prod from Costa and a whisper of 'one beat will do it'. The successful application of this advice was followed by another prod and 'a most un-Costa-like wink'.[31]

Davison linked his skill in bringing an orchestra or choir back into line to his 'amazingly quick ear, decision, promptitude'.[32] Costa was said to have stopped a rehearsal during a particularly loud section to enquire why one of the piccolos was not playing. This was a common theme in musical hagiography, quoted about Berlioz, Mendelssohn and many others. But it is significant that it was the Costa version which became a staple illustration for Victorian church sermons ('Are not two sparrows sold for a farthing?') The *Morning Post* remarked on 'his naturally quick and intelligent method of detecting, and above all of correcting, mistakes'.[33] Santley attributed this to his unusual habit in rehearsal of reading scores a bar behind the musicians: 'it is much easier to correct mistakes after hearing them

---

24 *Musical Times* (1 Jun. 1884), 321.
25 *Times* (30 Mar. 1884).
26 *Graphic* (24 Jun. 1871).
27 Haweis, *Pall Mall Gazette* (2 May 1884).
28 Klein, *Thirty Years*, 73.
29 *Times* (30 Mar. 1884).
30 *ILN* (19 Jan. 1850), 42. See also *Times* (12 Jan. 1850).
31 Stanford, *Pages from an Unwritten Diary*, 202–3.
32 *MW* (21 Aug. 1847), 538.
33 *Morning Post* (Mar. 1836).

than before'.[34] For performances, however, he appears to have relied on meticulous preparation and a good memory. The *MW* commented on his 'most retentive memory, if we may judge from the manner in which he has accompanied a variety of vocal compositions during the past season, without a copy'.[35]

Beat

One of the earliest French attempts to describe the role of an orchestral director highlighted the importance of a precise beat.[36] Many early conductors, such as Musard, used an exaggerated beat, often marking each note and stamping their feet – a legacy perhaps from the old *batteur de mesure* and the military bandmaster. One writer said that many went to Jullien's concerts 'more for the sake of watching his beat than hearing the music'.[37] Fétis advised conductors to 'avoid foot-stamping or tapping the baton, except when a single stroke will bring the band back to tempo'.[38] But for men like Costa, Chélard and Hummel, during the experimental phase of the 1830s, continuous time-beating was necessary in order to drill orchestras to play the increasingly complex scores which came into the repertoire.

As noted in Chapter 4, Costa began with an over-emphatic technique. A vigorous beat remained one of his trademarks. Stanford recalled that, since rehearsal time was short, much had to be left to chance and a 'belief in Field-Marshal Costa's right arm'.[39] In the 1830s, it was still seen as a virtue that Costa could 'indicate the due execution of the smallest fraction of a bar', just as critics marvelled that Musard's 'indefatigable bow marks every note, from whole notes to sixteenths'.[40] But as fashion and baton-practice evolved, he seems to have developed a more economical and relatively refined baton technique. By 1841 Lucas, one of the Philharmonic 'conductors' was being advised to learn from Costa and Mendelssohn that:

> There is no necessity for him to indicate with his baton every division of every bar in every composition … These musicians will teach him that to beat once in a bar is sufficient for all practical purposes.[41]

---

34 Santley, *Student and Singer*, 149.

35 *MW* (26 Aug. 1836), 175.

36 'Des qualités qu'on peut exiger d'un directeur d'orchestre d'opéra', Correspondance des professeurs et amateurs de musique, signed TDL, 1803. Cited in Southon, 349 et seq.

37 Wilhelm Kuhe, *Musical Recollections*, 88.

38 Fétis, *Manuel des compositeurs*, 127.

39 Stanford, *Pages from an Unwritten Diary*, 110.

40 *Le Ménestrel*, describing Musard in the 1830s, cited by Southon, 63.

41 *MW*, vol. 9, no. 118 (14 Jun. 1838), 111. *Morning Post* (18 May 1841).

As a specialist of the Italian repertoire, Costa was sensitive to the need for flexibility, especially in handling rallentandos and fermatas and in using different tempi for repeats. It took longer to convince the critics that he was not importing the bad habits of the Italian opera house into performances of the German classics. In an 1837 performance of Beethoven's *Adelaide*, he showed 'no idea of the style or spirit of the music … Mr Costa touched the keys as if they were red hot and as if he were accompanying a trifling Italian arietta'.[42] One of his most partisan opponents complained that, in an early concert at the Philharmonic, he took *A Midsummer Night's Dream* 'absurdly fast', showing that he was 'utterly unfitted by education' to perform the German classics.[43] But he gradually convinced most critics that he could handle the ultimate test of Beethoven's symphonies: the fifth ('new readings … evidently in perfect accordance with his intentions'), seventh ('many beauties previously little noticed')' and ninth ('from the admirable manner in which Costa brought out the author's intentions … the effect of the whole was much greater than on any former occasions').[44] Reviews of his first year at the Philharmonic stressed that, contrary to wide expectation, he was not 'metronomic'.

By the 1840s, Costa was being held up as the model for conductors. Moscheles was advised that: 'It is energy of mind that is required from the chief of an orchestra, and not energy of body'. A conductor should look not to the minutiae but to 'the general effect. He should be the orchestral master-spirit to echo the inspirations of the master mind … This is the secret of Costa's conductorship with the opera orchestra.'[45] In 1846, he was said to have 'established a system of conducting with the baton that is unequalled even in the most celebrated continental bands'.[46] The *Graphic* later wrote that he led 'by sympathy and power of character, not by the stick; indeed his baton hardly ever rises above his music; he seems merely to use it, as another would his forefinger, just to point or indicate'.[47] This suggests that his conducting style was evolving towards the modern concept of the baton as an extension of the arm. *New Grove* describes Jullien as 'the first truly stylised baton conductor who did not attain status as a composer.[48] But this title belongs more correctly to Costa. The hallmark of Jullien's conducting was not his baton technique but his combination of extravagant gesticulation with periods when he played an instrument taken up from nearby or sank exhausted in his ornate armchair. The *Examiner* contrasted Costa's 'usual firmness' with the 'stikulation

---

42 *Morning Chronicle* (28 Jul. 1837).

43 *Morning Post* (30 Jun. 1846).

44 *Daily News* (30 and 2 Jun. 1846 and 30 Mar. 1847).

45 *Morning Post* (25 Apr. 1843).

46 *Morning Post* (16 Mar. 1846).

47 *Graphic* (15 Apr. 1876).

48 *New Grove 2*, vol. 6, 266.

(sic) of the empiric Jullien school'.[49] Indeed, the first edition of *Grove* (1879–89) credited Costa with revolutionizing the method of beating time in England.[50]

In the opera house and the Philharmonic, Costa seems to have used what became the normal English on-the-note beat, rather than the habit, which became common in German opera houses, of beating just before the note.[51] For handling large-scale choral performances, however, he had to adopt a different technique, especially in the cavernous Crystal Palace, where there was an obvious time gap between Costa's baton and the entry of the choir. Here, after much experimenting, he gave a clearer and earlier signal, combining vigorous broad strokes of the baton with more fluid gestures of his left arm – another feature which anticipated later practice. With this and his efficient rehearsal regime, he achieved a novel level of precision without having to adopt the system of sub-conductors and Verbrugghen's electric metronome used, for example, by Berlioz.[52]

The first edition of *Grove* ascribed Costa's hold over his players in part to his long continuity with his orchestras. 'For many years there was not, in all England, an orchestral player of any reputation who did not comprehend the meaning of the slightest motion of his hand'.[53] In this he was contrasted with Julius Benedict (whose 'directions were not often attended to'), Henry Wylde (whose 'tremulous stick' was mocked by Gruneisen) and Joseph Surman (whose 'spasmodic gyrations' were described as 'perfectly inexplicable').[54] The main feature of Costa's beat was its simplicity and clarity. These were also features of Hallé and Manns, both of whom enjoyed similarly long tenure at orchestras with a low turnover.

Clarity was what most distinguished his nine years at the Philharmonic from Wagner's year there in 1855. Steady and unambiguous time-beating was seen as an essential virtue in a period when the simple beat patterns of Spohr's *Violin Schule* (1831) set the standard and when English orchestras still needed to be whipped into shape. But by the 1850s, when Berlioz was developing his more complex and fluid baton system and Liszt was merely marking the accents, the label of 'time-beater' became a term of abuse.[55] The suggestion that a conductor not only beat time but 'threshed' it – as Berlioz alleged against Costa – was becoming a common form of insult: Berlioz himself was accused by Wagner of sinking into 'the commonest rut of the vulgar time-beater'.[56] It was a charge which later damaged the reputations of all the early conductors. But, at the time, orchestras like the Philharmonic needed the precision and steadiness which Costa supplied, whereas his successor Wagner confused them with his fluid beat (Chapter 7). Shaw, often critical of Costa, praised

---

49 *Examiner* (25 Apr. 1863).

50 *Grove 1* under 'Conducting'.

51 *New Grove 2*, vol. 6, 272.

52 Cairns, *Berlioz*, 2 vols (London: Andre Deutsch, 1989 and 1999), vol. 2, 562.

53 *Grove 1* under 'Conducting'.

54 *Morning Post* (4 Nov. 1848) and (26 Apr. 1859). 'Tremulous stick', *ILN* (12 Jun. 1852).

55 Berlioz, Supplement to *Traité* (1855). On Liszt, see *Figaro* (18 Feb. 1843).

56 Wagner, *My Life*, 628; and Ganz, *Berlioz in London*, 108.

'the pointed steady unwavering beat of Costa who … never allowed the threads of the orchestral loom to become entangled'.[57]

One important aspect of baton-conducting, which the traditional Musical Director could not achieve from his seat at the keyboard, was the ability to communicate. This was a marked feature of the conducting of Mendelssohn, who was said to communicate 'as if by an electric fluid' and 'foreshadowed with his eye every spiritual nuance of the composition'.[58] The *ILN* critic wrote that Costa was the only conductor, apart from Habeneck, who possessed:

> the extraordinary faculty … of communicating his own feelings to his troops, inspiring them with his zeal, encouraging the timid, rebuking the too daring, rousing the sluggish … as if the spirit of the composer himself were animating the masses.[59]

His ability to convey his intentions to the players no doubt owed much to the fact that, from his first day at the Philharmonic, he faced them rather than the audience. This gave him the eye contact that later conductors such as Stokowski and Nikisch described as critical. It also explains what several writers identified as his 'magnetic flash' (Haweis), his 'special, perhaps magnetic, power' (Davison), his 'extraordinary magnetic control over his singers' (Klein).[60] At the Philharmonic:

> The effect of Signor Costa's presence seemed to have magnetised the whole orchestra. A wave of his arm and the expression he required were simultaneous. The secret of conveying his own feelings to the orchestra under his control has seldom been more thoroughly exemplified by a conductor.[61]

A fair judgement would be that Costa provided the clear, even heavy, beat that English orchestras and choruses most needed between 1830 and 1850. By the end of this period, the *Daily News* cautioned against his 'tendency to mark the points and the effects of light and shade rather too strongly'.[62] His four-square technique, essential for galvanizing the grand choral festivals, no doubt contributed to his later image as a metronomic time-beater. The *Times* obituary, commenting on his 'singularly decisive' beat, observed that 'he may sometimes have gone too far in this direction'.[63] Herman Klein considered that Joseph Barnby, the other major choral conductor of the period, scored over Costa because, although equally

---

57 *Shaw's Music*, vol. 1, 352; vol. 2, 322.

58 W.A. Lampadius, *Felix Mendelssohn* (Leipzig: 1886), 155.

59 *ILN* (17 Feb. 1849), 101.

60 Haweis, *Pall Mall Gazette* (2 May 1884); Davison, *From Mendelssohn to Wagner*, 109: Klein, *Musicians and Mummers*, 133.

61 *MW* (21 Mar. 1846), 131.

62 *Daily News* (12 Jan.1850).

63 *Times* (30 Apr. 1884).

precise, he was 'not quite so relentless in his beat; a trifle more plastic'.[64] But Klein credited Costa with having a perfect legato: 'he had the secret – which Richter also possessed – of absolute continuity, whilst indicating to a hair's breadth where the beat began and ended'.[65]

Tempo and Volume

Another feature on which fashion changed in the middle years of the century concerned tempo. Virtually all of the early conductors were criticized for setting too fast a pace. Fétis accused Habeneck in 1827 of too rapid tempi at the *Concerts Spirituels*.[66] English orchestras too were generally described as too brisk. Wagner claimed that, when he took over the Philharmonic from Costa in 1855, Mendelssohn's maxim 'chi va presto va sano' had become a 'fixed tradition'. This criticism implicitly extended to Costa, who had directed the orchestra for the previous nine years: 'The music flowed like water out of a fountain; to hold back was unthinkable; every *allegro* finished as a *presto* ... The orchestra played everything *mezzoforte;* a genuine *forte*, a genuine *piano* was never heard.'[67]

Costa's association with fast tempi became something of a joke. The *Examiner* observed that 'Homer sometimes nods and Costa occasionally gallops.'[68] Sterndale Bennett wrote sarcastically that, if Costa took over the Philharmonic, 'the only advantage would be that we might hear the whole of Beethoven's symphonies in one night and still have time to spare for supper'.[69] One critic reported that he took Meyerbeer's *L'Africaine* 'at the usual racing pace' and made the work on curtailing it almost unnecessary'.[70] Meyerbeer, who praised Costa's conducting of *Le prophète*, nonetheless felt that he took it 'too fast, as is the custom in England'.[71] Even supporters like Chorley accused him of pushing on the orchestra with so much vigour that an *accelerando* became 'an unintelligible *prestissimo*'.[72] The *Times* critic, presumably Davison, wrote that Costa's 'only fault as a conductor ... was a tendency ... to make his orchestra go faster than was conveniently practical'.[73]

Apologists for Costa argued that a brisk tempo was the only way to overcome the tendency of large choirs and orchestras to drag the time at the big festivals.[74]

64 Klein, *Musicians and Mummers*, 134.
65 Klein, *Musicians and Mummers*, 134.
66 Fétis, 'De l'execution', 248.
67 'What goes fast goes well.' Wagner, *On Conducting*, 59.
68 *Examiner* (31 Mar. 1849).
69 Bennett to Davison (24 Nov. 1836), Davison, *From Mendelssohn to Wagner*, 30.
70 *Pall Mall Gazette* (16 May 1865), Issue 84.
71 Quoted in Spark, *Musical Memories*, 57.
72 *Athenaeum* (2 May 1835), 339.
73 *Times* (12 Jan. 1850 and 16 Mar. 1847).
74 *Daily News* (19 May 1857).

The compensating benefit was that he brought 'a plain, bold and decided outline, filled in with vivid colours … He was never seen to more advantage than when riding on the whirlwind and directing the storm.'[75] Speed was one aspect of his ability to infuse his orchestra with 'an irresistible rhythm and real dynamic energy'.[76] It was this energy (what the *Examiner* called his 'gusto') that enabled him to re-animate the orchestra when he took over Spohr's *Faust* from the elderly composer.[77]

The other common complaint about the early conductors was that they allowed their orchestras, now larger and equipped with more powerful brass and woodwind, to play too loudly. Habeneck in Paris and Spontini in Berlin were regularly criticized for this. It was a charge which also attached to the next generation – Liszt, Berlioz and Wagner. Noise was a charge frequently associated with Costa and Jullien. Reviewing Rossini's *Le siège de Corinthe* in 1837, the *Examiner* commented that:

> there is little but braying of trumpets, beating of drums, clashing of cymbals: the whole of the orchestra playing fortissimo; the whole of the performers, principals and chorus, roaring like Bottoms's nightingales … Signor Costa … has become altogether a nuisance that must positively be abated.[78]

The *Times* also complained during this period about Costa's 'predilection for the noisy'; Costa had not yet learnt the 'nice distinction between loudness and noise'.[79]

Later in his career, Costa showed that he was capable of extracting *piano* as well as *fortissimo* effects. Hogarth noted that, at his first Philharmonic concert, 'such a *piano* was preserved that the voice of the singer was fully sustained and not drowned as formerly'.[80] In 1848, Hogarth remarked that the Philharmonic players were in seventh heaven because he had 'established that a real *piano* was to be obtained from an English band'.[81] Critics and soloists regularly praised his skill in adapting the orchestra to the needs of the singer. The *Morning Post* remarked that 'Every night you see his eye fixed on the singers; instead of making the orchestra drag them on, he attends upon them – nurses their voices, conceals their besetting defects as well as their casual errors.'[82] A rare case when he allowed the orchestra to overshadow Adelina Patti was noted with surprise: '(that we should have lived to hint at a fault in that most perfect of conductors!)'.[83]

---

75 *MW* (3 May 1884), 274–5.

76 Haweis, *Pall Mall Gazette* (2 May 1884); Davison, *From Mendelssohn to Wagner*, 109; 'dynamic energy' in Klein, *Musicians and Mummers*, 133.

77 *Examiner* (29 Apr. 1838). *ILN* (7 Aug. 1852), 98.

78 *Examiner* (15 Jun. 1834).

79 *Times* (26 Mar. 1838 and 12 Apr. 1837).

80 *ILN* (21 Mar. 1846), 193.

81 *ILN* (4 Jul. 1846), 11.

82 *Morning Post* (4 Aug. 1843).

83 *Examiner* (15 Jun. 1861).

Because of his tight control over the orchestra, Costa was not the worst offender in what was musically a noisy age. One critic reported that, at a concert by the Amateur Musical Society under Negri, the brass played with an 'overpowering loudness, in which the same gentlemen would not have indulged with the fear of Costa before their eyes'.[84] But overall, Costa remained, in Joseph Bennett's words, 'a noisy conductor'. 'That potent chief agreed with his brother-imperator Napoleon the Great in believing that Providence favoured the biggest battalions.'[85] Wagner and Stanford both commented that his orchestras mainly played *mezzoforte*.[86] The *MW* contrasted Costa's hostility to *piano* markings with the real *pianissimos* that Berlioz obtained from the New Philharmonic.[87] This was increasingly seen as a fault by critics who judged conductors on their ability to persuade large orchestras to play softly.

At the festivals, where volume was regarded as one aspect of the sublime, grandiose performances were a matter of national pride (Chapter 7). In a comment typical of the period, the *Examiner* commented that the loss of nuance at the Handel Festival was more than compensated by the overpowering sound and effect.[88] Here, as elsewhere, Costa was a man of his times. Writing to his librettist Bartholomew's wife with tickets for a concert at Exeter Hall in 1862, Costa stressed the size of the orchestra she would hear: 288 strings and 100 woodwind.[89] Spark noted Costa's enthusiasm for the basses at the Bradford Festival 'like a troop of organ pedal pipes'.[90] As he came to symbolize the mid-Victorian penchant for the gargantuan, this became another respect in which Costa, as the last survivor from the world of the 1830s, became the personification of its musical excesses.

Interpretation

Costa's interpretations were the product of his period. At the height of his career, in the 1850s, his performances in the opera house and concert hall were seen as revelatory in their precision and discipline. He brought this discipline to the large-scale choral performances at the big festivals. But he later fell foul of two conflicting ideologies.

First, as an opera conductor, he offended the literal school associated with Mendelssohn, which treated the score as a 'finished' work. One of his main tasks as Musical Director was to adapt scores to the forces available and to

84 *Daily News* (4 Feb. 1851).

85 *Musical Times* (1 Jun. 1897), 372.

86 Wagner, *On Conducting*, 59. Stanford, *Interludes, Records and Reflections*, 32; and *Pages from an Unwritten Diary*, 203–4.

87 *MW* (27 Mar. 1852).

88 *Examiner* (4 Jul. 1874).

89 Costa to Mrs Bartholomew (13 Aug. 1862), RCMA 3012.

90 Spark, *Musical Memoirs*, 3.

local tastes. This involved shortening overlong operas and oratorios, substituting arias into different scores, and re-orchestrating older works to accommodate new instruments. Such tampering was, however, beginning to be regarded as an aesthetic sin, especially in the case of German orchestral works and the operas of Mozart.[91] Costa was less guilty in this respect than many of his contemporaries, especially Bishop and Bochsa (who arranged Beethoven's Symphony no. 3 for ballet at the King's Theatre in 1829). He was often credited with restoring the scores of Rossini operas; and he refused to edit *Don Giovanni* when Gye insisted on casting Mario as a tenor Don (and Ronconi as a baritone Leporello). But, partly because of his dominant position in London, he attracted an undue share of critical censure for London malpractices. As the novel discipline and precision which he brought to the opera house and the Philharmonic came to be taken for granted, critics like Chorley and Davison increasingly fastened on Costa's every deviation from the score. Berlioz held Costa principally responsible for London practices in this respect (Chapter 8).

Costa's second ideological offence, which he shared with most of his contemporaries (including Hallé and Manns), was against Wagner's notions of interpretative flexibility and tempo modification based on *tempo rubato* and 'elastic beat' (*elastischer Takt*). Wagner, who had been astonished by the precision of Spontini and Habeneck, later dismissed them and 'the elegant tribe' of Mendelssohnian 'music brokers' as cold and uninspired for failing to penetrate the score's deeper intentions.[92] He predictably complained that Costa's Philharmonic played in a brisk Mendelssohnian style and lacked the fire of inspiration ('le feu sacré'); it was a 'skilled machine which I can never really get going'.[93] To his wife Minna, he described it as too machine-like – 'like Geneva music-boxes'. At the time, in the mid-1850s, this would have been taken in England as a compliment. The idea that a conductor should give novel interpretations beyond what appeared in the score had little traction during Costa's hey-day, when clarity and precision were the supreme virtues, and comparisons with Mendelssohn and Habeneck were still a mark of praise. Even at the end of his career, Costa's matter-of-fact approach to scores was regarded as typical of his period.

The *MW* obituary simply observed that:

> Sir Michael made no pretence to the elaboration and finesse which have come in with a passion for 'readings' – in other words for attempts at setting upon the music of the composer the stamp of the conductor … If he took in hand a

[91] José Bowen, 'The History of Remembered Innovation: Tradition and Its Role in the Relationship between Musical Works and Their Performances', *The Journal of Musicology*, vol. 11, no. 2 (1993), 140.

[92] Wagner, *On Conducting*, 50–56. On Hallé, see *Times* (11 Mar. 1888).

[93] Wagner to Liszt (16 May 1855). Cited in Richard Wagner, *Selected Letters*, ed. Stewart Spencer and Barry Millington (London: J.M. Dent and Sons, 1987), 341.

> symphony of Beethoven, he presented it just as it lay in the score, reproducing the master's recorded ideas, without seeking to put upon them a gloss of his own.[94]

Joseph Bennett, a generation later, commented that:

> No one … will ever write a chapter on Costa's 'readings' … His career was practically over when the new style of interpretative conductor, charged with finding new ideas in old scores, made his appearance. Costa had no such mission. He read the music as he saw it, without trying to read into it.[95]

But after his death, as the ideological war about conducting intensified, Wagner's doctrines and the prestige of the brilliant succession of conductors who developed them (Richter, von Bülow, Nikitsch, Hermann Levi, Felix Mottl and Anton Seidl) swept away Costa and the older school. Reflecting the Wagnerian spirit of the 1890s, Shaw damned the playing of Costa's orchestra as 'cold, brazen, correct'.[96] When Grove's *Dictionary* was revised in 1904–10, Vaughan Williams wrote that the Mendelssohnian style (which held *tempo rubato* 'in abhorrence' and aimed for no more than 'a fairly correct performance') was 'diametrically opposed' to that of Wagner (where 'correctness is the minimum from which [the conductor] starts').[97] The implication was that the earlier school was aesthetically out-of-date.[98] It was not until well into the twentieth century that this doctrinal bias began to be modified (Chapter 9).

The Protocol and Metaphors of Conducting

The rituals of conducting are a comparatively recent addition to Western art music. In 1830, there was no 'common practice' for baton technique, rehearsal methodology or podium manner. The composer-conductors had their own personal approaches, which their prestige enabled them to impose. But the professional conductors needed to show that they were making a contribution that justified interposing themselves between the audience and the orchestra. In 1843, the *Morning Post* wrote that two-thirds of the audience still saw Costa as 'nothing more than a man fancifully beating time with a stick'.[99]

This challenge, which eluded the old-style 'conductors' like Smart and Bishop, was first met in England by Costa and Jullien. It helped that they could show that, in addition to being professional conductors, they possessed other musical

94 *MW* (3 May 1884), 274–5.
95 Joseph Bennett, *Forty Years*, 53.
96 *Shaw's Music*, vol. 2, 102.
97 *Grove 2*, vol. 1, 402.
98 For a fuller discussion, Goulden, Chapter 9.
99 *Morning Post* (4 Aug. 1843).

qualifications. They made much of their status as composers. Jullien often included his own recent gavottes or polkas in his programmes and it was an important part of Costa's title that he was 'Conductor, Musical Director and *Composer*' (my italics). In addition, Costa performed at the pianoforte and Jullien played a range of instruments that he would snatch from nearby players. They also contributed, though in very different ways, to the evolving protocol of conducting.

First, the conductor began to be seen as representing the composer (who appeared less frequently in the proliferating opera houses and concert halls) and as mediating the score (which was becoming sacrosanct). He thus became an essential part of each performance – what Derrida later described as a supplement: 'someone in direct contact with lofty musical ideals that are unleashed at the flick of a stick, yet because they are mediated through him they are more contingent than they might otherwise seem'.[100] As the composer was increasingly elevated to the status of musical genius, this too boosted the image of the conductors who presented their works. Although Liszt wrote that 'the genuine task of a conductor consists in making himself manifestly superfluous', the trend was in the direction of making him the centrepiece of the performance.[101] Habeneck came to stand as the mediator of the emerging canon of orchestral classics; Costa was less well-placed to do this in the concert hall, but he credibly took on the role for the opera and choral works most associated with him (Rossini, Meyerbeer, Mendelssohn, Handel and later Verdi).

Second, the conductor began to assume a shamanic role, as the person who brought the inert notes on the page into musical existence. He acquired, in Roger Scruton's apt words, 'the charisma of his priestly office', managing his anonymously dressed players to present the works of absent composers to a passive and now silent audience.[102] Conductors exploited the notion that they, rather than the orchestra, were creating the music. Both Berlioz and Habeneck were described as 'playing' their orchestras. Using a metaphor which became one of the great musical clichés, the *MW* in 1847 remarked that Costa extracted every nuance of expression 'as though the entire orchestra were but one instrument, on which *he himself performed alone*' (my italics).[103]

Third, as the expanding audience struggled to understand what they were hearing, the conductor became the person who could demonstrate the music visually. More complex scores created a demand not only for programme notes and journalist-critics but also for conductors who could interpret them visibly as well as audibly. The conductor's use of body language and gesture supplied what the French conductor Deldevez later called 'le language du chef d'orchestre … une sorte de

---

100 Alastair Williams, *Constructing Musicology* (Aldershot: Ashgate, 2001), 38.

101 'A letter on conducting' (1853), cited in L. Ramann , ed., *Franz Liszt als Kunstler und Mensch*, trans. E Cowdrey, 3 vols (London: 1882), 232.

102 Roger Scruton, *The Aesthetics of Music* (Oxford: Clarendon Press, 1999), 439.

103 *MW* (10 Apr. 1847), 236–8; my italics.

langue muette'.[104] The conductor thus enabled the audience to witness as well as hear the performance of the music. D'Ortigue noticed that Habeneck's conducting involved an element of 'pantomime' and others compared him to the leading French stage actor, Talma.[105] As Davison noticed, people went to see Jullien as well as to hear him – 'the picturesque conductor, who … not only conducted but acted'.[106]

Fourth, the conductor took on some of the personality cult which had earlier been exploited not only by the instrumental virtuosi but also by composers who, like Mozart, Beethoven, Paer and Hummel, had put on concerts entirely of their own music. The professional conductor became a virtuoso himself and gradually emerged – like the opera singers– as a celebrity. Jullien achieved this through his florid dress, his extravagant podium manner and his acceptance of a jewel-encrusted baton on a tasselled cushion. Although the cognoscenti were repelled by this exhibitionism, it helped to impress the gullible that conducting was a vital part of music-making. Costa, the antithesis of the flamboyant Jullien, learnt to avoid such extravagance, which provoked mirth rather than respect. Reports of the opening of the Albert Hall in 1871 made fun of Costa's entanglement in his blue and gold court dress with an opera cloak and a sword. Instead, he embodied mid-Victorian notions of decorum and power to demonstrate his ability to control unprecedented forces with a minimum of gesture and fuss. He was a box-office draw in his own right, receiving curtain calls and bouquets at the opera.[107] His portraits were widely reproduced; and female members of the Birmingham Festival choir petitioned for his gloves to be cut up as mementoes.

Finally, conductors like Costa, Hallé and Manns, who commanded their orchestras for long periods, came to replace the leader as the personification of the orchestra. Even though he had no stake in the business, Costa was seen as the manager of his labour force, and thus symbolized the entrepreneurial businessman and the disciplining powers of modern capitalism.[108] In a way that would have been unimaginable in England a generation earlier, Costa's players were referred to as 'his' orchestra and even his 'myrmidons'.[109] This concentration of power affected the ways in which music was performed. It favoured more regimented playing, in contrast with the freer and more collegial style of the earlier decades of the century. It reined in the habits of ornamentation and improvisation which had been a prominent feature right up to the careers of Liszt and Mendelssohn. It also shaped the metaphors associated with conducting.

---

[104] Deldevez, *L'Art du chef d'orchestre*, 99.

[105] Southon, 116 and 127.

[106] Davison, *From Mendelssohn to Wagner*, 109.

[107] *Daily News* (23 Aug. 1847).

[108] Richard Leppert, 'Cultural contradiction, idolatry, and the piano virtuoso: Franz Liszt', in *The Sight of Sound: Music, Representation, and the History of the Body* (Berkley: University of California Press, 1993), 267.

[109] *MW* (21 May 1853), 315. *Morning Post* (20 Apr. 1843).

As the orchestra took shape in the eighteenth century, it was compared in particular to two metaphorical source domains: metaphors of command associated with the military and creative metaphors linked to civil society.[110] The composer-conductors combined elements of both since they were creative as well as commanding. Gounod, an occasional composer-conductor, saw himself as 'the driver of the coach'.[111] Berlioz viewed the orchestra as 'an immense keyboard, played by the conductor under the direction of the composer', with the players reduced to the status of instruments or machines.[112] The professional conductors too began to attract the metaphor of the performer who 'played' his anonymous orchestra in order to convert the composer's silent notation into vibrant sound.

For Costa, as for Spontini and Habeneck, the military was the metaphor of choice. It appealed to an audience which viewed performers in Napoleonic terms and was impressed by their ability to command large forces.[113] It favoured the Musical Director (with his phallic baton or 'truncheon'[114]) rather than the leader (who was, metaphorically speaking, merely a subordinate commander). Costa quoted the military analogy when he told the Philharmonic directors that, 'without the aid of good troops, no commander could be successful'.[115] Military images associated with Costa became one of the clichés of music-writing. He was 'a splendid drill-sergeant' (Grove), 'General Costa' (*ILN*), 'a Wellington' (*Musical Times*), 'GCO on his own territory' with 'the grip of a Field Marshal' (Stanford).[116] Explaining to Gye why dual conductorship was a bad idea, he used the metaphors of clockwork and the military: 'As well might it be expected that a clock should go with two springs or a battalion be commanded by two colonels.'[117]

Costa also attracted some newer metaphors. He was described as the 'great intelligence' and 'mastermind' of the Philharmonic; a scientist who 'set himself to raise the English orchestra from the condition of a concourse of atoms to that of a homogeneous body, subordinate to one will'; even as the leader of the players' trade union.[118] But the military metaphor predominated and continued to be applied to him long after conductors like von Bülow, Richter and Nikisch were attracting metaphors from nature with overtones of creativity and artistic interpretation.[119] By his last decade, Costa was out of date metaphorically as well as artistically.

---

110 Spitzer/Zaslaw, 515–18.

111 Quoted in Lydia Goehr, *The Imaginary Musical Museum* (Oxford: Oxford University Press, 2007), 275.

112 Berlioz, Supplement to *Traité*, 293. Southon, 156.

113 Elliott W. Galkin, *A History of Orchestral Conducting in Theory and Practice* (New York: Pendragon Press, 1989), xxix.

114 *Morning Chronicle* (15 May 1837).

115 *MW* (4 Jul. 1846), 309. Also *ILN* (4 Jul. 1846), 11.

116 Graves, *George Grove*, 125; ILN (21 May 1846), 193; Stanford, *Pages from an Unwritten Diary*, 206; *Musical Times* (1 Jun. 1884), 321–3.

117 ROHC, Costa to Gye corr. (27 Jan. 1869).

118 *ILN* (7 Feb. 1846), 98; Bennett, *Forty Years*, 51.

119 For the change in musical metaphors see Spitzer/Zaslaw, 520.

Comparisons with Other Orchestras and Conductors

In the absence of extant recordings or of a reliable performance tradition, it is difficult to form an assessment of conductors from music criticism and memoirs of the period which, when they mention conducting at all, are often partisan or formulaic. But there are several broad comparisons that can be made between Costa's and other orchestras, and between him and other conductors.

Costa's orchestra at Her Majesty's Theatre (1832–46) was judged superior to the Philharmonic under Bishop, Smart, Loder and Moscheles, despite the fact that the two orchestras largely shared the same players. The *MW* wrote of the Philharmonic's 'inferiority in discipline and musical intelligence to the admirable corps of foreign and native talent comprising the Italian Opera band'.[120] It even expressed the heretical opinion that Costa's opera orchestra was better structured to perform the Overture to *A Midsummer Night's Dream* than the Philharmonic under Mendelssohn himself.[121] Only after Costa's second season at the Philharmonic did the *ILN* consider that it could 'compete in some degree with his matchless band at Covent Garden'.[122]

After Costa moved to Covent Garden in 1847, his orchestra there was generally described as better than the band he left behind at Her Majesty's (Chapter 6). He had of course taken many of the best players with him, but he was also more skilful than Balfe in building up and retaining good players. It became a common boast that the Covent Garden band was 'the best ever assembled in England'.[123] Even Berlioz, a friend of Balfe, admitted that the Covent Garden orchestra and chorus were superior to those of Her Majesty's.[124] In 1862, the *Times* wrote that 'To compare the *Huguenots* and *Robert le diable* of Her Majesty's Theatre with [those] at another house would, under actual circumstances, be absurd.'[125] When Gye and Mapleson amalgamated their two orchestras in 1869, Covent Garden's players provided all five of the principal players.[126] When Costa later moved from Gye's to Mapleson's company in 1871, Shaw remarked that 'he had of course taken the orchestral supremacy with him'.[127]

Costa's orchestras and choirs were distinguished from others in enjoying a new profile as one of the opera house's main assets, though never at the high level of the star singers. Costa acted on the premise that, as he explained to Gye when they separated: 'The orchestra and chorus are the two primary elements of an

120 *MW* (19 May 1839), 23.

121 *MW* (24 Apr. 1845), 181.

122 *ILN* (1 Jul. 1848), 424.

123 Cox, *Musical Recollections*, vol. 2, 168.

124 *Feuilleton* (1 Jul. 1851) on 'l'insuffisance d'une exécution à peine ébauchée' of *L'Enfant prodigue*.

125 *Times* (1 Sep. 1862).

126 Gye 15 Feb. 1869.

127 *Shaw's Music*, vol. 1, 498.

operatic performance.'[128] This was a controversial assertion, but the critics – and, significantly the rival manager, Lumley – came to see the Covent Garden orchestra and chorus as the mainstay of the house.[129] There are frequent comments from the 1840s that Costa's orchestra was the best part of the evening, often redeeming mediocre performances.[130] Acute amateurs like George Eliot began to single out the virtues of the orchestra: 'I went to hear the *Huguenots* on Saturday evening. It was a rich treat, Mario, Grisi and Formes and that finest of orchestras under Costa.'[131]

It is more difficult to assess how well Costa's orchestras compared with equivalents on the Continent. English travellers betray either their musical inferiority complex or an anxiety to show that England was no longer a Land Without Music. Visiting foreigners, aware of these complexes, are often unduly polite, at least in public. Allowing for the bias on both sides, it appears that until the 1840s the orchestras of Her Majesty's and the Philharmonic were judged inferior to the leading Continental ones (the Paris Conservatoire, Meiningen, Vienna, Leipzig). But from the late 1840s Costa's bands were rated among the best in Europe.

In 1840, the *Morning Post* wrote that the Paris Opera orchestra under Habeneck was infinitely beyond any of the English theatres 'except, of course, the Italian Opera house band which, under Costa's baton, I still consider on the whole unrivalled'.[132] After a continental tour in 1846, John Ella ranked Covent Garden third after Paris and Vienna (but ahead of Berlin, Munich and Leipzig).[133] Following the 1848 revolutions, standards fell at the theatre orchestras of Paris, Berlin, Vienna, Munich and Frankfurt and, according to Chorley, foreigners began to speak of Covent Garden's 'superior brilliancy, its amazing readiness in reading at sight, and its entire subjugation to its conductor'.[134] In 1863, the *Times* claimed that Covent Garden had 'the foremost orchestral company in Europe'.[135] A decade later, the *Morning Post* judged that the Vienna Opera orchestra was unequalled except for that of Covent Garden.[136] Costa's orchestra was regularly compared favourably with that of the *Théâtre-Italien* in Paris, which Berlioz frequently denounced.[137] In 1848, the *ILN* critic contrasted the Covent Garden orchestra in *La donna del lago* ('unprecedented') with that of the *Théâtre-Italien* ('indeed terrible').[138] A year earlier, the Paris critic Fiorentino, attacking a production at the *Théâtre-Italien* in Paris, commented that 'To appreciate *Don Giovanni* one

---

128 ROHC, Costa to Gye corr. (27 Jan. 1869).

129 Chorley, *Musical Recollections*, 333. Lumley, *Reminiscences*, ix.

130 *Times* review of *Masaniello* (27 Jul. 1849).

131 Eliot to Charles Bray (5 May 1852), Haight, *Letters*, vol. 2, 25.

132 *Morning Post* (20 May 1840).

133 *Athenaeum* (21 Feb. 1846), 130.

134 Chorley, *Musical Recollections*, 333.

135 *Times* (3 Aug. 1863).

136 *Morning Post* (10 Feb. 1873).

137 For example, article in *Berliner Allgemeine musikalische Zeitung* (27 Jun. 1829).

138 *ILN* (29 Apr. 1848), 280.

should have heard the Royal Italian Opera in London, the magnificent finale of the first act, with a triple chorus, conducted by Costa, with its numerous chorus and a dazzling *mise-en-scène*.'[139] In the 1870s, the *Morning Post* critic judged Costa's last orchestra at Drury Lane as superior to that of the Vienna Opera.[140]

These are selective and partial witnesses. The consensus on the Continent would not have placed Costa's players above the best foreign orchestras. What is significant is that the only English orchestras and choirs held up as comparable with those in Paris and Vienna were those run by Costa and that his musicians generated a pride which would previously have been unimaginable. The other conclusion from the admittedly unreliable evidence is that the three main musical bodies in Victorian London – the Opera, the Philharmonic and the SHS – achieved and maintained a higher level of discipline and efficiency under Costa's control.

The sources for conductors are if anything even more partisan, tinged as they are by personal rivalries: for example, von Bülow's harsh criticisms of Manns and Richter, Weingartner's of von Bülow, Wagner's of Mendelssohn and many others. Moreover, many of the qualities claimed for Costa were common clichés of musical writing about conductors – as in Bruno Walter's description of his first experience of hearing von Bülow: 'It became at once clear to me that it was this one man who was producing the music, that he had transformed those hundred performers into his instrument and that he was playing it as a pianist played the piano.'[141]

The inferiority of the main London-based 'semi-conductors' of the older generation (Smart, Bishop, Potter, Moscheles) has been described in Chapter 3. In relation to conductors of his own generation, Costa was, at least for his first three decades, in a class apart. His monopoly of the main rostrums meant that few contemporaries had a proper opportunity to conduct, which may indeed have encouraged others to set up elsewhere – Zeugheer Hermann in Liverpool and Hallé in Manchester. Shaw commented that Costa's undisputed 'foremost place' was achieved within the 'very thin ranks' of English conductors.[142] Henry Wylde, who directed the New Philharmonic from 1858 to 1879, was derided by Berlioz as well as British critics.[143] Julius Benedict conducted with his head buried in his score, rarely gave a cue until it was too late and lacked 'the magnetic power and sense of ensemble that should be the primary gifts of a great conductor'.[144] Cusins, though Master of the Queen's Music, was described as 'an extraordinarily bad conductor' (Shaw) and as lacking 'the necessary working skills regarding

139 Quoted in *MW* (6 Nov. 1847), 702.

140 *Morning Post* (10 Feb. 1873).

141 Bruno Walter, *Theme and Variations*, trans. J.A. Galston (New York: 1946), 39.

142 *Shaw's Music*, vol. 1, 169.

143 *ILN* (12 Jun. 1852). *Morning Chronicle* (21 Mar. 1859).

144 Klein, *Thirty Years*, 13. See also *Examiner* (29 Apr. 1838). Klein, *Musicians and Mummers*, 90.

the orchestra' (Joachim).[145] Alfred Mellon was considered by some to be 'second only to Costa' but his sphere was the less prominent one of the ballet and English Opera.[146] Sterndale Bennett was recognized as a serious musician; the violinist Dando said that the ideal would be to combine 'Costa beating the time and Bennett telling him how to do it'.[147] But Bennett was primarily a teacher and composer; 'on the rostrum he was neither powerful not inspiring'.[148]

One test of Costa's conducting is that critics frequently noted that the standard of performance dropped on the rare occasions when deputies stood in for him.[149] Davison wrote that 'Our orchestral performers will not pay the proper attention to other conductors', though he blamed this in part on Costa's 'despotic monopoly'.[150] Shaw commented that 'If Sir Michael Costa could only realise the manner with which his orchestra takes advantage of his absence, he would probably never entrust M Sainton with the baton again.'[151] There was a fall in orchestral standards at the Philharmonic and Covent Garden after Costa's departure. The *Daily News* noted that, when the opera players performed at the Liverpool Festival under Hermann, they were 'not quite themselves in the absence of Costa'.[152]

Apart from brief appearances by foreign composers, Costa had no serious rival on the opera scene. Balfe's less impressive record is discussed in Chapter 6. Conducting was not his forte and his relative weakness is clear from Lumley's efforts to persuade Costa and Verdi to replace him at Her Majesty's. Of the other opera conductors, Arditi was certainly the best stand-in for Costa at Covent Garden, described as 'a very good conductor, second indeed perhaps only to Sir Michael Costa'.[153] But the other Italians who shared the rostrum with him – Enrico Bevignani, Auguste Vianesi and Li Calsi – were dismissed as very indifferent.[154] As late as 1891, Shaw held up Costa in order to berate conductors like Arditi, Bevignani, Vianesi, Logheder and Mancinelli, who made him think back 'almost regretfully to the pointed steady unwavering beat of Costa'.[155]

The other area where Costa was pre-eminent was that of choral conducting. His predecessor at the SHS, Surman, was 'a conductor whose forte is decidedly not conducting. The gyrations of his baton are perfectly inexplicable.' Klein described Costa as 'in his time the greatest choral conductor that England possessed', though

145 Joachim to Brahms, 13 Feb. 1877, cited in Ehrlich, *First Philharmonic*, 113. *Shaw's Music*, vol. 2, 366 (10 Jun. 1891).

146 *Morning Chronicle* (15 Sep. 1858).

147 Bennett, *Life of Bennett*, 288.

148 Elkin, *Annals*, 64.

149 *ILN* (17 May 1851), 416 and (23 Feb. 1850), 129.

150 *MW* (29 Jul. 1854), 504.

151 *Shaw's Music*, vol. 2, 164; also 148. *Morning Post* (18 Jun. 1877).

152 *Daily News* (29 Aug. 1849).

153 *Morning Chronicle* (15 Sep. 1858).

154 *Pall Mall Gazette* (14 Nov. 1870). *Athenaeum* (1 May 1869), 612; (8 May 1869), 644; (24 Jul. 1869), 122.

155 *Shaw's Music*, vol. 2, 322 and 1, 490.

he later placed Joseph Barnby on the same pedestal as Costa.[156] But Barnby, like Macfarren and Cusins, was excluded from the premier festivals by 'the supreme claims of Costa'.[157]

The *Musical Times* obituary commented that Costa 'towered above the petty folk who were his rivals'. The *MW* said that 'Better composers have lived and still live, but as a *chef d'orchestre* he stood, like Saul the son of Kish, head and shoulders above his fellows.'[158] He became a benchmark for other conductors. Johan Franz Herbek was praised as 'the Costa of Vienna'. Theodore Thomas was described as 'the American Costa'.[159] Benedict was judged 'as bad a conductor as Costa was a good one'.[160] Shaw commented that 'The [Bayreuth] orchestra, conducted by Felix Mottl, played with an absolute precision which reminded me of Costa.'[161] The *Morning Post* wrote that Jullien played Beethoven 'with a precision and a readiness which would not have disgraced Costa or Habeneck'.[162]

Costa faced more severe competition from the next generation of orchestral conductors. Even in the amateur choral world, there were able rivals in the 1870s, notably Henry Leslie, whose choir won first prize at the 1878 Paris Exhibition. But the most serious challenge came in the realm of concert conducting, which Costa largely abandoned after 1854, except insofar as symphonic music appeared in his mixed opera concerts. Hallé and Manns, as full-time concert conductors, had the advantage of long tenure with their dedicated orchestras through whom they left enduring legacies (in the Hallé Orchestra and the Crystal Palace Concerts). Manns had the added prop of a strong propagandist in George Grove, whose advice won him the credit of a much more progressive repertoire than Costa's[163] He was also able to use his mid-week concerts to prepare more finished performances at the more important Saturday concerts.[164] Manns was generally regarded as a better orchestral conductor than Costa, though the latter was judged to have outclassed him when they both performed Beethoven's Overture Leonora No. 3 in 1875.[165] But Manns too had his weaknesses. As a former bandmaster, his beat was sometimes too emphatic – what Shaw described as 'a vigorous broadsword exercise' – and was criticized by Cowen as unclear.[166] He was also 'a bundle of nerves' and

---

156 Klein, *Thirty Years*, 55. Klein, *Musicians and Mummers*, 134.

157 Joseph Bennett, *Forty Years*, 318.

158 *Musical Times* (1 Jun. 1884), 321–3. *MW* (3 May 1884, 274–5).

159 Ella, *Musical Sketches*, 266.

160 Klein, *The Golden Age of Opera* (London: G. Routledge & Sons, 1933), 120.

161 *Shaw's Music*, vol. 1, 726.

162 *Morning Post* (16 Jan. 1846).

163 Hueffer, *Half a Century*, Chapter 1.

164 *Pall Mall Gazette* (30 Apr. 1875).

165 Klein, *Thirty Years*, 56. Stanford, *Interludes Records and Reflections*, 19. Hueffer *Half a century*, Chapter 1. *Pall Mall Gazette* (12 Apr. 1875).

166 Cowen, *My Art and My Friends*, 31. *Shaw's Music*, vol. 1, 352.

'oversensitive'.[167] Von Bülow's public criticisms (including the comment that Manns' only skill was to ensure that the orchestra started and finished together) prompted a long exchange of insults between these two hyper-sensitive men.[168]

Hallé was mainly known in London for his piano recitals.[169] But by the time he appeared in London as a conductor, in 1880, he had built up a national reputation over 20 years of conducting in Manchester. He was described as not a born leader but 'very intelligent, very correct, very musicianly, and not altogether wanting in … receptive passion … he keeps his orchestra well in hand … .'[170] Like Costa and Manns, he had a decisive beat and did not use exaggerated gestures or try to impose his own interpretations.[171] Berlioz saw him as 'le musicien sans peur et sans reproche', and reported that impartial observers thought him superior to any London conductor.[172] Von Bülow, who dismissed all the other concert conductors in England as inept, considered Hallé the only capable conductor in England.[173]

The broad conclusion of the evidence is that Costa was superior to all of the other conductors in Britain until the arrival of Hallé and Manns half-way through his career. *New Grove* rightly remarks on the contrast between him and the 'technical ineptness of his contemporaries Bishop, Smart, Balfe and Benedict'.[174] Overall, Costa scored highly on the qualities demanded of the early professional conductors by the first theoreticians of conducting. Kastner prescribed musicality, perspicacity, *sang-froid*, perseverance, patience and firmness; Fétis called for animation and *sang froid*.[175] The *Morning Post*, discussing Costa and Habeneck in 1843, wrote that the pre-requisites of a conductor were respect, courage, energy, a corrective glance and a vigorous arm.[176] This combination was essential for securing the well-integrated ensemble playing which Fétis identified as one of the requirements of new music of the period.[177]

The rise in the standard of conducting in the middle decades of the century was not, of course, solely due to Costa. It reflected improvements across the music industry: better teaching, more concert facilities, a rising level of musical criticism, and higher standards in the larger provincial cities. But in the absence

---

167 Joseph Bennett, *Forty Years*, 117–18. Grove to Bennett (30 Jan. 1874), cited in 1820–1900, Percy M. Young, *George Grove* (London: Macmillan, 1980).

168 *MW* (12 Jan. 1878), 42–4 and Manns' reply 'HOW I OUGHT NOT TO DO IT', *MW* (21 Dec. 1878).

169 Klein, *Musicians and Mummers*, 158–9.

170 *Times* (11 Mar. 1880).

171 *Times* (11 Mar. 1880) and *Grove 2*, vol. 2, 276, Fuller Maitland on 'Charles Hallé'.

172 *Journal des Débats* (31 May 1851).

173 'Autocritical Notes of a Journey in a Fog', Leipzig *Signale* (Nov. 1878), reprinted in *The London Figaro*.

174 *New Grove 2*, vol. 6, 525.

175 G. Kastner, *Supplement to Cours d'Instrumentation* (1844) cited in Carse, *Beethoven to Berlioz*, 338. Fétis, *Manuel des compositeurs*, 125.

176 *Morning Post* (18 Apr. 1843).

177 Fétis, *De l'execution*, 424.

of any rival conductor of real status until Hallé and Manns began to make their mark in the late 1850s, the new level of orchestral and choral performance was rightly associated with Costa. Later in his career, even the cliché-addicted critics began to tire of repeating the same formulaic praises of the precision and energy which he brought to his performances. In the next generation, different yardsticks were advanced – for creative interpretation, more demonstrative conducting and progressive programming. These were standards by which, as will be discussed in Chapter 8, Costa and his generation were found lacking.

Chapter 6
Opera

Costa was, first and foremost, an opera conductor. For 47 years, he was the leading opera conductor in Britain. The only local competition in the first three decades was from Julius Benedict, a pianist who directed occasionally at the minor houses, and Michael Balfe, who conducted competently in adverse circumstances at Her Majesty's Theatre for seven seasons but was primarily a composer. Thereafter in the 1860s and 1870s there were several middling Italian conductors, of whom only Luigi Arditi was effective. Costa was the sole conductor at the houses where he worked, except for brief appearances by composer-conductors (Vaccai, Berlioz, Spohr, Gounod) and rare occasions when the leader Sainton deputized for him. The evolution of opera conducting in England was therefore almost exclusively in Costa's hands. The critic Haweis credited him with creating the modern operatic orchestra.[1] As discussed in Chapter 4, it was in the opera house that he laid down the template which he later applied at the Philharmonic and on the oratorio circuit.

For 32 years of Costa's London career, from 1847–69 and 1871–80, he was at the centre of the intense rivalry between Her Majesty's Theatre and Covent Garden. The struggle in what Chorley entitled 'the cauldron of scandal' between 'London's Montagu and Capulet opera houses' is fascinating in political and personality terms, but it has been told in detail elsewhere and can be summarized briefly here.[2]

By 1837, when the King's Theatre became Her Majesty's, Costa's reforms were largely in place. For the remaining four years of Laporte's management, the theatre enjoyed a golden age, with a reformed orchestra, an outstanding ballet and a repertoire of long-running bel canto hits. Its prime asset was a cast of brilliant Italian singers (including the sopranos Giulia Grisi and Fanny Persiani, the tenors Giovanni Rubini and Giovanni Mario, the baritone Antonio Tamburini and the bass Luigi Lablache). When Laporte died in 1840, his former assistant, Benjamin Lumley, tried with some success to reassert managerial authority over the Old Guard. But he foolishly alienated Costa in 1845 by invoking his contract to prevent him from taking on the prestigious Philharmonic concerts. Costa resigned in 1846 and was joined the next year by most of the Old Guard (and of the band and chorus) in a rival opera house at Covent Garden.

---

1 *Pall Mall Gazette* (2 May 1884).

2 The detailed history of the broader rivalry between the managers and their respective casts is described in Ringel; Gabriella Dideriksen, 'Repertory and Rivalry'; Rosenthal, *Two Centuries of Opera at Covent Garden* (London: Putnam, 1958), 72–123. Chorley, *Musical Recollections*, 73–381. Also Goulden, chapters 6 and 7.

Figure 6.1 Statue of Gye – still honoured at Covent Garden (courtesy of the Royal Opera House)

The next six years saw a bitter battle between Lumley's company and Covent Garden, where the first two impresarios went bankrupt before the management was taken over by Frederick Gye (Figure 6.1). Despite some impressive successes, notably with Jenny Lind, Lumley was defeated by Covent Garden's stronger cast, better orchestra and Gye's superior management. Lumley was declared bankrupt in 1856 and again in 1858. Her Majesty's was taken over by the wily 'Colonel' Mapleson whose effective competition during the 1860s placed Gye under increasing financial pressure. A fire at Her Majesty's in 1869 gave Gye the chance to entice Mapleson into a merger and create an operatic monopoly. He used this to wrest control over the orchestra and chorus from Costa, who predictably resigned, only to be brought back as Mapleson's Musical Director when the Colonel – equally predictably – fell out with Gye in 1871. Competition resumed for the next nine years, with Mapleson and Costa enjoying a slight musical edge over Gye and his succession of middling conductors.

In the course of these long struggles, the practical business of opera production underwent a significant evolution. A canon of operatic works was slowly taking shape.[3] Grand opera became entrenched at the centre of the repertoire, feeding a demand for more spectacular effects, larger orchestras, and singers capable of competing with these forces. The opera business was profoundly affected by the trend to professionalization in musical training, publishing, journalism, marketing and stage management.[4] For the first time, the in-fighting between rival companies was described in detail by the new breed of music-critic, avidly courted (and sometimes bribed) by the theatre managers. Press coverage, though unreliable, provides for the first time extensive material about conducting and the orchestra.[5]

These changes and the intense public competition between the houses provided the backcloth to Costa's relations with his four managers – relationships that were strained by the usual day-to-day tensions of opera management and by the poor inter-personal skills of the participants. In a business marked by insecurity and egotism, Musical Director and managers found it hard to coexist on a basis of equality. Laporte, an ineffective manager who 'does not pretend to any acquaintance with music', could not prevent Costa from building up unprecedented powers in the late 1830s.[6] Lumley was a more resilient manager, capable of great charm, but he emerges in his *Reminiscences* as devious and self-deluding. His alienation of Costa in 1845, having already quarrelled with the Old Guard, was reckless and self-destroying. In 1847–50, the first three years at Covent Garden, Costa came into conflict with all the other principals.[7] The relationship between Gye and Costa between 1848 and 1869 – a working partnership *faute de mieux*, leading to a bitter estrangement – is considered in more detail below. The final partnership with Mapleson, the smoothest of his career, was conducted largely on Costa's terms.

Tensions between conductors and managers, inevitable in the opera business, were in practice usually short-lived because conductors were transient and

---

[3] William Weber, 'The Rise of the Classical Repertoire in Nineteenth Century Orchestral Concerts', in Peyser, ed., *The Orchestra*, 373.

[4] On the structural changes see especially Katharine Ellis, 'The Structure of Musical Life', ed. Jim Samson, *Cambridge History of Nineteenth-Century Music* (Cambridge: Cambridge University Press, 2002), 343–7; Roger Parker, 'The Opera Industry', ibid., 87–118 and David Carew, 'The Consumption of Music', ibid., 237–59; Christina Bashford, *The Pursuit of High Culture*; William Weber, *Music and the Middle Class: The Social Structure of Concert Life in London, Paris and Vienna between 1830 and 1848* (Aldershot: Ashgate, 2004); Simon McVeigh, 'The Benefit Concert in 19th-Century London: From "tax on the nobility" to "monstrous nuisance"', in Bennett Zon, ed., *Nineteenth-Century British Musical Studies*, vol. 1 (Aldershot: Ashgate, 1999), 242–66.

[5] On the defects of the musical press and evidence of bribery, Goulden, 31–4.

[6] Ayrton, commenting on criticisms by Fétis, 'Music in London', 245.

[7] For Costa's rows with the lessee Delafield and Mario, see Gye, 27 Mar. 1848. and 3 and 7 Sep. 1850.

expendable. There were six Musical Directors at the King's Theatre in the decade before Costa's arrival. Costa's case is unusual in that he was Musical Director for 47 years – longer than anyone before or since – and dealt with managers who were themselves remarkably long-lived: Laporte ran his theatre for 13 years, Lumley for 17, Gye for 30 and Mapleson for 20. More remarkable than their squabbles was the fact that Costa and the managers were able to pull together for such long periods.

The key to understanding the evolution of the opera houses in the mid-nineteenth-century, and of Costa's relationships with the managers, lies less in personality or aesthetics than in the commercial context. The tribulations of what Frederick Gye called 'the dreadful business of opera management' have been eloquently described by Gabriella Dideriksen and Matthew Ringel.[8] Managers struggled to cover the cost of high rents, the spectacular stagings that public taste demanded, and the expanding wage bill for orchestras, choruses, and especially the few singers who could handle the heavy roles of grand opera. They were all involved in expensive litigation and suffered from the effects of epidemics, riots, royal mourning and economic slumps.[9] They also saw the erosion of the privileged semi-monopoly status of Covent Garden, Drury Lane and Her Majesty's as smaller theatres invaded their territory, especially after the deregulation of the theatres in 1843.

It is questionable whether the opera was as fundamentally insolvent as managers claimed and as the long roll-call of fleeing bankrupts suggests. Gye's claims of poverty contrasted with his life-style and the evidence of creative accounting. Jullien claimed that, while his own Promenade concerts struggled, Gye came to collect his rent, first on foot, then in a cab and later in a carriage.[10] By the late 1820s, when the term 'entrepreneur' first entered the language in the context of musical management, a new breed of businessman was trying to run the opera on a more commercial basis. In this they hoped to avoid the aristocratic 'committees of support' which had in the past generated some financial underpinning, but at the price of extensive interference in programming and casting – as Lumley experienced in 1852.[11]

Operating without any form of subsidy, the London manager was compared by Berlioz to 'a man carrying a barrel of gun-powder, which he can't get rid of, pursued by men with lighted torches'.[12] Managers aspired to social prestige but their preoccupation was economic survival. To survive, they needed to sell as many subscriptions as possible, which in turn depended on their ability to offer the prospect of lavish new operas and ballets and star artistes able to perform them. The high cost of these items meant that as little as possible was spent on the 'inferior departments' – the rank-and-file players and chorus. These

---

[8] Ringel; Ringel and Dideriksen.

[9] On Chartism, Lumley, *Reminiscences*, 219; on cholera, Gye, 4 Aug. 1849; on financial crises, Cairns, *Berlioz*, vol. 2, 309.

[10] On creative accounting, Dideriksen, 'Repertory and Rivalry', 85, n. 93.

[11] Hall-Witt, *Fashionable Acts*, 270.

[12] *Feuilleton* (1 Jul. 1851).

business pressures, which Fétis identified as 'the radical evil of music in London', guaranteed a fraught relationship between managers and Musical Directors.[13]

Costa's Power Base

The adverse business climate makes it the more remarkable that Costa was able to build up the unprecedented powers described in Chapter 4. Lumley and Costa, both autocratic by temperament, had drawn incompatible lessons from their careers: Costa wanted the power to prevent the musical anarchy that had blighted his first years at the opera house; Lumley's experience as Laporte's right-hand man had left him with 'one fixed rule – that a manager must be the sole master in his own theatre'.[14] Lumley tried in 1842 to take back the management of the musicians' contracts. But he abandoned this when opposed by the players and criticized by the *Athenaeum*.[15] The *MW* ascribed their divorce in 1846 to the fact that 'the jealous lessee of Her Majesty's Theatre, proud of his managerial prerogative, 'could not brook' Costa's extensive powers.[16] Gye too found Costa's power personally and financially threatening.

Before examining the range of Costa's authority in the opera house, it is worth noting that there were extensive areas where he exercised little or no influence. He was too financially cautious to follow Gye's suggestion that he should invest in Covent Garden.[17] He had only a limited role in managing the solo singers. He was too busy with his conducting duties – at the Philharmonic and the SHS as well as the opera house – to accept Gye's request that he should go recruiting on the Continent or compose occasional pieces to fill out shorter opera evenings: he wrote no operas after the failure of his Don Carlos in 1844.[18]

More surprising is his passivity towards the repertoire. Costa was musically conservative – a result in part of his training under the reactionary Zingarelli in a city dominated by opera seria and bel canto. He shared this conservatism with the English musical audience and most critics.[19] These prejudices inevitably influenced the managers, whose experience convinced them that novelties, such as Halévys *La Tempesta* (1850) and Berlioz's *Benvenuto Cellini* (1853), were unprofitable. The mid-nineteenth century saw a stagnating repertoire. At Her Majesty's Theatre, the number of contemporary works performed fell from four per season in the

---

13 Fétis, 'Music in London', 245.

14 Cox, *Musical Recollections*, vol. 2, 130.

15 *Athenaeum* (7 May 1842), 411.

16 *MW* (12 Feb. 1848), 99.

17 Gye, 10 Sep. 1849, 1 Aug. 1850 and 23 Jun. 1866.

18 Gye, 2 and 25 Apr. 1849, 20 Mar. and 18 May 1848, 23 Jun. 1866. He appears to have done some recruiting for Mapleson: *Morning Post* (8 Sep.1875); *The Era* (12 Sep. 1875).

19 There are good analyses in Temperley, 'Xenophilia in British musical history', 3–19; and Weber, *The Great Transformation of Musical Taste*. See also Goulden, Chapter 9.

1820s to two in the I840s and even lower in the 1860s and 1870s.[20] Moreover, the average age of the operas presented rose from 14 years (1826) to 27 (1860). One side-effect of an emerging operatic canon was that each of the two main houses devoted a third of its performances to only five operas.[21] Despite its promise to put on the best operas 'without distinction of country', Covent Garden's first nine years were dominated by Meyerbeer (228 performances), Donizetti (185), Rossini (172), Bellini (98), Mozart (73) and Verdi (52).[22] These trends were also largely true of Paris.[23]

But, even in this cautious climate, Costa's conservatism stood out in two respects. The first is his notorious refusal to take on works by composers for whom he felt personal distaste (Sterndale Bennett) or contempt (Jullien) – and his unwillingness to commit himself to directing any new operas except those by Spohr and Meyerbeer.[24] Not surprisingly, Gye found this attitude incomprehensible as well as frustrating.[25] According to the composer John Francis Barnett, Costa's caution reflected his wish to avoid a repeat of the misunderstanding with Sterndale Bennett over the latter's *Parisina* (Chapter 7). But Costa seems to have been more concerned about how much effort was involved in mounting new works. He told Walter Macfarren that, 'Few people know what it is to have to get up and direct the first performance of an entirely new work.'[26] The adaptation of Meyerbeer's operas for London required not only arduous rehearsal but also much rewriting, not least of recitatives. His preparation of unfinished works like Mendelssohn's *Christus* or Balfe's *Talismano* and of little known Handel oratorios added to a conducting burden heavier than that of any of his contemporaries. George Hogarth was surely right when he concluded that Costa's responsibilities at the Philharmonic, the SHS, opera and private concerts left him 'physically unable to give that time and attention to the production of new works which they absolutely require'.[27]

The second striking fact about Costa's attitude to the repertoire is that, despite his anxiety to control the production side of the house, he seems to have made little effort to influence the content of the opera programme. Drafting the theatre's prospectus was traditionally the manager's task and it was the manager was who was blamed for the deficiencies of programming.[28] Gye did, however, consult Costa before finalizing his prospectus, at least in the early days of Covent Garden. In 1850, Costa 'persuaded me against my wishes to announce 5 operas to be done

20 Goulden, Appendix E.

21 Ringel, 60.

22 Hall-Witt, *Fashionable Acts*, 298.

23 The process of repertoire stagnation is well discussed by Ringel, 10 and 71.

24 Costa's Covent Garden contract of May 1858, Goulden, Appendix A.

25 ROHC, Gye to Costa (14 Jan. 1869).

26 Macfarren, *Memories*, 153.

27 *ILN* (27 Aug. 1853), 170.

28 Busby, *Dictionary* (1806), under 'Director'.

instead of 6'.[29] In 1851, Gye wrote from Berlin with six 'ideas for next season', but Costa decreed that *La clemenza di Tito* and Rossini's *Otello* were not ready.[30] The following year, Gye wrote: 'I look forward to having a talk soon about plans for next season'.[31] Costa also influenced the repertoire indirectly in other ways. He advised Gye about the performability of specific works (Verdi's *Don Carlos* or Gounod's *Roméo et Juliette*), their suitability for the house's singers (a comic opera that would suit Ronconi) and especially their state of readiness for performance.[32] His known antipathy to certain works also influenced the programme: Mapleson claimed that it was fear of offending Costa that prevented him from putting on Offenbach's operas in the 1870s.[33]

But there is little evidence of any constructive input from Costa. Gye recorded a discussion in 1865 during which Costa 'for a wonder made no unpleasant remarks about the prospectus of the season', which suggests that Costa's role was largely detached and critical.[34] After Costa's resignation from Covent Garden, Gye told the Prince of Wales that 'no opera, during the whole 20 years that I have had the theatre, was ever done at Costa's recommendation'.[35] The only example of him actually proposing an opera for performance was when he suggested Donizetti's *Dom Sebastien* in 1862.[36] One partial explanation for Costa's passivity is that he and the managers shared the same conservative tastes; significantly, there was little change of repertoire following his departure from Her Majesty's or Covent Garden.

Despite these exceptions, Costa clearly dominated the musical management, at least until the late 1860s. There was simply no London-based conductor who could fill his shoes and no major foreign conductor willing to take the considerable risk of a London contract. Laporte, Lumley and Gye – all beset by legal and financial troubles and sporadically at war with the Old Guard – relied on Costa to keep the show on the road. Costa alone could manage the players and chorus, through his personality and his control of their contracts and of their access to concerts and the festivals. The managers also needed him to handle the truculent Italian singers and mediate in their disputes. In a typical incident, when Grisi announced that she was too ill to sing in *Semiramide*, it was Costa who went to her house and persuaded her to perform.[37] He was the intermediary through whom Luigi Labache, the only member of the Old Guard who stayed with Lumley, eventually joined Covent Garden in 1854. Another benefit was his ability to ensure that the leading singers

29 Gye, 20 Feb. 1850.

30 Gye, 21 Feb. and 25 Mar. 1850. ROHC, Gye to Costa (10 Feb. 1851).

31 ROHC, Gye to Costa (15 Oct. ?1852).

32 ROHC, Gye to Costa (15 Jun. 1858 and 5 Dec. 1866).

33 Mapleson, *Memoirs*, 306.

34 Gye, 21 Mar. 1865.

35 Gye, 22 Jun. 1869.

36 Gye 3 Mar. 1862.

37 Gye, 3 Apr. 1848.

attended rehearsals and to curb their tendency to over-act or introduce too much ornament. Patti contrasted the freedom she enjoyed when performing as Norina (*Don Pasquale*) in Paris with the regime in London, where 'Costa would allow no upsetting of furniture, no vigorous slaps on the face, administered to Don Pasquale by his insubordinate ward'.[38]

Costa's services were in some ways costly to the management. His high credibility with the players and singers rested on his readiness to defend their interests against a management which saw them as an easy target for economies. There were explosions between Costa and the investors at Covent Garden in the late 1840s when he 'advised the band and chorus to press their claims'; when he paid the chorus for Passion Week concerts, which were usually performed gratis; and when he refused to sign his own contract for 1850 unless the rank-and-file players were paid for Easter performances.[39] He infuriated Gye by advising the bass Attri not to deputise in *Les Huguenots*, since it might harm his reputation.[40] But overall the management benefitted from having someone who could persuade the musicians to perform reliably in often stressful conditions. During his 22 years at Covent Garden, Costa averaged over 70 performances per season – 59 different operas in all.

Most important of all, Costa's conducting was a key factor in ensuring that Covent Garden beat off the competition from Her Majesty's. In 1863, George Eliot and her husband saw both theatres' productions of *Faust* in a week and greatly preferred Covent Garden's because of its 'superior, well-conducted orchestra'.[41] Gye's willingness to pay Costa more than anyone except Patti, Pauline Lucca and Mario is a mark of his anxiety to retain his services. Lumley's attempts to entice Costa back were a reminder to Gye that he could not afford to lose his conductor. When Covent Garden's standards fell in the early 1870s, Gye was urged to re-engage him. When Gye and Mapleson split in 1871, the latter's first act was to engage Costa.

In addition to his reputation as a conductor, Costa kept together the best orchestra and chorus in London. After 53 players and 47 choristers migrated with Costa to Covent Garden in 1847, Lumley and his conductor Michael Balfe never managed to recruit the 160 well-trained players and singers needed to perform the new repertoire of Meyerbeer, Halévy and Verdi. This became a central element in the competition between the two houses (Figure 6.2). In theory they claimed to pursue distinct cultural agendas, with Covent Garden promising to provide a progressive alternative to 'the wishy-washy Italian masters'.[42] But contrary to its progressive manifesto, Covent Garden's first six years gave more weight to Italian (51 per cent) and grand

38 Sutherland Edwards, *The Prima Donna*, vol. 2, 85.

39 Gye, 22 Nov. 1849, 7 and 24 Apr. 1849, 17 Apr. and 18 May 1850.

40 Gye, 5 May 1864.

41 Eliot to Francois D'Albert-Durade (18 Jul. 1863).

42 Hall-Witt, *Fashionable Acts*, 182–4 and 232–47. Yates, *Recollections*, 180.

Figure 6.2 *Punch* cartoon of the Battle of the Operas, showing Costa and Balfe fencing with their batons and their casts arrayed for conflict (*Punch Almanach*, 1849) (courtesy of Westminster City Libraries)

opera (33 per cent) than to the Austro-German school (13 per cent).[43] In a pattern that became common, it also copied two of Lumley's new Verdi productions.

Costa gave Covent Garden an important edge over Her Majesty's in the 1850s, especially through his mastery of the bel canto repertoire and his ability to bring together the complex scores and effects required by Verdi and especially Meyerbeer. Looking back at the production of *Dinorah* in 1859, for example, Chorley observed that 'Nothing of the kind is now attainable in any other European theatre'.[44] *Don Giovanni* in 1861 (with Patti, Tamberlik, Ronconi, Grisi, Formes, Tagliafico and Csillag) was remembered by Herman Klein 'as a treasured memory, as in a sense the operatic *clou* of the mid-Victorian era'.[45] Insofar as there was a cultural difference between the two houses, it was to be found not in the repertoire but in how it was performed. Lumley relied on the drawing power of Jenny Lind, who saved Her Majesty's Theatre financially in 1847–48 but at the heavy artistic cost of accepting the 'pernicious star system', which was 'utterly destructive of every other artist in the company'.[46] Covent Garden survived the epidemic of Lindmania by relying on 'the excellence of the ensemble, rather than

43 Hall-Witt, *Fashionable Acts*, 298.

44 Chorley, *Musical Recollections*, 395.

45 Herman Klein, *The Reign of Patti* (London: Fisher Unwin, 1920), 85.

46 *ILN* (21 Aug. 1852), 134; *Athenaeum* (28 Aug. 1847), 917; *MW* (4 Sep. 1847), 565.

the preponderating influence of any one particular star'.[47] The key element in this ensemble was Costa's orchestra.

The realization that an orchestra was a central element of an operatic production can be mapped in the embryonic music press. In 1837, a review of Costa's opera *Malek Adhel* mentioned the orchestra among 'the accessories'.[48] The *Times* critic James Davison reflected the same view when he commented in 1846 that 'Mr Lumley can get another band and another chorus, but he cannot find another Grisi and another Mario.'[49] The later consensus that Covent Garden's orchestra and chorus were one of its greatest strengths thus represented a major shift of attitude.[50] Chorley expressed this notion in striking terms when he wrote in 1841, after a tour of the Continent: 'first should come the chorus and orchestra; then the singers in combination; then the stage arrangements; lastly the singers individually considered'.[51] In a thoughtful review of the 1848 season, Davison drew attention to 'the growing importance of the orchestral and choral departments … The success of an opera now not infrequently depends on the efficiency of the orchestra and the chorus … .'[52]

This became a common theme among the critics as Covent Garden demonstrated its superior ensemble playing.[53] The *ILN* pointedly reminded Lumley's successor at Her Majesty's, John Smith, that 'the orchestra and chorus … are *not mere accessories*, they are the life and soul of the opera'(my italics).[54] Chorley later recalled:

> That the Italian Opera at Her Majesty's Theatre never recovered the loss of Signor Costa is a matter of operatic history … our world had been educated up to a point at which the entire performance was felt to be the real object of interest … .[55]

Through the 1860s it was a commonplace that 'without Signor Costa the Royal Italian Opera would never have been what it is'.[56] This perception was reflected in the new fashion for including Costa in curtain calls and for referring to him and his players as 'one of the leading attractions of the season'.[57] Significantly, Lumley's boastful prospectuses after 1847 virtually never referred to his orchestra

---

47 *Times* (24 Aug. 1848).

48 *Morning Post* (18 Jan. 1837).

49 *MW* (26 Sep. 1846), 458.

50 *ILN* (10 Apr. 1847), 233–4.

51 Henry Chorley, *Music and Manners in France and Germany* (London: Longmans, 1841), vol. 1, 289.

52 *Times* (25 Aug. 1848).

53 For example, *Morning Chronicle* (6 Aug. 1860).

54 *ILN* (28 Jul. 1860).

55 Chorley, *Musical Recollections*, 174.

56 *Morning Post* (23 Mar. 1863).

57 On Costa and the band see, for example, *Morning Chronicle* (18 Aug. 1857); *Morning Post* (16 Aug. 1858); *Daily News* (24 Jul. 1868).

and its conductor. The superiority of Costa's musicians remained one of Gye's key asserts during the more taxing competition that he faced from Mapleson in the mid-1960s. The *Examiner* complimented Arditi on having worked hard to match 'the perfect orchestra under the rule of Signor Costa'. But Covent Garden still had 'the advantage in the rare perfection of the instrumental performance of every piece that is produced'.[58]

Costa's indispensability was especially obvious during Covent Garden's two greatest crises. In 1849, when the manager Beale decided to close the company after the bankrupt Delafield fled to France, it was Costa and Gye who agreed to continue to the end of the season. Gye noted: 'Costa saw the chorus and between us we got all to play without pay.'[59] Although the 'Commonwealth' of 1850 was notionally a partnership with the main singers, Costa was 'the supreme musical as Gye was the chief financial president'.[60] Covent Garden survived artistically in 1850 because Costa was able to put on 68 performances of 17 operas to a standard that eclipsed those at Her Majesty's.

In the second major crisis, after fire devastated Covent Garden in 1856, Costa spurned Lumley's invitation back to Her Majesty's and adapted the company's programme to the Lyceum, which was too small for the company's Meyerbeerian money-spinners. He cut the orchestra from 80 to 50 but rotated the players and thus ensured that no one deserted. He also kept the company afloat by persuading the musicians to accept salary cuts and putting on a profitable series of concerts in the reopened Crystal Palace at Sydenham. Gye had feared that, if Costa declined to conduct these concerts, the singers would also refuse and the company would flounder.[61] In the event, 'the band came and Costa settled with them'.[62] Costa sustained the company in 1857–58 when Gye, overcome by his exertions after the fire, took to his bed and did not visit the opera for eight months. He supervised the opening of the rebuilt Covent Garden in 1858, with 44 performances. For the Queen's visit in June 1858, Gye wrote from his bed (in a shaky hand) 'Would you be kind enough to make out the programme and as attractive as you can. I need not say how much obliged I should be if you would conduct'.[63]

Costa and his musicians were not the sole reason for Covent Garden's success over Lumley. Gye's pragmatism, his canny financial management and his remarkable luck were important factors. By recruiting and holding together a broad cast, Gye was better placed than Lumley to handle the inevitable last-minute changes of cast and opera. In 1855, he boasted he had 46 operas in his repertoire, many of which could be substituted 'at a few hours' notice'.[64] But his

58 *Examiner* (3 Jun. 1865).

59 Gye, 14 Jul., 2 Aug. and 28 Jul. 1849.

60 Cox, *Musical Recollections*, 237.

61 Gye, 17 Mar. 1856.

62 Gye, 4 Apr. 1856.

63 ROHC, Gye to Costa (4 Jun. 1858).

64 1855 Prospectus.

ability to juggle a large cast in this way depended crucially on Costa's discipline and organizing ability.

It was a sign of Costa's importance that he was the only person to whom Gye revealed his plans to take over the lease: 'Don't mention to anyone that I have the theatre. Not yet certain.'[65] The proprietors of Covent Garden granted Gye his lease only after he had a written commitment from Costa and Mario; they abandoned their attempts to revise the terms when told that Costa had already approved the contract.[66] Costa was also the only member of the company with whom Gye shared his plans for the Lyceum after the 1856 fire. Gye reported from Paris on the singers he had signed up: 'I thought you would like to hear how *our affairs* progressed' (my italics).[67] He consulted Costa about the options for what he called the 'risorgimento' of Covent Garden. With Costa's encouragement, he tried to lease Her Majesty's before eventually deciding to rebuild Covent Garden.[68]

Costa was also a useful sounding board, especially on the manoeuvres of the artistes and the opposition. He wrote from his holiday retreat in Folkestone to warn that the lawyers of Gye's ex-partner, Colonel Knox, were trying to persuade him to sign a hostile affidavit.[69] He tipped Gye off about Lumley's and Mapleson's manoeuvres to entice Mario and Grisi back to Her Majesty's and about Gye's partner and part-time manager Frederick Beale 'telling all sorts of lies about me to Grisi and Mario'.[70] Costa's reports about Lumley's efforts to draw him back to Her Majesty's no doubt reminded Gye that he could not take his conductor's services for granted.[71]

Since the late 1830s, thanks to his role as organizer of royal concerts (Chapter 7), Costa had become the opera's main channel of contact with the Queen. Victoria's adviser Baron Stockmar reported to her that Costa was going to get Laporte to free singers for a concert. 'Mr Costa will be at 5 o'clock this evening at Baroness Lehzen's, to receive Her Majesty's commands.'[72] Costa interceded with the Queen not to demand the orchestra when they were needed for the dress rehearsal of *Robert le diable*; and not to press for Pauline Viardot to sing in *Fidelio*, as she had dropped the part.[73] Royal favour was a barometer of success in the opera business. In 1847, the Queen went to Covent Garden only nine times, compared with 27 visits to Her Majesty's. But, after Jenny Lind's retirement in 1848, the success of Costa and the Old Guard musicians in Victoria's favourite bel canto and Meyerbeer operas gradually secured a change of court favour. In the

65 ROHC, Gye to Costa (10 Feb. 1851).
66 Gye, 13 and 18 Sep. 1849.
67 ROHC, Gye to Costa (31 Mar. 1856); Gye, Jun–Nov. 1856.
68 'Risorgimento' in Gye, 29 Jun. 1856. Gye, 13 Feb. 1857.
69 Gye, 30 Jan. 1863.
70 Gye, 4 Jul. 1863 and 13 Nov. 1850.
71 Gye, 7 Jul. 1852, 18 Apr. 1853, 30 Mar, 1854, 30 May 1854.
72 RA VIC/Y 152/3 14 Aug. 1837.
73 Costa (Mar. 1849, n.d.), RA VIC/Add C 4/117. Gye, 12 Apr. and 17 May 1851.

next 14 years, she attended Covent Garden 78 times, against only 37 visits to Her Majesty's.[74] Gye needed Costa's close links with the Royal Family, for example to make arrangements for the State Visit of Napoleon III in 1855 (see Chapter 4, Figure 4.12).[75]

Because of his reliance on Costa, it was Gye who made the running to preserve the relationship. They had begun on bad terms: Costa suspected that Gye wanted to interfere with the musical department; and Gye found Costa jealous and inflexible. But Gye increasingly acted as a peacemaker between Costa and the rest of the management. When Costa was not on speaking terms with the lessee, Gye persuaded Delafield to write an apology.[76] It was Gye who stopped the manager Beale from taking Costa at his word in April 1849 when he threatened to resign. Gye continued to treat Costa with kid gloves after he took over the company in 1851 When Costa complained about his interference, Gye took him aside 'in a conciliatory manner' and did not react when Costa responded brusquely. Gye climbed down after Costa objected to his hiring the Czech composer Max Maretzek, whom Costa described as 'a Lumleyite', to compose music for the ballet.[77] When he noticed that Costa was sulking, 'I called on him and, after hearing a number of petty *amour-propre* grievances all meaning nothing, made things smooth again.'[78] Gye turned aside Costa's periodic threats of resignation with that mixture of half-apology and flattery at which he was so accomplished. 'Your letter has quite frightened me … Do please come and fill that place which no other can as yours. I hope it is not too late to send the tickets for your friends.'[79]

It was mainly thanks to Gye's tact and forebearance that they gradually learnt to work together to keep Covent Garden afloat. According to Dideriksen, there was a 'distinct possibility' of Costa's appointment being terminated as early as 1855.[80] Gye's Diary sometimes reveals his extreme irritation with Costa's:

> intolerable *amour propre* ... This man wants to be the incarnation of Covent Garden and for no one else to appear in the management of it – and the tyranny he would exercise would be fearful. *He told me I was a great deal too much at the theatre!!!!!!!* However I must for the present put up with all this, smile, be courteous – what a dose![81]

74 PhD diss by M.J. Budds, cited by Hall-Witt, *Fashionable Acts*, 350.

75 Gye, 12 Apr. and 17 May 1851.

76 Gye, 26 Jul. 1849.

77 Gye, 25 Apr. 1849, 18 May 1848 and 20 Mar. 1848.

78 Gye, 19 Aug. 1853.

79 ROHC, Gye to Costa (7 Aug. 1854).

80 Dideriksen, 213.

81 Gye, 16 Nov. 1854; emphasis in original.

But, although he resented Costa's 'wretched temper and arrogance', there is plenty of evidence that he recognised the need to 'smooth' him and retain his services.[82] When Costa was absent from the theatre without notice in 1865, Gye wrote 'I had a great mind to have a row with him but thought it more prudent not.'[83] On another occasion, 'He was rather inclined to be nasty but I would not quarrel.'[84]

Sources of Conflict

Although Gye was pernickety about legal contracts, he had little choice but to allow Costa to build on the terms he enjoyed as a founder member of Covent Garden. By the time of the 'Commonwealth' between Costa, Gye and the main singers in 1850, there was a clear division of authority: Gye managed the theatre, except for the musical side which fell to Costa.[85] Costa's contracts with Gye marked the high point of authority to which the new professional conductor could aspire. But the division between music and management in an opera house is cloudy. Conflicts of authority manifested themselves in six areas: rehearsals, moonlighting, a second conductor, extra night performances, and issues of musical judgement and authority.

Rehearsals

Disputes about the time allowed for preparing performances, a feature of London's musical life, continued throughout their partnership. By 1858, Costa had persuaded Gye to add a significant clause to the contract under which he had functioned at Her Majesty's:

> Mr Gye is to give Mr Costa the name & order of appearance of every new opera he may intend to bring out at least 6 weeks before the actual performance thereof in order to give Mr Costa time to have it fully rehearsed without interruption & prepared for & also to give Mr Costa a week's notice of every other he may think fit to perform so as *to enable Mr Costa to prepare it to his satisfaction* (my italics).[86]

Gye chafed under Costa's terms, even though he knew that they gave him an edge over Her Majesty's. Costa's caution saved Gye from making Lumley's mistake of promising what could not be delivered or of putting on productions whose

---

82 Gye, 16 May 1865.

83 Gye, 18 Apr. 1865.

84 Gye, 3 May 1864.

85 Gye, 14 Feb. 1848. *Times* (25 Feb. 1850).

86 Contract of 24 May 1858, ROHC.

'glaring deficiencies' were due to 'want of rehearsal'.[87] In 1861 Gye's delayed staging of *Un ballo in maschera* was commended after Mapleson had hurriedly mounted a mediocre production. When persuaded by Costa not to commit himself absolutely to doing Meyerbeer's *Dinorah* in 1859, Gye won credit in the press for his honesty.[88]

But there were frequent clashes when Costa demanded postponement to ensure proper rehearsal – a concern shared by some of the singers, for example by Grisi over a production of *La favorita* in 1850. Gye suffered financially from deferred performances, as when Mapleson scooped his production of *Faust* in 1863: 'the letting is very good and this postponement will be very injurious … I at last put the music off til Thursday to my great loss.' But Covent Garden won in the comparison.[89] In 1864, Costa demanded six rehearsals of *La fille du regiment*, 'which we gave last year and now only change one character. I have put off [Flotow's] *Stradella* twice to please him.'[90] Gye complained frequently about Costa's inflexibility and obstruction, alleging that he 'made all sorts of difficulties about rehearsals. He always finds difficulties and never suggests a remedy.'[91]

Meyerbeer's and Halévy's operas, with their heavy demands on numbers and orchestral effects, brought Costa's perfectionism into sharper conflict with Gye's business exigencies. In 1864, Costa decreed that *L'Etoile du nord* was not ready. 'I told him the Etoile must be done. He tries to thwart everything.'[92] They 'nearly came to words' over the preparation of *L'Africaine*. Gye had seen the Paris version and recognized that it would need 'an immense deal of altering and cutting'.[93] But he became so impatient about delays that he began to suspect that Costa was unsympathetic to Meyerbeer's operas and wanted 'to get out of doing the Africaine'.[94] This seems improbable. Meyerbeer enthusiastically endorsed Costa's conducting of his works and was one of the two modern composers whom Costa contracted to conduct. He put on 155 Meyerbeer performances in his last decade at Covent Garden, 22 of *L'Africaine*. Indeed the 'completeness and excellence' of these performances were described in Gye's obituary as the 'distinctive feature' of the house.[95]

The coordination of rehearsals was another source of friction, especially when Costa took his musicians off to rehearse for the festivals (see below). They had a major row in 1866 when Costa called a morning rehearsal that threatened to run

87 Unidentified review of 9 Aug. 1852, Victoria and Albert Museum Collection, London.

88 *Athenaeum* (5 Mar. 1859), 327.

89 Gye, 25 and 26 Jun. 1863. Eliot to D'Albert-Durade (18 Jul. 1863).

90 Gye, 24 May 1864.

91 Gye, 31 Mar. 1864 and 10 May 1865.

92 Gye, 16 Jun. 1864.

93 Gye, 11 Jan. 1865.

94 Gye, 9 Jun. 1865.

95 *London Standard* (5 Dec. 1878).

over into a concert that Gye had arranged for the afternoon. Gye's account shows how quickly minor issues could flare up between them:

> Costa said in his disagreeable way 'I have got my rehearsal and when I have finished the band will go. (There is no band for the concert). What's that to me, your concert?' I said of course the theatre must be cleared before the concert people can come in. He said 'That's nothing to me. I know my business and I shall finish my rehearsal'. I ought to have knocked him down! But the rehearsal was going on and I left him … It is almost impossible to put up with him.[96]

On this occasion, Costa uncharacteristically gave way, bringing his rehearsal forward by half an hour to avoid a clash. But their disagreements became more acute in the later years of the partnership. In July 1868, Costa stormed out after Gye accused him of saying that Auber's *Le domino noir* was ready, despite the fact that the leading soprano had not rehearsed once. Gye later 'found him pacing up and down Hart St waiting for a cab' and asked him to name a date for the first night, but received no answer.[97] When Costa dropped a rehearsal of Auber's *Fra Diavolo* because Mario had failed to apologize for skipping an earlier rehearsal, Gye told him that private affairs should not interfere with the programme of the house.[98]

Moonlighting

Gye's frustration about delayed productions added to his irritation at Costa taking players away from the opera house to perform on the festival circuit. Absences for duties at the Philharmonic and the Ancient Concerts had long been sanctioned.[99] By the 1850s, however, the growth of the festival phenomenon and Costa's central place in it meant that members of the opera orchestra were in greater demand elsewhere. Gye naturally resented these absences, for which he received no compensation. In 1854, he went down to Sydenham to try (unsuccessfully) to withhold permission for his orchestra to play under Costa for the reopening of the Crystal Palace.[100] He calculated that he lost over £600 from the orchestra's absences at the 1862 Exhibition.

In May 1865, Costa asked to change the opera because he needed to rehearse the players for the SHS premiere of his oratorio *Naaman*. Gye grumbled that: 'This is too bad and cannot last!'[101] In June of the same year, Costa missed a performance before the Prince of Wales, arguing that he was too tired to conduct

96 Gye, 12 Jun. 1866.

97 Gye, 14 Jul. 1868.

98 Gye, 16 Jun. 1865.

99 Ella's contract of 21 Aug. 1846, Faculty of Music Library, The Bodleian Library, Oxford, Mss 163.

100 Bowley, *Re-opening of the Crystal Palace*.

101 Gye, 9 May 1865.

three nights in succession, but Gye discovered that he had been rehearsing the Handel Festival chorus.[102] Two days later, the players were not available to rehearse because they were at the Handel Festival. Gye complained that he 'had given them no permission to go … But Costa having accepted the conductorship, I am to be sacrificed.'[103] The orchestra was absent for three days in the following week. 'The fact is the fault is all Costa's. He knew perfectly well … that it would stop my rehearsals; but, as he most improperly had engaged *himself*, he *winked* at the band going.'[104]

From 1866, Gye tried to set a new pattern, telling Costa that the opera orchestra 'must be at my call whenever I needed them'.[105] But the next year, when the players petitioned Costa to negotiate on their behalf, he forced Gye to add to their contracts a provision that 'they shall be at liberty to attend music festivals'.[106] This problem, intimately linked to Costa's control over players' contracts and his own availability for extra opera nights (see below), was insoluble while Gye had only one conductor at his disposal.

Deputy Conductor

To reduce his dependence on Costa's availability, Gye repeatedly 'begged' him to engage a subordinate at the theatre's expense – 'but as usual uselessly. And so I am sacrificed.'[107] Gye called at Costa's house in 1866 to suggest engaging 'a M. Gianelli, *maestro al piano* at Madrid, to help him, but he was against it'.[108] Later in the year Gye appointed Giovanni Bottesini, assuring Costa that he would conduct only at concerts. But, according to Arditi, 'poor Bottesini … was, as a matter of fact, never for one night allowed the privilege of wielding the Wand'.[109]

Gye's concern to install a deputy was sharpened by the sporadic rumours (and hints from Costa) that he might take on the Paris Opera or retire altogether.[110] In 1864, he said that Gye would be able to do as he liked the following season, 'meaning probably that he would not remain with me'.[111] In 1866, the Prince of Wales mentioned to Gye that Costa was going to be appointed Director of the proposed National Training School of Music, the precursor of the Royal College

[102] Gye, 17 Jun. 1865.

[103] Gye, 19 Jun. 1865.

[104] Gye, 22 and 23 Jun. 1865; emphasis in original.

[105] Gye, 5 Jun. 1866.

[106] Memorandum of 8 Jan. 1867, ROHC. Text in Goulden, Appendix A.

[107] Gye, 20 Jun. 1865.

[108] Gye, 7 Feb. 1866.

[109] Arditi, *Reminiscences*, 235.

[110] Gye, 7 Jul. 1852, 18 Apr. 1853, 30 Mar. 1854, 30 May 1854, 4 and 28 Apr. 1864. Mapleson, *Memoirs*, 29.

[111] Gye, 6 and 18 May 1864.

of Music.[112] But, after discussing the following year's arrangements with Costa, Gye commented 'This does not look as if he has thoughts of leaving me … Yet I heard that Costa had said something of the kind to Strakosch and Mario 2 or 3 weeks since.'[113] Gye's determination to reinsure by appointing a second conductor for 1869 was to become a major reason for Costa's resignation.

Extra Nights

In his quest to raise revenue, Gye sought to put on performances on Mondays (from 1861) and, at the height of the season, on Fridays (from 1864) and Saturdays (1867), exploiting the fact that the musicians were paid monthly and could not demand pay for extra nights. Having averaged 65 performances a season in the 1850s, Gye put on 78 a year in 1861–67.[114] This became another issue with Costa, who wanted to keep Mondays and Fridays free for the SHS and the festivals. When Gye complained that Costa was skipping Monday performances, despite the fact that his salary had been raised to £1,500 to cover them, Costa blandly replied that the salary rise was agreed because he *often* conducted on Mondays.[115] The following year, they again clashed when Gye billed Costa to conduct on a Monday without consulting him. Costa told a member of Gye's staff 'I shall conduct on Monday, but mind you never take a liberty with me again, neither you nor Mr Gye!!!'[116] They eventually agreed in 1866 to make Monday a regular Covent Garden night in exchange for raising Costa's salary to £2,000.

Musical Judgement

As a newcomer to the opera house, Gye at first treated Costa's musical domain with tact. He wrote from Berlin 'I have the names of several musicians who could come in case you should have found any difficulty with our people – yet you would of course have written me if any had existed.'[117] When Alfred Mellon proved unable to handle the Covent Garden concert series, Gye wrote diplomatically to make sure that Costa approved the engagement of a successor. But as he grew more confident about his own judgement, Gye began to interfere in the musical side. He advised Costa how to handle the singers – holding them to ambitious deadlines: 'I have often told C that the only way to make them study is to say the opera must

[112] Gye, 25 Jun. 1866. Costa accepted the post but the project fell through. Bennett, *Life of Bennett*, 350.

[113] Gye, 28 Jun. 1866.

[114] Ringel, 92.

[115] Gye, 3 May 1864.

[116] Gye, 12 May 1865.

[117] ROHC, Gye to Costa (10 Feb. 1851).

be given.'[118] In 1864, he ordered the librarian to transpose Zerlina's aria 'Vedrai carino' (*Don Giovanni*) for Nantier-Didiée, which Costa had refused to do.[119]

Gye initially recognized that Costa was 'the most competent judge' of the singers.[120] Costa remained influential not only with the Old Guard but also with the next generation, especially Adelina Patti, who wrote at the end of her first season thanking him for 'how much you have done for me'.[121] But as Gye became more self-confident, he began to criticize Costa's judgement. 'Costa advised me not to engage Pischek … he said he sang very badly in Italian, but *had never seen him act* – he also advised me against Bosio I remember!!' After the success of *L'Africaine,* Gye noted that 'Lucca and Wachtel had the honours altho' Costa wanted me to take their parts away saying they were both so stupid and they could never sing them'.[122] Such point-scoring is typical of Gye's Diary in the 1860s. It needs to be balanced against Mapleson's admission that he suffered a 'dismal fiasco' when he cast an Italian soprano for *Faust*, against Costa's advice.[123]

Management of the Opera House

As noted in Chapter 4, Costa's obsession with orderly programming led him to want to control all aspects of the music. In 1848, for example, he countermanded the lessee's decision to change the curtain time.[124] His insistence on receiving at least six weeks' notice of new operas (and one week's notice for revivals) speaks eloquently of his wish to constrain Gye's frequent changes of programme, which happened on average for one production in six during the 1860s.[125] By then Costa had more power than any London conductor, before or since. This not only jarred with Gye's own autocratic personality, but also trespassed on his commercial domain (see below). As early as 1854, Gye complained that 'Costa treated me in a very extraordinary manner, almost as if I were his servant instead of he mine.'[126] The illusion that Costa was Gye's servant – or vice versa – provides a clue to the central power struggle at the core of their relationship. The extent of Costa's power – and Gye's resentment – emerges in a letter written after their divorce in which Gye asked the critic Gruneisen whether it was reasonable for a conductor to have:

---

118 Gye, 4 Jun. 1866.

119 Gye, 17 Jun. 1864.

120 Gye, 10 Jan. 1850.

121 Letter of 24 Aug. 1862, quoted by J.F. Cone, *Adelina Patti Queen of Hearts* (Hants: Scholar Press, 1994), 49.

122 Gye, 12 May 1854 and 22 Jun. 1865; emphasis in original.

123 Mapleson, *Memoirs*, 93.

124 Gye, 8 May 1848.

125 Ringel, 214.

126 Gye, 19 May 1854.

> the uncontrolled management of orchestra, chorus, *maestro al piano*, chorus master and even the music librarian, at salaries which you could be bound not to alter? and would you strip yourself of the power of discharging any of these 180 persons, no matter what their conduct might be? Would you … be debarred from entering the room in which a rehearsal was taking place?[127]

Costa's contractual authority over the *mise-en-scène* raised issues of demarcation that were harder to resolve as the management of the house became more specialized. In 1852 Gye took on an experienced stage manager, Augustus Harris, who increasingly acted for him as a fixer and recruiter on the Continent – tasks that Costa had declined. Harris and the scenic artist Beverley began to attract press attention; they were described, along with Costa, as 'those most efficient and important members of the establishment'.[128] As Harris became *de facto* deputy manager, it was inevitable that he would come into conflict with Costa, who accused him of being Gye's spy and of extorting money from the singers in exchange for their engagements.[129] Gye described a blazing row in which Costa 'complained of Harris, Beverley simply because they did not bow to the ground to him and be entirely his servants.!!!'[130] Mapleson claimed that Costa extended this vendetta to Harris's son.[131]

The Rupture

By the time Covent Garden burnt down in March 1856, Costa and Gye were clearly the twin pillars of London's only successful opera house. Costa's newly demonstrated skill in grand opera coincided with the kudos he was gaining at the Philharmonic and the SHS. The next decade marked the high point of a partnership that was, for both men, the most important of their respective careers and the longest in the history of opera in England. Gye's correspondence shows a warmer tone after the fire, moving from 'My dear Sir' to 'My dear Costa' or 'My dear friend'.

But it remained a marriage of convenience and they were never socially close. Gye noticed that he had not seen Costa from the end of one season to the start of another. Moreover, their partnership was founded on an unequal relationship. Struggling in competition with Mapleson and Her Majesty's Theatre, and preoccupied with financial and legal worries, Gye had no choice but to humour Costa and rely on him to oversee the day-to-day running of the opera. Gye's Diary often makes no mention of the mainstream business of the opera – the casting,

---

127 Gye to Gruneisen (26 Mar. 1869), in Gruneisen, *Opera and the Press*, 53.

128 *Morning Post* (5 Aug. 1861).

129 Gye, 22 Jun. 1858 and 18 May 1863.

130 Gye, 16 Nov. 1854.

131 Mapleson, *Memoirs*, 306.

rehearsals and performances. He commented rarely on the quality of Covent Garden productions, often simply noting the daily house takings.

Personal chemistry was critical in the battle between Covent Garden and Her Majesty's, which continued through the 1860s and 1870s, since the outcome depended not on their repertoires (which remained very similar) or their casts (which were often evenly matched) but on the quality of their managers and conductors and the complex relationship between them. Lumley's weaknesses in this area led to his losing most of his cast, his conductor Balfe and the support of his lessor Lord Ward.[132] Personal animosity was a major obstacle to cooperation between Gye and Mapleson. Lack of mutual sympathy was, along with financial strain, the issue on which the Gye–Costa partnership eventually collapsed.

From the start, their personalities contrasted vividly. Costa was introverted, inflexible, cautious and obsessed with the authority that he needed to ensure orderly productions. His dedication to his musical duties was almost monastic and his hobbies were private – silverware, horses and collecting clocks.[133] Gye by contrast was extraverted, entrepreneurial, suspicious and interfering. He had a large family and numerous business and intellectual interests outside the theatre. Although not musically adventurous, he was the most successful of the mid-Victorian opera managers, thanks to his remarkable energy, tact, business flair and tenacity. He was a pragmatist, for example allowing Carl Rosa's wife Parepa to sing *Norma* in exchange for Rosa taking £300 worth of boxes and stalls.[134] When he needed someone's services, he could flatter and humour with gifts of grouse, eggs, strawberries and opera cloaks. He was described by Maurice Strakosch, Patti's brother-in-law, as 'le modèle des directeurs … un peu rude de formes, très autoritaire, mais esclave à sa parole qui valait tous les écrits et sa signature'.[135] But his Diary also reveals a man ruled by suspicion. His shabby treatment of Mario and Grisi at the end of their careers showed that he could be brutal when he no longer needed them. There was also a crude side to Gye's personality which may have jarred on the fastidious Costa: when asked whether he might find a job for Mapleson at Covent Garden, Gye replied that Mapleson 'could hold up Therèse Tietjens' dress and see her bed warmed at night'.[136]

Given their deep differences of personality and their hunger for power, it is surprising that Costa and Gye managed to work together effectively for two decades in such a turbulent environment. The picture that emerges is of two autocrats cooperating well enough to contain the sensitive issues of finance and authority, and creating productions of a quality and polish that were, in some

---

132 Lumley, Benjamin, *The Earl of Dudley, Mr Lumley and Her Majesty's Theatre: A Narrative of Facts Addressed to the Patrons of the Opera, his Friends and the Public Generally* (London: Bosworth and Harrison, 1863).

133 *Vanity Fair* profile of 1872.

134 Gye, 16 Jun. 1872.

135 Maurice Strakosch, *Souvenirs d'un Impresario* (Paris: Ollendorf, 1887), 28.

136 Gye, 15 May 1863.

styles, never exceeded. During the decade after the reopening of Covent Garden in 1858, however, their personal relations became increasingly fractious.

Much of their mutual exasperation was due to the normal strains and misunderstandings of running an opera house. Gye was put out to receive a letter of thanks from the Amateur Musical Society for lending them three musicians, which he had refused but Costa had authorized.[137] There were plenty of people keen to feed Gye's suspicious nature. In 1854, a contact reported to Gye that Costa was behind defamatory rumours against him and was 'a great enemy of mine'.[138] When Lucca created difficulties about her part in Verdi's *Don Carlos,* Gye speculated that Costa had put her up to it.[139]

From the mid-1860s, a note of tetchiness – never far from Gye's pen – crept more frequently into his entries about Costa, revealing that minor issues were becoming harder to manage. As they approached their 60s each man, under acute but different strains, was less ready to make allowances for the other. It was then that the lack of personal warmth between them began to tell. In 1865, when Costa declined to audition the tenor Hilaire because Gye had not asked him in person, Gye exploded: 'The man's arrogance is beyond all belief and I would have given him a devil of a blowing up, but such pride is too pitiable.'[140] A month later, Gye recorded bitterly that Costa had not sent him a ticket for the first night of his oratorio *Naaman*, 'although I am constantly giving him opera boxes besides the one I give him for the season'.[141] Several pages of Gye's Diary are taken up with a quarrel over whether Costa needed to ask Gye for permission for Patti to sing at the 1864 Birmingham Festival. Gye said that 'as a matter of business I did not wish her to sing there, but as it was for him she might go with pleasure'. But Costa's 'absurd pride' prevented him from asking or even thanking him.[142]

It was a sign that relations were deteriorating that Gye increasingly recorded stories to Costa's discredit (as indeed he did about other musicians). The soprano Marguerite Artot 'innocently committed the *enormous indiscretion* of telling Costa the other day that the chorus did not sing in tune with her!!! She little knew the tender ground she was treading on; it has doubtless made the gentleman her enemy for life.'[143] When Costa complained about the soprano Fioretti, Gye heard from Harris that 'she had written something to Graziani which had offended Costa's pride'.[144] When Costa tried to replace Hermione Rudersdorf in the part of Donna

---

137 Gye, 22 Jun. 1852.

138 Gye, 21 Apr. 1854.

139 Gye, 5 Jun. 1867.

140 Gye, 31 Mar. and 6 Apr. 1865.

141 Gye, 12 May 1865.

142 Gye, 13–24 May 1865.

143 Gye, 28 Jun. 1864; emphasis in original.

144 Gye, 10 May 1865.

Elvira, 'I found out that he had had some row with Rudersdorf at Exeter Hall about his Oratorio'.[145]

Gye's many anxieties aggravated his health and morale. His Diary reveals his vivid fear that he was about to be arrested for debt or in connection with his legal battle with Lumley over the services of Wagner's niece Johanna.[146] A long-standing sufferer from the 'brown ague', he began in the late 1860s to complain of fatigue. He had always shown a misanthropic strain. He was not on speaking terms with his own father, who tried repeatedly to dun him for money. Although capable of charm, he regarded nearly everyone in the opera business with suspicion or contempt. His feud with Colonel Knox went through the Chancery Division to the Lords, leaving a bitterness so deep that Knox sought to harm Gye by investing in Mapleson's company. Gye saw his partner Mitchell as 'perfidious', Lumley 'the most dreadful rascal', the impresario Jarrett 'a traitor', the manager Beale 'a very undecided slippery chap', Mapleson 'untrustworthy', Meyerbeer 'an intriguer', the soprano Jeanne Cruvelli and her brother 'cormorants', the bass Joseph Tagliafico a 'devil' and Grisi and Mario 'mean-spirited wretches'. He even suspected his favourite Patti of being 'up to some tricks'. Increasingly intolerant of criticism, Gye began in 1869 to keep a press cuttings scrapbook in which he annotated objectionable reviews.[147] By then, according to Mapleson, he was physically unwell and in a state of nervous irritability.

In the late 1860s, the balance of power was shifting in ways that changed the chemistry of their relations. Gye was the dominant manager in London. He no longer needed Costa as a link to the Queen, who had ceased to attend the opera after Albert's death in 1861. Although Costa retained his contacts with the royal family, Gye was able to develop his own close relationship with the operaphile Prince of Wales, for whose mistress Pauline Lucca he occasionally rescheduled the programme.[148]

In this situation, it became more difficult to handle the underlying issues of finance and authority which had lain like a land-mine at the base of their relations. Having taken over Covent Garden on the verge of collapse, Gye proved to be an effective manager, dropping expensive singers and drastically cutting the ballet. But he remained financially vulnerable. The opera accounts, admittedly unreliable evidence, suggest that he made an average loss of about £3,000 a year in 1851–54 and a modest net profit in 1855–58.[149] He had no choice but to pay progressively more to his top soloists, who ceased to see him as a partner in a battle for survival and regarded him as the manager of a flourishing opera house. In 1853, he begged his bankers, Coutt's, to carry over his loan because of 'the many contrary

145 Gye, 25 May 1865.

146 Gye, 11 Jan. 1854

147 Gye, 1869–73, ROHC.

148 Gye, 14 Jun. 1867.

149 Gye, 12 Feb. 1865. Dideriksen and Ringel, 28. Gye versus Knox PRO, C16/31/K27 29 Apr. and 15 Sep. 1861.

circumstances of the last opera season'. Three years later, he had to pledge his family jewels as security for a loan.[150]

Costa knew that Gye's cash-flow problems were real, but he was exigent about payment of his salary, which rose from £1,200 (1851) to £1,500 (1862) and £2,000 (1866) – the same as Gye claimed to be taking.[151] In a typical exchange in 1866, Gye explained that he could not pay the last instalment of Costa's salary because some subscribers had gone away without paying: 'I am very very sorry but I really cannot help it. Believe me.' Under pressure from Costa's solicitor, he later sent a cheque for £200 and a box of grouse, but losses on Covent Garden's concert series forced him to carry the remaining £200 into 1867.[152] The next year Gye expressed surprise when Costa's solicitor threatened a writ for non-payment.[153]

More serious for Gye than Costa's salary was his inability to control the cost of the musicians whom he saw as an easier target for economies than the top singers. Gye understood that the grand opera repertory called for larger numbers of capable musicians. But he continued to press for ways of reducing their wages. For Costa, this raised issues of musical standards and welfare as well as authority. John Ella may have been exaggerating when he claimed that salaries of soloists had doubled and of musicians halved between 1830 and 1870. But the rank-and-file musicians were dangerously close to what Dickens and Thackeray called the 'shabby-genteel people', obliged to maintain a middle-class image on the basis of a frugal salary.[154]

As early as 1849, Gye thought he had persuaded Costa to cut the musicians' rates by a quarter, but he discovered that Costa had not done so for fear of losing some of his best players.[155] Gye warned that 'he would be the ruin of the theatre' and tried to negotiate direct with the chorus, but significantly it was Costa who persuaded them to sing.[156] After the 1856 fire, Gye secured a salary cut of one-eighth, but Costa and the musicians saw this as a temporary concession and it remained a vexed issue between them. In 1865, Gye rejected the band's demand to restore the one-eighth, 'but of course as usual he took their part'.[157] Costa's day-to-day management of the orchestra enabled him to evade Gye's fiscal austerity, as when he opened the chorus pay-list a day earlier than Gye wished in 1866.[158] But Gye appreciated that Costa's regime was cost-effective for him. When the players demanded an increase in 1866, Costa advised him correctly that they would not

---

150 Gye 15 Jan. 1853 and 9 Jan. 1856.

151 Gye, 25 Jan. and 1 Feb. 1868.

152 ROHC, Gye to Costa (12 and 17 Aug. 1966). Gye, 12 and 17 Aug., 17 Sep. and 5 Dec. 1866.

153 Gye, 12 Oct. 1867.

154 Dickens, *Sketches by Boz* (1836), vol. 3, chapter X; Thackeray, *A Shabby-Genteel Story*, (1840 unfinished).

155 Gye, 22 Nov. 1849 and 5 Mar. 1851.

156 Gye, 7 Apr. 1849.

157 Gye, 11 Jan. 1865.

158 Gye, 7 Feb. 1866.

press their case.[159] They gradually found their way to an arrangement under which Costa drafted the musicians' contracts and sent them to Gye for signature.

Gye's financial position appears to have worsened during the 1860s. The cost of rebuilding Covent Garden raised his debts to £145,000 in 1860, forcing him to borrow at high interest rates, which kept him 'in constant anxiety and hot water'.[160] After a brief monopoly in opera during 1861 and the Great Exhibition season of 1862, he was hit by the decline in foreign visitors during the American Civil War and the costs of his continuing lawsuits (particularly with his ex-partner Knox). He lost important sources of income when his main autumn tenant, the English Opera Association, collapsed in 1866 and the Floral Hall concerts made a loss in 1866–67.

Meanwhile, the running costs of Covent Garden escalated. To perform his grand opera repertoire, he had to increase the number of soloists from 23 (before 1856) to 28 (in 1861–67). Growing competition from Mapleson at Her Majesty's and from Drury Lane meant that he was in an escalating auction for the services of the leading singers. When Costa objected to putting on second team singers in *I Puritani* in 1868, Gye told him that he 'could no longer pay for perfection as the public would not pay for it'.[161] He even considered in 1863 taking over the *Théâtre-Italien* in Paris to secure a monopoly of the singers' services, but concluded that he was too independent to 'bow and scrape to Ministers'.[162] In 1865 he seriously contemplated selling his Covent Garden investment, admitting in his Diary that he did not care whether he remained as manager afterwards.[163] In 1867, he overdrew his account – 'a thing I never did before'.[164]

In a renewed effort to reduce the cost of the orchestra, Gye tried to negotiate directly with their leader. He described exultantly in his Diary that he had settled the orchestra's contracts before finalising Costa's.[165] But this coup failed: 69 players petitioned Costa to get Gye to accept 'our fair and full claims'.[166] Gye was reduced to pleading with Costa to scale the chorus back to 80 and taking on part-timers when necessary.[167] He was increasingly worried by the competition from Mapleson, who relied mainly on a diet of Italian operas, which could get by with a smaller cast and orchestra.[168] Mapleson was Gye's equal in tenacity and guile and had stronger musical credentials, having been a violinist, music critic and second-rank singer. But by 1867 Mapleson's financial position was even

159 Gye, 3 Aug. 1866.
160 Gye, 2 Aug. 1861.
161 Gye, 6 Apr. 1868.
162 Gye, 9 Feb. 1863.
163 Gye, 14 Jul. 1865.
164 Gye, 5 Aug. 1867. Details in Ringel, 185–6.
165 Gye, 28 Jul. 1867.
166 Memorandum of 8 Jan. 1867 in the ROHC.
167 ROHC, Gye to Costa (31 Jan. 1867).
168 Ringel, 116.

more precarious than Gye's and there were rumours that he would barely survive the season.[169] He proposed, through an intermediary, a pact not to poach each other's singers and to pay them only 'curtain salaries'. Gye replied that he could not rely on Mapleson's word.[170]

Thanks mainly to Gye's tact, Covent Garden's 1867 season opened on a cooperative note. Costa finalized the orchestral engagements at his house after persuading the players that Gye could not afford to reinstate the one-eighth salary they were demanding. During Christmas week, Gye allayed Costa's suspicions about Augustus Harris and his fear that Gye planned to open the house five nights every week. 'He had evidently conjured up all sorts of things in his mind in consequence of Bottesini's engagement, who he said was a great blackguard … We however parted very good friends when I had reassured him.'[171] They compared notes about the Paris premiere of Gounod's *Roméo et Juliette* and the royal command performance during the visit of the Turkish Sultan in July. Having found a new modus vivendi, Costa largely disappeared from Gye's Diary and concentrated on the 15 operas in the 1867 prospectus, including premieres of Verdi's *Don Carlos* and *Roméo et Juliette.* They agreed a contract for 1868 on the usual terms. But on 7 December 1867, the situation shifted dramatically when a fire at Her Majesty's destroyed much of Mapleson's uninsured properties.

Gye's first reaction to the fire was to try to book Drury Lane in order to deny Mapleson an alternative theatre, but Mapleson beat him to it by one hour. Gye's readiness to pay £4,000 simply to frustrate Mapleson showed how anxious he was to end their ruinous competition. A third-party proposal to revert to a single Italian opera company brought them face to face for the first time in February 1868.[172] Gye commented that Mapleson 'seems a good natured but a wild harem scarem fellow and I fear … that his word is not in the least to be depended on.'[173] But he calculated that an Italian opera monopoly would yield a gross profit of about £20,000, and was therefore disappointed when this project petered out.[174]

Gye's finances deteriorated further in 1868. With no more surety to offer the bank, he could not pay Costa and the singers, and feared that one of them might start bankruptcy proceedings against him.[175] He again pressed Costa to reduce the expenses of the orchestra, which had risen from 12 per cent of the budget in 1861–67 to 15 per cent in 1868.[176] Costa 'allowed that the singers were too

169 Gye, 6 and 21 May 1867.

170 Gye, 24 Jun. 1867.

171 Gye, 22 Dec. 1866.

172 Gye, 31 Mar. 1868. The negotiations for Gye and Mapleson to be bought out by a consortium are fully described in Ringel, 227–32.

173 Gye, 6 Feb. 1868.

174 Gye, 1 Feb. and 31 Mar. 1868.

175 Gye, 28 May, 11 Jun., 25 Jun. 1868.

176 Ringel, 241.

highly paid, but the moment I talked upon the orchestra, he as usual opposed any reduction'. Gye warned him again that 'things could not go on as they are'.[177]

Gye's financial embarrassment helped to overcome his antipathy to working with Mapleson. In late June, feeling 'very unwell ... I wrote to Mapleson about joining the two operas'.[178] They began to meet secretly at Gye's house in Wandsworth. Gye remained suspicious of Mapleson who, according to Harris, was still trying to lure Costa.[179] Merger offered Gye the chance to neutralize the threat from Mapleson, tame the singers and musicians, and restore his bank credit with Coutts. Desperation rather than policy drove both parties to sign a confidential agreement on 11 August 1868 for a three-year partnership from 1869. Only one house, in practice Covent Garden, would perform Italian Opera, under the management of Mapleson.

With Mapleson signed up in a virtual Italian opera monopoly, Gye was for the first time in a buyer's market for musicians. This prospect seems to have triggered a change in his behaviour. For 20 years, he had gone to enormous lengths to humour his artistes, putting up with their tantrums, fake illnesses and exorbitant demands, and even – in the case of Mario and Grisi – paying their taxes. He took advantage of his agreement with Mapleson to offer Mario a shorter contract at a lower salary. Mario left the company, commenting that, after all his sacrifices, it was unworthy to bargain over the last notes of a singer's career. The alliance with Mapleson also marked a decisive shift in the balance of power between Gye and Costa. Gye no longer feared losing Costa to his rival and now had access, though Mapleson, to another conductor. Luigi Arditi, although not in the same league as Costa, was competent and pliable.

There is conflicting evidence about whether Gye wanted to retain Costa in the new circumstances. Mapleson maintained that Gye was 'most anxious to be rid alike of his services and of his tyranny'.[180] By July 1868, Gye was sufficiently serious about finding an alternative to Costa that he sounded out Patti's brother-in-law Maurice Strakosch.[181] Gruneisen stated that there had been no prospect of Costa staying since it was 'known full well that Mr Costa would never consent to ... not having the proper rehearsals and the control of the executants'.[182]

On the other hand, Gruneisen had earlier implied that Costa might stay: 'if Costa and Arditi will consent to work together, they are to be alternate conductor'.[183] Moreover Gye's Diary suggests that he went to some lengths to retain Costa, who was still the leading opera director in London and whose services could allow another rival house to emerge. Costa was the first person to be told in confidence

177 Gye, 8 Jul. 1868.
178 Gye, 19 Jun. 1868.
179 Gye, 3 Aug. 1868.
180 Mapleson, *Memoirs*. 82.
181 Gye, 29 Jul. 1868.
182 *London Standard* (25 Feb. 1868).
183 Announcement in *The Queen*, cited by Santley, Student and Singer, 271.

of the agreement with Mapleson.[184] Gye devoted much care to his negotiations with Costa, despite many other worries: he was complaining of chest pains and his father died that month. He took a whole day over drafting the key letter explaining his proposals to Costa, assuring him 'I will do all in my power to render your position as agreeable to you as possible and I trust that the 20 years we have been together may receive an addition of many more.'[185] Gye also abandoned several of the changes which he had initially written into Costa's new contract, including a cut in Costa's salary. He assured Costa that his 'recommendations' about musicians to be hired would be taken seriously.

It is fair to conclude that Gye wanted to keep Costa – but on his own terms. He stood firm on 'the *principles* I have laid down' (emphasis in original): there would be two conductors and the impresarios would have the final word in the management of the musicians. Gye may well have doubted whether Costa would accept these terms, which Gruneisen claimed would reduce his position to that of 'a call-boy'. Whatever his aim, Gye handled the exchanges adroitly, with an eye to not putting himself in the wrong with Costa's many admirers, including the royal family. He was thus able later to claim that 'notwithstanding the awful life he has led me for some years, I did all I could to enlist his services for the coming season'.[186]

Costa seems not to have grasped that a fundamental change had occurred. He did not comment on Gye's proposals, but simply stamped his old contract and sent it back for signature in the usual way. At the age of 61, was not prepared to yield the powers he had accumulated over 40 years. His reputation was high. He had, belatedly, been elected to the Athenaeum Club and rumours of a knighthood were in the air. He knew that, as Mapleson observed, Gye was afraid of his 'mere force of will'. For Costa, the central issue was the one that had governed his whole career: the need for total control over the musical resources necessary for disciplined performances. As he wrote to Gye:

> The Director of the Music, the Conductor and the Superintendent of the *mise-en-scène* is clearly responsible for the efficiency of the performances, and … it is out of all reason that he should be interfered with or subject to the control of others in the exercise of his functions.[187]

But for Gye the balance of power had changed: he was now in a position to bend the musicians to his will. To Mario as well as Costa, he pretended that his hands were tied by his deal with Mapleson. But it looks as though Mapleson was telling the truth when he wrote that Gye was the prime mover. Gye was determined to seize the chance to restore his finances by establishing an Italian Opera monopoly

184 Gye, 9 Jan. 1869.

185 ROHC, Gye to Costa (14 Jan. 1869).

186 Gruneisen, *Opera and the Press*, 44 and 53.

187 ROHC, Costa to Gye (27 Jan. 1869).

under firm managerial control. For Gye, Costa had ceased to be a necessary solution to his problems and become someone whose existing contract was an obstacle to his financial salvation. As their acrimonious correspondence leaked to the press, Gye offered Li Calsi the role of stand-in conductor at the derisory salary of £42 a month, but 'he was evidently afraid of Costa'.[188] On 22 February, Gye and Mapleson made the decisive move of engaging Vianesi and Arditi.[189]

Did Costa resign (as Gruneisen claimed) or was he dismissed (as recent scholars have argued)?[190] Neither seems to have been the case. Costa wrote to the *Daily News* on 20 February clarifying that he had not resigned. But he made clear to Gye on 27 January that he would not renew his engagement if Gye insisted on his new terms.[191] Gye in turn told Costa on 2 February that he would offer no further concessions. On the following day, Costa stated that, unless Gye confirmed his contract in its traditional form by 5 February, he would consider himself free of all obligations. Gye did not do so, but sent a further proposal three days after that deadline.[192] It is fair to conclude that they had reached an impasse in which it was obvious to both that Costa's position as conductor on the old terms could not continue.

The simplest explanation for the break was that, once Gye had an operatic monopoly, there was not room in the company for two ageing autocrats who had drawn incompatible lessons from their bruising early years at Covent Garden. Paradoxically, their main point in common – their hunger for control and efficiency – was the recipe for friction. The issue of who ultimately 'owned' the musical side of the venture resurfaced later in 1869 when Costa was asked to hand the performing score of *Dinorah* to Arditi.[193] Gye was incensed that Costa removed 'his' cuts from the score before handing it over. This was the sort of issue that a conductor could never expect to win. Given the commercial pressures on the opera house, it was inevitable that, when Costa's imperatives (efficiency, preparation, professionalism) came into stark conflict with Gye's (economic viability and control of expenditure), the latter would prevail. Costa's power at the opera house was not sustained by his successors. A letter from Vianesi in 1875 shows that Gye had successfully reduced the conductor's role at Covent Garden to that of an employee and intermediary.[194]

It is a sign of the bad blood between them that Gye recorded avidly in his Diary any points to the discredit of 'that rascal Costa'.[195] He circulated a folder

---

188 Gye, 9 Feb. 1869.

189 Gye, 22 Feb. 1869.

190 Ringel, 241. Cowgill and Dideriksen state that he 'sacked Costa'. 'Opera orchestras', 273. Ringel and Dideriksen state that Gye 'frequently considered releasing Costa', 23.

191 ROHC, Costa to Gye (27 Jan. 1869).

192 Gye, 8 Feb. 1869.

193 ROHC, Gye to Costa (5 and 15 Apr. 1869).

194 Vianesi to Gye, 1 Dec. 1875, RAM, 2007.928.

195 Gye, 25 Feb. 1871. Gye, 29 Mar. 1871.

of 'the Costa correspondence' and took a copy to the Prince of Wales to explain his side of the story.[196] Costa enjoyed a more immediate and public revenge, with acclamations at his next concerts and press articles lamenting the decline of the orchestra at Covent Garden.[197] Costa's knighthood in April 1869 particularly riled Gye – an entrepreneur on the fringe of social respectability. He later commented bitterly to the Prince of Wales' Secretary that the Queen clearly did not know how much money he had lost by catering to her wishes 'or else I felt that the Queen would not have made Costa and Benedict Knights & have passed *me* over, who had done more for the Lyric Drama in England than any other man'.[198]

Unlike Lumley in 1846, Gye did not face a mass-exodus of musicians. The senior of the new conductors, Arditi, acknowledged that there was 'much discontent and irritation' among the players, who maintained 'a dogged silence' on his opening night.[199] But most stayed on, though 14 players, the chorus-master (Smythson) and the leading soprano Christine Nilsson followed Costa when he joined Mapleson at Drury Lane two years later. Gye was correct in his belief that he could now impose his will on the musicians. He reduced the orchestra's share of expenditure from 14.64 per cent to 9.2 per cent, and forced the chorus to restore an earlier agreement to perform without pay on Mondays or Fridays, which Costa had opposed.[200] More important to Gye, he made sure that he always had first call on the players during the festival season.

Over the next three years, Gye employed four Italian conductors, of whom the most capable, Arditi, left after one season, in protest against dual conductorship and six performances a week.[201] Gye's experiment was roundly criticized, especially by the pro-Costa *Athenaeum*: it was:

> absurd to believe that the musical organisation, discipline and efficiency of an opera, the work of 22 years, could be transferred from the hands of a thorough disciplinarian, a consummate musician and an incomparable conductor to the rule of two professors with divided authority.

With too little time for rehearsal, 'haste, hurry and flurry' were 'the disorder of the day and inefficiency of the night'.[202] Without Costa's iron control, it proved hard to merge the two theatres' musicians and singers in a single company. There were 21 changes of programme out of 80 performances.[203] The musical side was sufficiently

---

196 Gye, 22 Jun. 1869.

197 *ILN* (24 Apr. 1869), 422. *The Orchestra* (30 Jul. 1869).

198 Gye, 30 May 1871; emphasis in original.

199 Arditi, *Reminiscences*, 181.*Pall Mall Gazette* (31 Mar. 1869).

200 Cowgill and Dideriksen, 'Opera orchestras', vol. 1. Gye, 8 Mar. 1869.

201 Gye, 6 Jul. 1869. Arditi, *Reminiscences*, 76 and 186.

202 *Athenaeum*, (23 Jul. 1870), 123 and (6 Aug. 1870), 185.

203 Ringel, 249. *Athenaeum* (1 May 1869), 613.

fragile for the bookseller Mitchell to suggest that Costa should be invited back. But such was the bitterness between them that Gye would not consider it.[204]

Although artistically undistinguished, Gye and Mapleson's first monopoly season netted a profit of about £29,000.[205] They failed to consolidate their monopoly by bringing in the manager of Drury Lane', which scored better reviews during the 1870 season, though neither company made a profit.[206] The Gye–Mapleson merger agreement had provided that Gye would 'take no part in the management unless he wished to do so'. But, as Mapleson observed drily, 'the wish came upon him after about a fortnight'. Mutual mistrust broke their partnership a year earlier than envisaged. Mapleson returned to Drury Lane, 'my first act being to secure the services of Sir Michael Costa'.[207]

Costa's nine-year collaboration with Mapleson at Drury Lane and later Her Majesty's was the smoothest of his career. Mapleson, a fellow mason, put up with Costa's 'despotic' nature because he valued the discipline that he brought to the orchestra, which the *Athenaeum* puffed as his best orchestra.[208] As usual Costa had 'full powers to regulate the musical doings according to his pleasure'.[209] Costa remained an exigent partner: the pianist Eugenio di Pirani described how Costa, at the request of the German Empress, forced Mapleson to hire him by threatening to resign.[210] After his disputes with Harris at Covent Garden, it was significant that the stage manager was appointed 'at the instance both of Mr Mapleson and Sir Michael Costa'.[211] Costa's musicians were frequently credited with redeeming Mapleson's middling cast.[212]

At Covent Garden, Gye used his unchallenged authority to adopt a new programming policy, based on a handful of stars (Patti, Emma Albani and later the baritone Victor Maurel) and a greatly increased number of performances. Unlike Costa, Gye's conductors (Vianesi and Bevignani) could be brow-beaten to perform five or six times a week, to suit his timetable.[213] In 1874, Gye put on 81 performances of 31 operas, compared with Mapleson's 19. The *Graphic* commented that the Covent Garden orchestra had lost the *esprit de corps* for which they had been distinguished under Costa and were 'hopelessly demoralised'

---

204 Gye, 28 Jul. 1869.

205 Gye, 15 Jul. 1969.

206 *Athenaeum* (12 Nov. 1870), 633.

207 Mapleson, *Memoirs*, 82 and 86.

208 *Athenaeum* (22 Apr. 1871), 503.

209 *Graphic* (25 Mar. 1871).

210 *Etude Magazine* (Jan. 1915), http://scriabin.com/etude/1915/01/well-known-composers-of-to-day-eugenio-di-pirani.html.

211 *Morning Post* (18 Apr. 1871).

212 For example *Examiner* (9 Aug. 1879). *Athenaeum* (15 Jul. 1871), 88 and (28 Jun. 1879), 833.

213 *Athenaeum* (18 Mar. 1871), 343. On too frequent performances, see also *ILN* (27 Jul. 1872), 94. On the deficiencies of Vianesi and Bevignani and divided control, *Athenaeum* (18 Mar. 1871), 343 and (29 Jul. 1871), 152.

by their two conductors.[214] Another critic wrote: 'Muster his forces as he will, Mr Gye cannot get the old galaxy or anything like it together. Think what the Italian Opera was in Costa's palmy days!'[215]

It was a period marked by artistic inertia for both theatres – 'five years perhaps unmatched for dullness in London's operatic annals'.[216] Drury Lane was generally judged the stronger when the two houses competed: in *Fidelio* and *Les Huguenots* (1871–72);[217] *Semiramide, Fidelio* and *Lohengrin* (1875);[218] *Robert le diable* (1876);[219] and *Aida* (1879).[220] But, while Gye claimed to make a profit of £15,000 a year in the period up his retirement in 1877, Mapleson invested disastrously in the abortive construction of a National Opera House at Millbank. Money was the trigger of his split with Costa, who had agreed to join him at a lower salary of £1,500, but resigned in 1879 when Mapleson was unable to meet back-payments that were overdue.

By then, Costa had been the leading operatic conductor in England for 47 years. He faced no challenge on his home ground, except for Richter's brief *Ring* performances in 1877. But there was growing competition in the other three main spheres of his career: concerts, the oratorios and the festivals. These fields are the subject of the next chapter.

---

214 *Graphic* (27 Jul. 1872).

215 *Pall Mall Gazette* (6 May 1884).

216 Davison, *From Mendelssohn to Wagner*, 291.

217 *Graphic* (20 Apr. 1872). *Athenaeum* (13 May 1871), 599 and (20 May 1871), 630.

218 Klein, *Thirty Years,* 44–7. *Examiner* (19 Jun. 1875). *Graphic* (20 Apr. 1872).

219 *Examiner* (3 Jun. 1876).

220 *Athenaeum* (28 Jun. 1879), 833.

Chapter 7
Concerts, Oratorios and Festivals

Concerts

Whereas Costa dominated the opera scene and set the pattern for opera conducting in London, he had to fit into a concert structure which was already burgeoning. In 1826–27 London, with more than twice the population of Paris and four times that of Vienna, was supporting 125 concerts, compared with 78 in Paris and 111 in Vienna.[1] Fétis estimated in 1829 that there were three or four concerts a day in the Easter-to-August season. By 1845 'the season is now all year round' and in 1863 the *Times* claimed that there were about 500 concerts a year.[2]

Concerts expanded more rapidly than the theatre and the opera, helped by the fact that they were less regulated and (from 1837) less heavily taxed. Concerts were more accessible to a wider social base.[3] As the audience expanded, the variety of concert models was extended. Virtuoso 'recitals' enjoyed a vogue from Paganini's first London concert in 1831; chamber concerts started in 1835; promenade concerts in 1838. Lenten oratorios broadened out to include secular and operatic works. One off benefit concerts increased from 15 in 1795 to 30 in 1825, 42 in 1828 and 61 in 1855. There was also a resurgence of private salon concerts, in reaction to the socially mixed benefit and promenade concerts.[4]

Composer-conductors from abroad, such as Mendelssohn, Hummel and Spohr, provided strong role models. But there were also numerous London-based musicians putting together concerts and 'conducting' them from the piano. The most significant was Sir George Smart, who presided at 49 Philharmonic concerts and in 1825 alone took 59 concerts. Because there were no permanent orchestras outside the Opera, sponsors of concerts had to recruit scratch orchestras, which they promoted as being 'chiefly selected from the opera band'.[5] Except for a small number of high-earning virtuosi – Paganini, Liszt, Thalberg – they worked to small profit margins and sought to attract their audience by offering *pot pourri*

---

1 William Weber, *Music and the Middle Class*, 262–3 and Tables 1–4. More work is needed to establish accurate concert patterns. Carnelley, 'George Smart', cites 78 in 1825, excluding private concerts.

2 Fétis, 'Music in London', 278–9. *Morning Chronicle* (26 Dec. 1845). and (4 Jul. 1863).

3 Pierre Bourdieu, cited in Weber, *The Great Transformation*, 91.

4 McVeigh, 'Benefit concert', 243 and 253. On Lenten Concerts, Howard Smither, *The Oratorio in the Nineteenth and Twentieth Century* (Chapel Hill: University of North Carolina Press: 2000), 281.

5 *Morning Post* (21 Jan. 1805).

programmes and novelties outside the current opera programme, often seriously under-rehearsed. The pianist Julius Benedict's annual benefit comprised 30 varied pieces and ran for four and a half hours.[6]

Costa's first appearance in a concert seems to have been at a benefit at the King's Theatre, with Malibran and Hummel, in 1830.[7] Six years later he was conducting a Classical Chamber Concert series in Willis' Rooms, performing Beethoven and Hummel Septets, with 'the full band' of the Philharmonic.[8] He later appeared in joint programmes at the opera house with Paganini (as accompanist), Liszt (as extra pianist) and Chélard (as co-conductor). By the end of the decade he had become the leading conductor of benefit and salon concerts. His prominence on this circuit was helped by his position at the opera house, which supplied most of the players and singers for these concerts. Operatic excerpts also made up an increasing share of the programmes: from 17 per cent in the 1820s, to peak at 24 per cent in the 1830–40s.[9]

Part of Costa's job as Musical Director was to conduct the opera house concerts, trading on the appeal of the house's stars and favourite arias. These concerts helped to demonstrate the superiority of Costa's musicians over Balfe's, when the latter ventured into the same field[10] (Figure 7.1). They were also an

Figure 7.1 Balfe conducting a concert at Her Majesty's (*ILN,* 26 Oct. 1850) (courtesy of Westminster City Libraries)

6 *MW*, vol. 33 (1855), 334. Also *Times* (27 Jun. 1848).

7 *Morning Chronicle* (5 Jul. 1830).

8 *Morning Post* (4 Feb. 1836).

9 McVeigh, 'Benefit concert'.

10 Lumley, *Reminiscences*, 290.

important source of income for the opera house: it was Costa's series at the Crystal Palace in 1856–67 which kept the company afloat after the Covent Garden fire. Like benefits and private *soirées*, opera concerts lacked the aesthetic cachet of abstract music. The *Times* complained in 1850 that a programme of 'a couple of hackneyed overtures and the accompaniments of a string of Italian cavatinas and duets … differs in nothing from the fashionable monster concerts'.[11] Although Costa gradually passed most of this work to Alfred Mellon and Bottesini, his reputation suffered from his association with this less weighty fare. After a good performance of Beethoven's Symphony no. 7 in 1878, the *Times* regretted that he had in the past 'wasted his splendid orchestra's resources on the performance of hackneyed overtures'.[12] But during the 1840s, by including a few symphonic and choral pieces, he was able to show that he was qualified to conduct the repertoire of the Philharmonic and the SHS.

Private Aristocratic Concerts

The *QMMR* noted in 1823 the rapid growth of private musical parties, as wealthier patrons separated themselves from the socially mixed benefit and promenade concerts.[13] Initially the most frequent 'conductors' at these social occasions were Smart, Greatorex and a Signor Scappa.[14] But Costa was well placed to become the leading organizer of these concerts. He was not only a member of the Old Guard, who were the most sought-after performers; he alone had the authority to ensure that these prestigious events did not suffer from the lack of rehearsal and ill-discipline that marked most benefit concerts.[15] His dominant role in this market gave him early social exposure in a central part of the London season.

Between 1835 and 1860, he conducted, directed or 'presided at the pianoforte' at more than 80 concerts at Kensington Palace, Buckingham Palace and other aristocratic residences.[16] The list of his clients is significantly more aristocratic than Smart's from the previous generation. A handwritten programme shows him acting as both impresario and accompanist for one of many concerts he organized for Victoria in consultation with the royal family.[17] His position as gate-keeper gave him leverage over the opera stars, for whom these events were lucrative and prestigious. Fétis remarked that private concerts were 'the curse of the Italian manager', since the singers rushed from the opera to attend soirées, often refusing to sing heavy parts on concert nights and missing rehearsals the

11 *Times* (25 May 1850).

12 *Times* (28 Aug. 1878 and 3 Jun. 1879).

13 McVeigh, 'Benefit concert', 253–4.

14 *QMMR*, vol. 18 (1823), 252.

15 *QMMR*, vol. 10 (1828–30), 90.

16 Author's data, based on concert programmes and press announcements.

17 Vic addl mss 1585 (18 May 1835).

next day.[18] Laporte called them 'those theatrical indignities which it is my provision to endure'.[19] Costa, as director of the opera and impresario of these concerts, must have been in a highly ambivalent position.

The Philharmonic

The *laissez-faire* diversity of the London market discouraged the development of a specialized concert orchestra of the kind that dominated Paris (the Conservatoire) or Vienna (the Philharmonic). From its start in 1813, the London Philharmonic drew extensively on the opera house players. Founded in a mood of self-conscious innovation – even the name was new – its ethos was idealistic and high-brow. Its programmes initially excluded vocal or instrumental solos and concentrated on orchestral works of 'the Greatest Masters', which were beginning to be labelled 'classical' and would later be considered 'canonical'.[20]

The most marked characteristic of the early Philharmonic was its egalitarian and collegial make-up. Its first prospectus forbade any 'distinctions of rank' and a second prospectus laid down that 'the station of every performer shall be absolutely determined by the Leader of the Night' – a post which itself rotated.[21] The instrumentalists who dominated the Philharmonic Society tried to function as a cooperative, initially without pay or professional management, but found themselves increasingly at odds with the specialization that was beginning to shape London's musical life. By the 1840s, the Philharmonic was suffering from falling subscriptions and beset by internal feuding. There was growing criticism of its sclerotic programming and of untidy performances under the system of divided control (Chapter 4).[22] Whereas Costa's system had brought clarity to the opera house in the mid-1830s, use of the title of 'conductor' at the Philharmonic (from 1820) and of the baton (from 1833) simply made the continuing competition between the conductor and leader more obvious. The Society thus became the focus of the controversy about conducting.

The first group of Philharmonic 'conductors' (Bishop, Smart, Moscheles, Loder) took up the baton too late to develop an effective technique and lacked 'that firmness with which a conductor should control his orchestra'.[23] They also lacked the continuity enjoyed by the orchestra's violin-leaders: the three violinists who led the 48 Philharmonic concerts between 1840 and 1845 easily eclipsed the seven

---

18 Fétis, 'Music in England', 245.

19 Laporte to Bunn (9 Jun. 1835), Bunn, *The Stage*, 237.

20 Temperley, 'Xenophilia in British musical history', 3–19. For a full discussion see Ehrlich, *First Philharmonic* and Weber in, inter alia, *The Rise of Musical Classics*, 337–55.

21 BL RPS MSS K.6.d.3.

22 *Spectator* (2 Jul. 1842). Ehrlich, *First Philharmonic*, Chapter 4, 'The Quest for Leadership'.

23 *Athenaeum* (16 May 1840), 403.

ad hoc 'conductors', except for Mendelssohn.[24] The *MW* identified divided control and lack of continuity as the main obstacles to improvement. It pointed to the obvious remedy: 'We need but compare the orchestra of the Italian theatre under one head with that of the Philharmonic Concerts under many to prove the error of the system pursued at the latter.'[25]

The Philharmonic directors swallowed their collegial principles to the extent of appointing Mendelssohn for most of the 1844 season.[26] But even he had to share control with leader Tom Cooke and complained about 'the radical evil which I have this time amply experienced … [which] must prevent the Society continuing to prosper – the canker in its constitution – musical rotten boroughs etc.'[27] The Philharmonic was still allergic to the dictatorship implicit in conducting: many believed that a conductor was merely an 'animated metronome', without any executive power.[28] The *Athenaeum* observed that the players, who 'hardly endured Dr Mendelssohn', were 'even less disposed to submit to a resident'[29]

These undercurrents cast doubt on the accepted narrative that, having knocked the opera house into shape, Costa was seen as the natural candidate to do the same for the Philharmonic. He had been blackballed as a Philharmonic member. There was strong resistance from the 'native talent' lobby, led by Davison who saw his close friend Sterndale Bennett as 'by far the best' for the job, but privately worried that any London-based conductor would attract 'displays of ill-feeling and petty prejudice'.[30] In addition both Chorley and Davison took the view that Costa lacked the pedigree to conduct the German 'classics' which provided the core of the Philharmonic repertoire. Chorley wrote in 1844 that the appointment of Costa would be 'outrageously unpopular, both with Germans and Englishmen'. As an Italian, he was already liable 'to spoil by exaggeration the operas of Mozart'; a similar approach to Beethoven's symphonies would be fatal.[31] Davison's *MW* had long decided that 'Signor Costa is not at home in the German school of music.'[32] But, even in that austere organ, opinion was divided. The editor ('MW') did not endorse the view of one editorialist ('JG') that 'If M. Costa's appointment takes effect … then adieu to the fame of the Philharmonic.'[33]

---

24 The leaders were F Cramer (10), Loder (21) and Cooke (17); the 'conductors' were Moscheles (11), Smart (9), Bishop (8), Potter (6), Mendelssohn (6), Lucas (6) and Sterndale Bennett (2). Statistics from Foster, *Philharmonic Society*.

25 Leader in *MW* (26 Mar. 1840), 185–8 and (26 Mar. 1840), 187.

26 *MW* (25 Apr. 1844), 141.

27 Mendelssohn to Paul, *Felix Mendelssohn's Letters*, ed. Paul Elek (London: Cole, 1946), 182–3.

28 *QMMR*, vol. 8, no. XXX, 438. *ILN* (9 Aug. 1845), 90. *Athenaeum* (2 Aug. 1845), 772.

29 *Athenaeum* (12 Jul. 1845), 697.

30 *ILN* (9 Aug. 1845), 90. *MW* (24 Jun. 1836), 22 and (25 Apr. 1844), 141–2.

31 *Athenaeum* (16 Nov. 1844), 1051.

32 *MW* (24 Jun. 1836), 22.

33 *MW* (30 Jan. 1845), 50.

With Mendelssohn unavailable for 1845, the Philharmonic was in crisis. Ella, the leader of the second violins, wrote in his diary that only 'total regeneration' would save the Society from decay.[34] After being turned down by Spohr and Habeneck, the Society in desperation invited Costa to take on the 1845 season. When Lumley refused to release Costa from his contract at the opera, they appointed Henry Bishop, who again demonstrated his 'want of a presiding spirit … the conductor had no control over his orchestra and the orchestra did not seem to understand the gyrations of the conductor's baton'.[35] As criticism crescendoed, Bishop resigned after three concerts and the season was lamely continued under Lucas and Moscheles. Invitations were hurriedly sent to Marschner, Lindpainter and Guhr for 1846 but to no avail.

The resistance to structural reform within the Philharmonic was apparent when the Society turned again to Lucas, only to reject his demands for 'more rehearsals and absolute power, without the interference of leaders'.[36] Costa was now free of his contract with Lumley and was being encouraged by Prince Albert to take on the Philharmonic, But it was obvious that Costa would be at least as demanding as Lucas.[37] Moreover, a performance by Costa of Beethoven's Symphony no. 6 in May 1845 confirmed Chorley's doubts about his suitability. Although well-disciplined and correct in most of its tempi, Costa's conducting showed too much of the Italian spirit:

> a disposition to exaggerate every passing *swell* of tone into an *emphasis* which destroys flow … A conductor of German music can only be satisfactory so far as he is able to germanise himself; and this neither Signor Costa nor M. Habeneck seems able to do. We have better hopes of the former however because, besides being the younger man, he studies deeply.[38]

But two months later, Costa's conducting of *Cosi fan tutte* at Her Majesty's led Chorley to detect 'an increased temperance' and 'that universal comprehension of music to which few attain – and *very* few Italians'.[39] Costa was clearly trying to demonstrate his credentials with performances in the opera house concerts of the overtures to *A Midsummer Night's Dream* and Weber's *The Ruler of the Spirits*, which the *MW* reviewed enthusiastically.[40]

---

34 *RMU* (11 Mar. 1845).

35 *MW* (24 Apr. 1845), 183.

36 *ILN* (9 Aug. 1845).

37 *ILN* (4 Jul. 1846), 11.

38 *Athenaeum* (10 May 1845), 469; emphasis in original.

39 *Athenaeum* (26 Jul. 1845), 744; emphasis in original.

40 *MW* (24 Apr. 1845), 181.

In the summer of 1845, the Philharmonic again approached Costa, offering a salary of 10 guineas an evening, twice the rate paid to Moscheles and Bishop.[41] His characteristically strict conditions were at first rejected but, when Costa then declined the job, the directors conceded most of his demands, while reserving to themselves control over the repertoire.[42] He was still not even an associate of the Society and had to be hurriedly elected as member.

Chorley described Costa's 'absolute power' as 'the most important announcement of the season'.[43] He immediately changed the lay-out, rationalized the orchestra's pay-scales and demoted the leader, who was listed in programmes simply as a section principal. Later, he banned outsiders from rehearsals and stopped lead players from sending substitutes to rehearsals. Around 1850 he standardized 'Philharmonic' pitch at the level of the Covent Garden orchestra. He also used his authority to introduce a more restrictive policy towards encores, frequently refusing repeats that interrupted the plot of an opera or oratorio or which tired a singer or unduly prolonged a concert.[44]

In two areas he had more difficulty at the Philharmonic than elsewhere. He rarely escaped the rule of one rehearsal per concert. The *Times* described it as 'preposterous' that he was allowed only a single rehearsal for a marathon concert involving Spohr's Symphony in C minor, excerpts from Mendelssohn's *St Paul*, Beethoven's Mass in C and his Symphony no. 9.[45] The other area where he met opposition was over weeding out less competent players. This had to be approached gradually and with tact, since good players were still in short supply and some elderly instrumentalists were protected by directors.

Overall, Costa's were the most radical reforms that the Philharmonic saw in the nineteenth-century. He was able to carry them out because the Society needed services that only he could provide. He imposed a tighter discipline on the players, most of whom were from his opera house orchestra. He coordinated rehearsals and performances between the Philharmonic and the opera house, which had in 1841 prevented its players from attending the Philharmonic's morning rehearsals.[46] He also brought back to the Philharmonic the opera stars, whose services had been with-held by Laporte since 1836.[47] He saved rehearsal time by importing pieces that had already been performed at Covent Garden. The Philharmonic archives contain

41 His salary was raised to 15 guineas in November 1851. Costa to Watts (12 Nov.1851), BL PRS MSS 339/223.

42 Costa letter (16 Aug.1845), Foster, *History of the Philharmonic Society*, 193.

43 *Athenaeum* (3 Jan. 1846), 18.

44 For example, from the *Times*: to rest Mario and preserve 'dramatic propriety' in *Les Huguenots* (20 May 1850); to sustain the plot in *Elijah* (28 Aug.1862); to avoid over-running a long Philharmonic programme (22 Jun. 1847). He was, however, occasionally overruled by Queen Victoria: *Daily News* (18 Jun. 1857).

45 *Times* (30 Mar. 1847). Foster, *Philharmonic Society*, 71. Pamela J. Willets, *Beethoven and England* (London: British Museum, 1970), 51–2, 209.

46 BL, Lbm Loan 48, 2/3, 4 Feb 1841.

47 *MW* (15 Apr. 1836), 80. *Athenaeum* (30 Apr. 1836), 315.

many requests to him to negotiate the appearance of individual soloists and to supply scores.[48] He had the loyalty of the first violin, Tom Cooke, and was popular with the players, who cheered his first appearance.[49] He arrived at the Philharmonic with growing prestige. The *ILN* commented on his closeness to the royal family and their regret at his departure from Her Majesty's.[50] In February, the Queen pointedly complimented Costa at a state banquet by commissioning the band to play selections from his opera *Don Carlos*.[51] She also made a more public gesture at his second Philharmonic concert, praising his conducting and his new lay-out.[52]

These assets help to explain the remarkable impact of Costa's first season. As always, the critics, especially Hogarth as Secretary of the Philharmonic, need to be interpreted with scepticism. But one past detractor, Chorley, was quick to eat his earlier criticisms:

> the first Philharmonic Concert established Signor Costa in the foremost rank of conductors … we have heard no Philharmonic performance to compare with Monday's … We felt conscious of an alertness and a submissiveness, a delicacy and a spirit new to the Hanover Square rooms; of a near approach to the highest continental style of finish, such as is produced at Leipzig under Mendelssohn and at Paris under Habeneck.[53]

His first test, a trial run-through of the *Missa Solemnis*, impressed an audience of sceptical connoisseurs. 'They were literally playing from sight; and yet so clearly and firmly were they guided by Mr Costa … that they not only moved together with a precision and smoothness which rendered it seldom necessary to interrupt them for the sake of correction, but gave the nicest graduations of sound and the most delicate orchestral effects.'[54] His first concert had a typically overloaded Philharmonic programme: Weber's Overture to *Oberon* (which was encored), two Haydn symphonies, Beethoven's Symphony no. 3 and a Spohr violin concerto. The *MW*'s verdict was one of 'unqualified satisfaction'.[55] At the second concert before the Queen, Beethoven's Symphony no. 6 'excited the auditory beyond measure'. There were three encores at the third concert, which offered Spohr's Symphony in D and Beethoven's Symphony no. 8. Chorley detected 'a much freer and more expressive handling of the music than we had expected … an increase

---

48 Hogarth to Costa (15 May 1854) about Castellan, Lablache and Thalberg. BL RPS MSS 330/95.

49 *MW* (21 Mar. 1846), 130–31. *ILN* (14 Feb. 1846).

50 *ILN* (7 Feb. 1846), 96.

51 *ILN* (21 Feb. 1846), 130.

52 *ILN* (4 Apr. 1846), 226.

53 *Athenaeum* (21 Mar. 1846), 298.

54 *Daily News* (13 Mar. 1846).

55 *MW* (21 Mar. 1846), 131.

of temperance … The power which Signor Costa has already gained over the orchestra was notably displayed … .'[56]

At the fourth concert, Costa risked his reputation by performing Mozart's Symphony no. 40, followed by Beethoven's *Choral Fantasy* and the first complete London performance of the *Missa Solemnis*. He was unusually allowed three rehearsals. The *Spectator* pronounced the performance far better than Spohr's at Bonn', for which there had been three months of rehearsal.[57] Chorley commented that:

> his was no case of a German master directing German singers who had all their choral lives been nibbling at portions of the work – but an Italian *maestro* called upon to beat the comprehension of its novelties into the overwrought and ill-paid music-manufacturers of a London season.[58]

The remaining four concerts repeated the pattern: efficient performances of Beethoven, Haydn and Mozart, interspersed with a diet of overtures, arias and concertos (including Marie Pleyel playing Weber's *Konzertstück*). The Philharmonic secretary, Hogarth wrote that Costa had shown 'beyond a doubt that he is one of the greatest conductors – if not the greatest in the world … it has been acknowledged by all factions in London … the symphonies and overtures of Beethoven, Haydn, Mozart, Weber, Cherubini, Mendelssohn, Onslow etc. have never been so superbly rendered'. To celebrate a surge in subscriptions and a profit of £300, the directors gave him a whitebait dinner and a piece of silver plate.[59]

The 1847 season, when he had to combine eight Philharmonic concerts with his arduous first season at Covent Garden, confirmed the changes that he had effected. He shared the platform with Mendelssohn at what was to be the latter's last appearance. The Queen described the concert as 'one of the best I ever remember. Costa conducted admirably Beethoven's very fine [8th] Symphony.'[60] The Philharmonic again publicly thanked him 'for services during the last two seasons, through which the Society was saved from destruction'.[61]

For the next four years, the turnaround at the Philharmonic was helped by a surfeit of talented refugees from the Continent. Most of the critics reviewed Costa's Philharmonic conducting enthusiastically. There were ritual reports of ovations for Costa – the 'Atlas of the Society' – and favourable comparisons with Habeneck. Amid the plaudits, some remained unconvinced. The implacably hostile *Morning Post* largely boycotted the Philharmonic, objecting that he was 'utterly unfitted by

[56] *Athenaeum* (25 Apr. 1846), 434.

[57] *Spectator* (1 May 1846). *Morning Post* (6 May 1846).

[58] *Athenaeum* (9 May 1846), 485.

[59] *ILN* (4 Jul. 1846), 11.

[60] QVJ 26 Apr. 1847.

[61] *ILN* (26 Jun. 1847), 410.

education … altogether out of his element'.[62] Davison, also taking sides against Costa in the battle of the opera houses, criticized his 'hyperboles of expression' and excessive rallentandos, sticking to his belief that 'Costa is always safer with Haydn and Mozart than with Beethoven and the modern writers'. But by 1852 he pronounced the orchestra irreproachable, except for some 'passages where extreme delicacy and an absolute pianissimo are required'.[63] Chorley, always on the look-out for Italian foibles, warned that Costa, having freed himself from the English habit of ignoring accent and expression in the score, was now giving too much emphasis to the *sforzandos*.[64] But, after the first London performance of Cherubini's Symphony in D, Hogarth reported (in a dig at Chorley) that even his '*sforzando* critics were struck dumb by Costa's poetic readings'.[65] In 1853, Chorley wrote of 'a force, brilliancy and brio such as we now get from no orchestra save at the hands of Signor Costa. Ten years ago there was no such execution attainable in England.'[66]

For nine years, Costa conducted all but two out of 73 Philharmonic concerts – more than Smart (49) and Bishop (39) had undertaken. The Society enjoyed rising standards and financial success. Wagner described the Philharmonic as 'a magnificent orchestra, as far as the principal members go … strong *esprit de corps*', though he added that it showed 'no distinct style or fire of inspiration'.[67] When Berlioz shared the platform with Costa in 1853, his friend Ganz recalled that he expressed 'unbounded surprise' at the quality of the orchestra and declared diplomatically that 'one rehearsal will be ample with your orchestra'.[68]

As higher standards in the orchestra began to be taken for granted, the focus of the critics shifted to the Society's 'Philharmonically orthodox' programming. In 1854, the *Athenaeum* summed up a season 'suicidal in its exclusion of novelty' and redeemed only by 'the beauty of orchestral execution … '.[69] Some of the blame for this rubbed off on Costa since it was widely believed that he had absolute power. But the seven Philharmonic directors jealously guarded their right to select the programmes and relations with them were too fragile for Costa to challenge this. Costa's nine years at the Philharmonic saw virtually no change of repertoire and no sign of the increase in the proportion of operatic works which some had feared.[70]

The conservatism of the Philharmonic spawned a rival in the New Philharmonic Society, which 'does not entertain the opinion acted upon by *an elder institution* that no schools but those which may be called classical are to be considered'

62 *Morning Post* (30 Jun. 1846).
63 *Times* (30 Mar. 1847); *MW* (3 Apr. 1852), 213.
64 *Athenaeum* (19 Mar. 1853), 359.
65 *ILN* (7 May 1853), 339; *Athenaeum* (19 Mar. 1853), 359.
66 *Athenaeum* (23 Apr. 1853), 506.
67 Nettel, *The Orchestra in England*, 185.
68 Ganz, *Berlioz in London*, 162 and Hogarth, *Philharmonic Society*, 230.
69 *Athenaeum* (25 May 1854), 658.
70 For statistics, Goulden, Appendix E.

(my italics).[71] The New Philharmonic began bravely, with Berlioz offering a revelatory performance of Beethoven's Symphony no. 9 (after an unheard-of six rehearsals) and of parts of his own *Romeo and Juliet* Symphony and *The Damnation of Faust*. Clara Schumann performed her husband's Piano Concerto in 1856, 10 years before the old Philharmonic tackled it. The New Philharmonic went through the familiar cycle of new ventures: a brave reformist agenda, backed by generous rehearsals and extravagant early reviews, leading to disenchantment as finances ran out of control, standards fell and the repertoire stagnated. But it damaged the old Philharmonic, which made a loss of £50 in 1854.[72]

A more serious challenge to Costa came from Sterndale Bennett, who had resigned after Costa's appointment in 1846. Their mutual antagonism became notorious when Costa declined to conduct Bennett's overture *Parisina* after Bennett had tactlessly sent him a note demanding that it be taken more briskly.[73] Although the directors took Costa's side, Bennett was re-elected as a director in 1853 and Costa stayed only on condition that he need not attend meetings or conduct pieces of which he did not approve.[74] Early in 1854 Costa sought again to resign but was persuaded to delay his departure until the end of the season. His ostensible reasons for resigning were ill-health and overwork, but it was no secret that he was frustrated by the Society's amateur ethos and the interference of its directors.[75] The *Examiner* was probably correct when it commented that Costa could not bear to be 'ruled in council by those who were in every respect very subordinate to him'.[76]

The directors approached Spohr and Berlioz before rushing to engaged Wagner on a one-year contract.[77] Wagner's demands for a subordinate conductor and generous rehearsals were predictably rejected. His unhappy season, which produced a deficit of £400, has been extensively analysed elsewhere.[78] He made a significant impact, not least with English premieres of his own works. But the common theme of criticism was the contrast between 'the strict military rule of Mr Costa' and Wagner's unfamiliar and variable style of conducting. The London critics objected to Wagner's 'wavering, fidgety, uncertain beat', which 'fails to indicated the divisions of a bar with anything like intelligible point'.[79]

71 P.M. Young, *The Concert Tradition* (Durham: Dobson Books Ltd, 1965), 208.

72 *MW* (7 Mar. 1852), 203, (29 Jul. 1854), 504 and (23 Apr. 1855), 255.

73 Ehrlich, *First Philharmonic*, 80 and 86–7.

74 Gye, 30 Jan. 1853. Costa to Watts (7 Jan. 1853), BL MSS. 339. MSS 330/75v.

75 *MW* (27 Mar. 1852), 202. Cox, *Musical Recollections*, vol. 2, 289. Letter from Philharmonic Society member to the *MW* in 1855, quoted by Carse, *Beethoven to Berlioz*, 387.

76 *Examiner* (17 Mar. 1855).

77 Letters of 27 Nov. 1854 (to Spohr) MSS 330/96v and 24 Dec. and 1 Jan. to Berlioz. BL MSS 330/97 v and 98.

78 Enrlich, *First Philharmonic*, 88–92. Hogarth, *Philharmonic Society*, 107–10.

79 Henry Smart, quoted in Elkin, *Annals*, 56. *MW* (30 Jun. 1855), 416–17.

This echoed the complaint of the Dresden authorities in 1848 that he had 'beaten time incorrectly'.[80]

The next three decades at the Philharmonic are described by Ehrlich in a chapter ominously entitled 'Plateau and Descent'. The tenures of Sterndale Bennett (1856–66) and William Cusins (1866–84) lie outside this book but they throw interesting light on Costa's achievement. Many of his services had been covert – rehearsal practice, tight ensemble, retention of talent and replacement of incompetent players. The Philharmonic missed these skills, and especially his ability to bring in the opera singers and coordinate opera and Philharmonic timetables. When the opera began to put on Monday performances from 1862, the Philharmonic lost 40 of its best players. It also suffered a serious loss of continuity: only 15 of its 66 players remained by the end of the decade. Above all, there was a decline of authority and discipline. It is impossible to imagine Costa tolerating the turf war that occurred in 1856 between four leaders; or allowing players to skip rehearsals; or accepting a reduction of the orchestra from 77 (1847) to 66 (1860); or agreeing to cut the Philharmonic season to six concerts.[81] Standards fell as the Society, without Costa's ability to manage the limited pool of able players, struggled to compete with the New Philharmonic and August Manns' Crystal Palace orchestra, which was to provide the main impetus for orchestral advance in the next two decades.[82]

Oratorios

The Handelian tradition of choral performance gave the role of directing the players 'when necessary' to the leader. As late as 1844, William Crotch stated that 'the conductor of a public performance should … play nothing but the voice parts'.[83] George Smart stated that, until late in his own career:

> The conductor then sat at the organ, with a harpsichord, later pianoforte, so placed that he could reach also its keyboard and … played on one or the other throughout the recitative, and likewise in the rhythmical pieces, adding in these latter independent counterpoint … .[84]

---

80 Köhler, *Richard Wagner*, 217.

81 Ehrlich, *First Philharmonic*, 105–8. Koury, *Orchestral Performance Practices*, 155.

82 On the decline of the Philharmonic into 'torpor, complacence and routine', Elkin, *Annals*, 66. On Manns, Michael Musgrave, *An Audience for Classical Music: The Achievement of August Manns at the Crystal Palace*, Inaugural Professorial Lecture, Goldsmith's College (7 May 1996).

83 Preface to G.F. Handel, *Anthems for the coronation of King George II*, ed. William Crotch (London: Handel Society, 1844), v.

84 Macfarren, recalling a 1866 conversation with Smart, *Musical Times* (1 Dec. 1872), 668.

This was the arrangement at the leading society, the Ancient Concerts (1776–1848), which was 'conducted' from the organ by Thomas Greatorex. A similar division of roles between 'conductor' and leader applied at the Vocal Concerts (from 1792 intermittently until 1838) and the SHS.

Since its formation by mainly middle-class Dissenters in 1832, the SHS flourished sufficiently to fill London's largest concert room, the Exeter Hall. Enjoying the support of Mendelssohn and the royal family, it bid fair to become the focus of England's burgeoning choral movement. By 1845 however subscriptions had fallen from 600 to 260. Its mainly amateur forces were finding it hard to master a wider range of works by Handel and new ones by Mendelssohn. Like the Philharmonic, the SHS had yet to adapt to the new style of conducting. (Figure 7.2). In his last performance of *Elijah* in April 1847, Mendelssohn struggled with the 'rough and uncertain' orchestra and the 'most unruly and inefficient chorus'.[85] Above all, there was growing criticism of the regular conductor, Joseph Surman, 'whose forte is decidedly not conducting'.[86] After an inept performance of *St Paul*, the *ILN* prescribed 'a conductor of great professional experience and tact and of moral weight with the orchestra'.[87]

Figure 7.2 An SHS concert in the Exeter Hall in 1840, the conductor facing the audience (courtesy of www.hberlioz.com)

[85] Julius Benedict, Sketch, 52–3, contested by the SHS Treasurer, Bowley, *Sacred Harmonic Society*, 22.

[86] *Athenaeum* (26 Feb. 1842), 195. Also *MW* (16 Apr. 1840), 242. and *Morning Post* (4 Nov. 1848).

[87] *ILN* (18 Mar. 1848), 185.

The SHS approached Costa not because of his experience in this field (which was limited to rare forays in the 1830s),[88] but because it needed a strong conductor, who could introduce the order that he was delivering at Covent Garden and the Philharmonic. He was too busy at both to take charge for 1847–48 but, as the crisis deepened and Surman was dismissed, he agreed to conduct the SHS for the following season.

He promptly applied his formula. The offices of leader and organist were abolished. 'New and stringent regulations' enforced punctuality at rehearsals and made it easier to weed out weak singers and players.[89] The orchestra pit was reconstructed and laid out on the lines of the Philharmonic. The strings, 'formerly very weak', were reinforced and the band 'beautifully balanced', with the cellos and basses deployed behind the violins. The organ was tuned to even temperament. The chorus was expanded and 'wonderfully improved' by the addition of women altos and boys 'to sweeten the whole body of choral sound'.[90] In *Elijah* this addition to the altos made 'a great improvement especially in modern music, in which the alto part is written higher than in the oratorios of Handel'.[91] In some respects Costa was building on the arrangements adopted by Smart at the 1834 Handel Commemoration, where he conducted 'at a desk' with a keyboard in front of him, facing the orchestra, 'not playing himself, but beating time with a baton', and with the leader invisible[92] (Figure 3.5 above). But Smart did not repeat his conducting experiment at Victoria's coronation in 1838.[93]

In his first year, Costa attacked the main works of the oratorio canon, including Handel's *Messiah*, *Judas Maccabeus*, *Israel in Egypt*, the *Dettingen Te Deum*, Haydn's *Creation*, Beethoven's Mass in C, and Mendelssohn's *Elijah, Hymn of Praise* and *Athalie*. English critics, who were connoisseurs of oratorio and pedantic about shortcomings, reviewed his first season enthusiastically. He was praised for producing a remarkable improvement in a very short time, thanks to 'the extra care now bestowed on rehearsal'.[94] The SHS's annual report announced a 'marked improvement' and a surplus of £244.[95] Significantly, the advance of the SHS under Costa coincided with the closure of the Ancient Concerts after 72 years. Smart had earlier resigned in protest against 'the appointment of several conductors to one orchestra'.[96] A performance in April 1845 under Bishop led the *MW* to comment that 'Nothing could have been more melancholy and less musical.'[97] John Ella

88 Poster for 'Grand Sacred Oratorio' at Drury Lane, 15 Apr. 1837, V&A.

89 *Daily News* (6 Feb, 1849).

90 *Daily News* (2 Nov. 1848).

91 *Morning Post* (2 Nov. 1848).

92 Mount Edgcumbe, *Musical Reminiscences*, 232. *The Mirror* (5 Jul. 1834).

93 *MW* (1838), 74.

94 *Times* reprinted in *Musical Times* (1 Feb. 1849), 109–10.

95 These and other quotations are from the SHS annual reports for 1846–48.

96 Leader in *MW* (26 Mar. 1840), 185–8.

97 *MW* (24 Apr. 1845)

later expressed the view that 'Had the directors nominated Costa, instead of the late Sir Henry Bishop … he would have reorganized the choral and orchestral forces and infused vitality into the venerable institution'.[98]

In 1849–50, Chorley reported that Mendelssohn's *St Paul* 'went more brilliantly, firmly and delicately than ever SHS choruses went before Signor Costa took them in hand'.[99] Davison criticized some departures from Mendelssohn's tempi, but judged a repeat performance of *St Paul* 'a nearer approach to the desired perfection than any previous execution of the work that we remember'.[100] The season ended with another profit and expanding subscription lists. The SHS's own review of the year noted that 'even works which had grown familiar by frequent repetition … yielded a new satisfaction and delight, both to performers and the auditory'. The seal of royal approval was added when Albert attended *Israel in Egypt* and Victoria went with him to hear Mendelssohn's *Athalie* 'which … Costa conducted splendidly'.[101] It was a sign of changing tastes that the *ILN* described Mendelssohn's *Elijah* as a landmark performance 'not so much from the effectiveness of the principal singers as from the choral and orchestral ensemble … The entire performance … is the greatest evidence of their extraordinary improvement under Costa's artistical guidance.'[102]

The hey-day of the SHS came during the five months of the Great Exhibition in 1851, when it put on 31 performances and made a profit of £1,227. Performances were praised for their no-nonsense English qualities – 'solid round tone in the chorus and no humbug in the orchestra'.[103] Reviews typically claimed that the great works of Handel, Bach and Mendelssohn had never before been so well performed. Even Wagner recalled 'the great precision of the chorus of seven hundred voices, which reached quite a respectable standard on a few occasions'.[104] Spohr wrote that his *Calvary*, under 'the excellent conducting of Costa', left him 'completely overpowered'; the impact was 'more immense than the composer himself had ever conceived'.[105]

Costa brought other benefits to the SHS. He widened the repertory, adding eight Handel oratorios and many first performances of other works.[106] He gave the SHS access to the leading singers from both opera houses, virtually imposing on them the young Adelina Patti.[107] He persuaded the choir to produce 'a beauty of tone and a delicacy of reading not hitherto obtained from such a mass of singers

98 Ella, *Musical Sketches*, 71.

99 *Athenaeum* (2 Feb. 1850), 137.

100 *Times* (12 Jan. 1850) and (16 Feb. 1850).

101 RA QVJ 22 Jun. 1849.

102 *ILN* (13 Apr. 1850), 247.

103 Nettel, *The Orchestra in England*, 142.

104 Wagner, *My Life*, 634.

105 Spohr, *Autobiography*, 304.

106 Details in Goulden, 331–2.

107 Klein, *Reign of Patti*, 95

in London'.[108] But, as a largely amateur body, the SHS's forte continued to be the *fortissimo*. There were sometimes false entries and the vast choir was occasionally 'unsteady' – a grave crime in the world of heavy choral artillery. Costa's struggles are reflected in frequent complaints about his 'too audible prompting'.[109] But deficient first performances often led to a better rehearsed second try – as with Mendelssohn's *Christus*, which was criticized in November 1852 but presented with 'marked improvement' two weeks later.[110]

For three decades from 1848, Costa was Britain's leading exponent of the oratorio, performing one or two concerts a week during the Winter season. The SHS came to be recognized as the leading oratorio society in Europe. Charles Lamoureux took it as the model for the *Société de l'Harmonie Sacrée*, which he founded in Paris in 1873.[111] The scale and quality of SHS performances became a source of national pride in an ethos where oratorio was highly esteemed.[112] The *ILN* described the SHS as 'among the most extraordinary instances on record of the development of musical resources'.[113] After attending performances in Belgium, Holland, Germany and France, Gruneisen wrote 'how proud I feel at the progress in my own country and how conscious I am that our advancement has mainly arisen from the … exertions … of the SHS'.[114] Overall, the SHS had an immense impact on amateur choral standards in throughout the country.

By the 1870s, however, its status was contested by the provincial choral societies and Costa's pre-eminence was challenged by new generation of choral conductors, such as Joseph Barnby, who conducted a successful British premiere of Verdi's *Requiem* in 1875. Past successes bred complacency and inertia.[115] The SHS depended unduly on Costa's prestige and his heavy infrastructure of support staff who, according to Grove, strained the SHS's resources.[116] In 1881, it had to leave the Exeter Hall for smaller premises in St James' Hall. After Costa bowed out in the early 1880s, there was a move to sustain the SHS under Hallé but 'Nobody could supply Costa's place under the conditions of the time' and it finally expired in 1883.[117]

---

108 *Athenaeum* on *Solomon* (5 Mar. 1859), 326.

109 *Graphic* (21 Dec. 1871).

110 *Times* (5 and 17 Nov. 1852).

111 Southon, 61.

112 Leanne Langley, `The musical press in nineteenth-century England', *Quarterly Journal of the Music Library Association*, vol. 46, no. 3 (1990), 589.

113 *ILN* (2 Jan. 1869), 19.

114 Gruneisen to SHS (12 Nov. 1853), RCMA 4059.

115 *Pall Mall Gazette* (29 Apr. 1882).

116 Grove, *Pall Mall Gazette* (1 May 1884).

117 Bennett, *Forty Years*, 334. *Times* (26 Feb. 1883).

The Festivals

The SHS was Costa's entrée to his most visible national role – as director of the major choral festivals. The growth of the choral movement vividly illustrates the explosion of musical interest across England, boosted by the tuition systems developed by John Hullah and John Curwen.[118] The choral societies fostered new orchestras, commissioned new works and, from 1844, provided the main readership of the leading musical journal, Novello's *Musical Times and Singing Class Circular* (my emphasis). They were a spectacular exception to the trend towards passive consumerism, identified by Habermas as a by-product of the Industrial Revolution.

They also fed the growing fashion for the gargantuan – what Spohr called 'the habitual English taste for massive instrumentation'.[119] Choral societies could not emulate the theatre by putting on long runs of the same work, but they could exploit the increasing size of the orchestras, choirs and concert halls. Costa became the leading purveyor of this peculiarly Victorian phenomenon. He was invited to conduct the Birmingham Festival in 1849, 20 years after his humiliating debut there. As usual, he conducted not from the organ but from a rostrum. He also made systemic changes: total authority for the conductor, more focused rehearsals, a new lay-out and tighter discipline.

The Birmingham Festival consolidated Costa's image as the rescuer of ailing musical institutions. The *Times* reported that his first Birmingham *Messiah* achieved 'a style of unparalleled excellence' and that the Festival had been obliged to set aside its traditional ban on applause.[120] Costa remained in charge for 33 years, raising its reputation and pursuing a modestly adventurous repertoire. In 1858, the *ILN* compared the pre-eminence of the Birmingham Festival (in 'the usual magnificent state') with the 'very far from successful' Three Choirs Festival.[121] The *Graphic* described the orchestra as 'the finest and most accomplished in the provinces' and the chorus was judged superior to any in Germany.[122]

His achievement in Birmingham led other cities to seek Costa's services. In contrast with George Smart's role in many minor festivals (Derby, Newcastle, Bury St Edmunds, Bath, etc.), Costa directed the more important festivals at Bradford (1853–57) and Leeds (1874–80) as well as the single Glasgow festival of 1873. He was the natural person to oversee the grandiose re-opening of the Crystal Palace at Sydenham in 1854 after the skimped arrangements under Smart and Bishop at the 1851 Great Exhibition (Chapter 4).

---

118 For the northern choral societies, see Brian Pritchard, 'The music festival and choral societies in England in the 18th and 19th centuries' (PhD diss, University of Birmingham, 1986), vol. 2, section C.

119 Spohr, *Autobiography*, vol. 2, 312.

120 *Times* (5 Sep. 1849).

121 *ILN* (4 Sep. 1858), 221.

122 *Graphic* (2 Sep. 1861 and 30 Aug. 1873).

The success of the 1854 experiment and of Costa's opera concerts at the Crystal Palace in 1856–57 encouraged plans to make it the home of a regular Handel Festival. After successfully demanding huge resources, Costa organized a trial event in 1857 in the revamped main nave, which became known as the Handel Auditorium (Figures 7.3 and 7.4). He assembled 1,200 singers from as far away as Limerick and put on three major concerts. The scale and precision of the 1857 concerts led the *Times* to call it the musical event of the year. Meyerbeer described the performance of *Israel in Egypt* as the most wondrous display of choral power he had ever heard.[123] Chorley reported that:

> The great mass of vocal sound seemed to sway to and fro, like a balloon when the inflation is consummated before it is allowed to break loose … it was no less evident that the mass was under control … The energy, mastery and animation of Signor Costa … were never more signally manifest … there was something vast and noble and boundless – a delicious amplitude and richness of sound … which amounted to a new and poetic experience which went far to satisfy us that … even such monstrous performances as these may have real depth and truth and life and beauty as regards music.[124]

From 1859, the Handel Festival became a triennial three-day event, usually consisting of the *Messiah*, another major work such as Mendelssohn's *Elijah* and a mixed programme of less familiar works by Handel and others (including Costa). Preparations began with the auditioning and intense rehearsal of amateur choristers in the provinces. The quality of performance benefitted from the ability of the orchestra and chorus to work together over four full days.[125] Artistic success was matched by financial reward: by 1868, the takings were more than £100,000.[126]

Contemporaries were astonished by the grandeur and discipline of these performances. The stage at the Crystal Palace was four times that of the Exeter Hall and 16 times the Philharmonic's Hanover Rooms.[127] The young Prince Arthur reported breathlessly to Queen Victoria on a performance of *Israel in Egypt* in 1865: 'Costa was there as conductor and I do not suppose anybody could lead a band of such an enormous number as 4,000 better than he did. It was the most splendid sight I ever saw.'[128] Even Shaw admitted that 'the effect was on the whole stirring and impressive'.[129] At the 1862 Festival, there were 3,120 singers, 505 players and an audience of over 67,000. Three years later, the *ILN* speculated whether there were any limits to what could be attempted. 'After what we have

---

123 Bowley, *Sacred Harmonic Society*, 42.

124 *Athenaeum* (20 Jun. 1857), 797.

125 *Morning Post* (20 Jun. 1857).

126 *ILN* (27 Jun. 1868), 642.

127 Bowley, *Sacred Harmonic Society*, 48.

128 Prince Arthur to Victoria (2 Jul. 1865), RA VIC/Add A 15/710.

129 *Shaw's Music*, vol. 1, 151.

Figure 7.3 The Handel Festival at the Crystal Palace (detail) (*ILN*, 27 Jun. 1857, 630–31)

Figure 7.4 Costa conducting Sims Reeves at the Handel Festival. Distin's 'monster drum' behind (detail) (*ILN*, 8 Jul. 1865, 1) (courtesy of Westminster City Libraries)

heard, we do not see why we may not have 10,000 voices at the next festival.'[130] But some were beginning to argue that more was not necessarily better: the move of the SHS to a smaller venue at St James' Hall in 1881 involved in reduction of forces which the *Musical Times* thought 'a distinct improvement'.[131]

The Handel Festivals demonstrated not only the Victorian capacity for the grandiose: they also showed the impressive advances in musical performance since the 1834 Handel Commemoration, when 'the orchestra and choral effects were not by many a degree to be compared with what has since been effected by the SHS'.[132] Hogarth gave the main credit to Costa 'without whose profound knowledge of his art, practical experience, firmness, energy and indefatigable perseverance the great design … could not have been accomplished'.[133] Chorley wrote that 'The orchestra was without a fault – strong, superb and brilliant … under any other conductor … must such a scene have become one of hopeless confusion.'[134]

The Reverend Cox described a morning rehearsal at the Crystal Palace. 'Costa took his place with his accustomed punctuality amidst a perfect furore of applause both from the audience and orchestra.' He rehearsed parts of *Messiah*, then focused on less well-known parts of *Saul*, *Samson*, the *Dettingen Te Deum* and *Judas Maccabaeus*, which some in the choir were singing from sight. The rehearsal audience demanded an encore of the 'Hailstone' chorus from *Israel in Egypt*, 'which Mr Costa yielded at once … with his usual grace and good humour'. There was a further ovation for Costa at the end, with the orchestra 'vying with the general public in their demonstration of respect'.[135]

With their huge scale and solemnity, the Festivals Victorianized Handel and took on the flavour of a national institution. The Queen and Albert could be seen beating time with a fan and a scroll; and the opera stars competed to reinforce the amateurs.[136] With their broad social composition, the Festivals were a symbol of cohesion in a country that many feared had fractured politically during the turbulent 1830–40s and was becoming aesthetically and socially polarized.[137] They demonstrated the importance of the middle classes as consumers and patrons of music. The *ILN* proclaimed: 'It is among … the middle classes of England that this divine art, in its best and noblest forms, is now making progress with a rapidity and sureness unequalled in any other country in the world.'[138] For the *Times* the Festivals showed how music could contribute to 'the moral and

---

130 *ILN* (13 Jun. 1868), 642.

131 *Musical Times* (1 Aug. 1881), 401.

132 Cox, *Musical Recollections*, vol. 1, 309.

133 *ILN* (2 Jul. 1859), 22.

134 *Athenaeum* (25 Jun. 1859), 849.

135 Cox, *Musical Recollections*, vol. 1, 333.

136 For a good analysis of the Crystal Palace phenomenon, see, Michael Musgrave, *The Musical Life of the Crystal Palace* (Cambridge: Cambridge University Press, 1995).

137 Weber, *Music and the Middle Class*, 24–5.

138 *ILN* (25 Jun. 1859), 22.

intellectual training of the middle and lower orders of this country'.[139] They were also the main musical opportunity for London to meet the industrial cities and for amateurs to come together with professionals – encounters that did not flatter the London professionals.[140]

At its height, the oratorio movement took on a religious and liturgical as well as a musical significance. Performances of the oratorios of Handel and Mendelssohn were part of 'the musicalization of Victorian Protestantism', reinvigorating the Protestant hymn tradition and blending national and civic pride with art and faith.[141] Davison described the audience at a performance of Mendelssohn's *Sleepers Awake* at the 1853 Bradford Festival as 'absorbed in one feeling of awe, united in one act of earnest and sincere devotion'; music, 'the handmaid of religion, placed its fingers on the lips of the scoffer'.[142] Wagner detected here 'the true spirit of English musical culture, which is bound up with the spirit of English Protestantism', remarking perceptively that 'an evening spent in listening to an oratorio may be regarded as a sort of service, and is almost as good as going to church'.[143]

Finally, the choral movement – and the Handel Festivals in particular – were evidence of English superiority in what Rokstro called the 'cathedral' of the arts.[144] Englishmen took pleasure in comparing their choral prowess with pedestrian performances in France.[145] The Festivals thus became the vehicle for a new musical confidence in a country that still smarted from the neglect and patronizing comments of its neighbours. They enabled English music-lovers to show, after all that had been said to the contrary, that 'England may justly be classed as a musical nation'.[146] Indeed, many saw England as the defender of the tradition of Handel and Mendelssohn, who were elsewhere in retreat before the 'Music of the Future' and the 'prophets of Baal'.[147]

Costa's handling of these monster festivals gave him a nationwide reputation. They reinforced his image as an all-powerful conductor and demonstrated beyond doubt that conductors made an essential contribution to musical performance. Klein described him as 'in his time the greatest choral conductor that England possessed'.[148] But for the musically sophisticated, the Festivals came to be seen

139 *Times* (30 Jun. 1862).

140 *Athenaeum* (5 Mar. 1859), 326 and (28 May 1859), 719.

141 Michael Ledger-Thomas, '"Lyra Germanica": German Sacred Music in Mid-Victorian England', *German Historical Institute London Bulletin*, vol. 29, no. 2 (Nov. 2007), 30–32.

142 *MW* (10 Sep. 1853), 577.

143 Wagner, *My Life*, 634–5.

144 *Grove 1*, under 'Oratorio'.

145 On the Paris 1862 Exhibition, Bowley, *Sacred Harmonic Society*, 53. See also *Athenaeum* (26 Mar. 1859), 427.

146 Cox, *Musical Recollections*, vol. 1, vi. *ILN* (25 Jun. 1859), 22.

147 Ledger-Lomas, 'Lyra Germanica', 23–5. *Times* (5 Nov. 1852). 'Baal-worship' in Albert-Mendelssohn (20 Apr. 1847), Ledger-Thomas, '"Lyra Germanica"', 37.

148 Klein, *Thirty Years*, 55.

as an expression of Victorian philistinism. Verdi dismissed such large-scale events as 'a gigantic confidence trick' (though that did not deter him from slipping over incognito to hear *Israel in Egypt* at the Handel Festival or from using 150 players and 500–600 singers at the London performance of his *Requiem* in London in 1875).[149] A later *Times* critic, Fuller-Maitland, said that they had 'no more to do with Handel's intentions than the Cup Tie'.[150] Writers like Shaw were especially scornful of the ritualization of state events characterized by the heavy instrumentation of hackneyed works.

Costa's leading role in the opening of the Great Exhibition (1862), the Albert Hall (1871) and the Alexandra Palace (1873) raised his national profile (Figure 7.5). But his close association with these pompous state occasions and their repetitive programmes tended to obscure the achievements of his earlier years in the opera and concert hall and thus to dim his later reputation (Chapter 8).

Costa directed the Handel Festival until paralysis forced him in 1883 to hand over to Manns. By his last decade, Costa was no longer the only person capable of redeeming England's faltering orchestras. Others like Hallé in Manchester, Manns at the Crystal Palace and Cusins at the Philharmonic, with their own cohesive orchestras and more modern repertoires, were becoming the benchmark conductors, especially for orchestral works. When the French conductor Jules Pasdeloup visited London in 1878, the *Times* wanted to compare him not with Costa but with Manns or Cusins.[151] Foreign conductors such as Richter were ready to take over the more prestigious festivals like Birmingham. Moreover, festival

Figure 7.5 Opening of the Albert Hall (1871)

149 Verdi to Escudier (28 Jun. 1874), Gerald Norris, *Stanford, the Cambridge Jubilee and Tchaikovsky* (Newton Abbot: David and Charles, 1980), 142. John E. Borland, 'Orchestral and Choral Balance', *Proceedings of the Musical Association*, vol. xxviii (1901–02), 14. 'incognito' in Klein, *Thirty Years*, 59.

150 *Shaw's Music*, vol. 1, 151.

151 *Times* (4 Jun. 1878).

organizers were beginning to find Costa's rigid terms expensive and irksome. The Leeds Festival balked at his reluctance to conduct Bach and Beethoven's Symphony no. 9. It was a symbolic moment when the Leeds committee invited Costa to return on the understanding that the committee would select the repertoire and the band – conditions which Costa predictably rejected.[152]

---

152 William Spark, *Musical Memories*, 8.

Chapter 8
Costa's Reputation and Legacy

Contemporary Reputation

By 1880, Costa was 72 years old, at a time when life expectancy for those who reached the age of 15 was still only 60. His letters frequently complain of fatigue and stomach troubles. His last portrait photographs show a man wearied by 50 years of effort (Figure 8.1). In the last five years of his life, ill-health meant that the previously vigorous and hyper-active Costa became progressively less prominent in England's musical life. By 1879, he was delegating increasingly to his first violin, Prosper Sainton.[1] He conducted his last Handel Festival in 1880 and his last Birmingham Festival in 1882. Early that year, Victoria recorded in her diary 'Poor Sir Michael Costa is very ill, having had a stroke. He was paralysed and could neither speak or use his left arm, but has partially recovered the use of both.'[2] Critics noticed that this illness had a detrimental effect on his conducting.[3] Hallé commented that 'Poor Costa looks awful, but gets through his work in spite of his illness. There is

Figure 8.1 Costa in 1882

1 *Athenaeum* (19 Jul. 1879), 90.

2 RA QVJ 2 Feb. 1882.

3 *Pall Mall Gazette* (5 Sep.1882).

indomitable pluck in the old fellow.'[4] He relinquished his masonic posts and moved to convalesce in Hove on the south coast. Daily bulletins in the *Times* reported his decline and an apoplectic seizure from which he died on 30 April 1884.

It is a comment on the relative status of musicians and music in London and Paris that Costa was not given the honours accorded to Habeneck, whose hearse-ribbons were held by Auber, Meyerbeer and Spontini.[5] After a Church of England service, he was buried next to his father at Kensal Green Cemetery. The cortege included the Duke of Wellington, Hallé, Sullivan, Benedict, Carl Rosa, Santley, Bevignani and the younger Gye brothers, as well as representatives of the musical institutions and the Italian community. He left his estate to his brother Raphael, with provision for it to be used on the latter's death to fund British students to study composition abroad. In view of Costa's Italian pedigree and his limited lyrical skills, it was ironic that the scholarships were for composers with strong melodic skills to study in Germany. The *Musical Times* described his legacy (£6,789) as the biggest musical bequest since Handel and a fitting sign of his gratitude to his adopted country.[6]

Costa's musical achievement had probably peaked in the 1850s when, having reformed the orchestra and chorus at the opera, he did the same at the Philharmonic (1846), Covent Garden (1847), the SHS (1848) and the Birmingham Festival (1849), before launching the Handel Festival (1857). Thereafter, his ubiquity, energy and longevity ensured that he remained the dominant practitioner on the Victorian musical scene. He rehearsed and conducted virtually every performance during his 47 years at the two main opera houses.[7] None of his contemporaries or successors carried a comparable workload. Klein described him as 'the once all-powerful Sir Michael Costa'.[8] Joseph Bennett commented that he was:

> at the top of the profession, organising, marshalling and directing the operating of the principal musical forces of England, conducting Meyerbeer's operas, Handel's oratorios and Beethoven's symphonies without a rival … he could hardly have risen higher.[9]

During his last two decades, Costa's career continued on a plateau, but he enjoyed growing celebrity and high status. Queen Victoria's bestowal of a knighthood in 1869 (the first for conducting) gave him a unique status until the epidemic of musical knighthoods in the following decades. He remained in favour with the

---

4 Hallé to Marie (28 Aug. 1882), Michael Kennedy, *The Halle Tradition: A Century of music* (Manchester: Manchester University Press, 1960), 84.

5 Escudier, *France Musique*, no. 7 (18 Feb. 1849), 49.

6 *Musical Times*, vol. 25, no. 498 (1 Aug. 1844).

7 The only exceptions were brief appearances by Vaccai, Berlioz and Spohr, and rare stand-in duties by Sainton and Alfred Mellon.

8 Klein, *The Golden Age of Opera*, 118.

9 Bennett, *Forty Years*, 50.

royal family, especially the Princess Royal (whom he had taught) and the Prince of Wales (the leading Mason). He was frequently mentioned in the press and media. As early as 1835, Costa figured in Thackeray's *Cox's Diary* as one of the musicians whom the *nouveaux riches* Coxes mis-pronounce – 'Mr Coster'.[10] Three months before his death, he was portrayed in Gilbert and Sullivan's *Princess Ida*, leading the serenading party to besiege the walls of the castle. His image was boosted by the wide dissemination of lithographs, photographs and caricatures that went with the celebrity culture of mid-Victorian England. There are probably more portraits of Costa than of any London musician of the period, except for Lind, Grisi and Patti. His images often copy the aristocratic portraiture from which Victorian studies derived, attesting not only to his public position but also to the rising status of conductors.[11] His prominent role in the festivals and major state occasions further boosted his national profile.

His reputation benefited from the positive image of the institutions that he had rescued. The opera house in particular changed from 'what John Bull would stigmatise with a sneer as a *foreigneering* concern' – associated with xenophiliac customers and effete Italian and French musicians – to that of a successful English institution, patronized by a reformed monarchy and a respectable, serious clientele.[12] The *ILN* described the first night of *Les Huguenots*, where nearly all the chorus and band were English, as 'a national triumph'.[13] The *Times* commented in 1844 that English audiences now had 'the remarkable satisfaction of saying, "It is we that have made it". This ever renders the opera an object of national satisfaction.'[14] In addition, Costa's position at the SHS identified him with the explosion of musical activity in middle England and brought him the kudos of directing 'the leading musical institution of its class in the world'.[15] If the English had not recently produced a major composer, they could at least thank Costa for showing that they were among the leading practitioners and consumers of music.

Costa attracted respectful obituaries, embellished with the fairy tale theme of the journey from his disastrous start in Birmingham to his successes in the opera house, concert hall and festivals. The *Athenaeum* stated that his 'wholly exceptional position' was due to the fact that he was not only a great conductor but also 'the first great conductor who has permanently resided in this country'.[16] The *Musical Times* wrote that he was 'certain to reach posterity in his quality as a

---

10 Thackeray, *Miscellaneous Prose and Verse* (London: Bradbury and Evans, 1835), 482.

11 Mathieson, 'Embodying music', 116–25.

12 John Murray, *The World of London* (London: Murray, 1851), 155. Hall Witt, *Fashionable Acts*, 349, note 202.

13 *ILN* (29 Jul. 1848), 55.

14 *Times* (19 Aug. 1844).

15 Cox, *Musical Recollections*, vol. 2, 61.

16 *Athenaeum* (3 May 1884), 576.

conductor'.[17] The *Times* predicted confidently that he 'will have a permanent place in the history of English music'.

Decline of Reputation

After his death, Costa's reputation sank with remarkable rapidity. Joseph Bennett commented in 1897 that 'The present generation knows little of Michael Costa.'[18] Shaw wrote of 'the once famous and now forgotten conductor'.[19] The third edition of Grove's *Dictionary* (1927) wisely removed the judgement in its earlier editions that 'his services … will not soon be forgotten'. By the fifth edition (1954), the entry had been cut by a third. There are many explanations for this speedy eclipse.

Some are personal to Costa. The claims made during his lifetime were often over-stated, such as the *Times*' description of him as 'the man who by universal consent is the greatest in Europe'.[20] Particular care needs to be exercised about the testimony of friends like Cox (that Meyerbeer thought him 'the greatest *chef d'orchestre* in the world') and Kuhe (that Rossini, Mendelssohn and Meyerbeer 'regarded Costa as a magnificent conductor').[21] The removal of Costa's domineering personality dissipated the aura of fear and permitted a less deferential assessment. The *Athenaeum* commented that 'Of late years there may have been too much of blind hero-worship.' Vaughan Williams echoed this a generation later: 'Perhaps the exaggerated respect paid to Costa during his lifetime has caused too violent a reaction.'[22]

Although he had a few loyal friends, he was essentially a loner. He did not create a 'school' or a durable institution (like Gye, Hallé or Wood).[23] The institutions that might have perpetuated his memory (Her Majesty's and the SHS) did not survive. Those that survived did not cherish his memory: Gye worked hard to deny him any credit for Covent Garden's achievements and the Philharmonic pointedly did not make him an honorary member. He wrote no memoirs, attracted no biography and left nothing to sustain his reputation, apart from the Michael Costa Scholarship at the RAM. He was never fully integrated into the musical Establishment. He lived aloof from his fellow-musicians, especially the influential cliques around Grove–Manns–Parry–Stanford and Macfarren–Davison–Sterndale Bennett. Despite his efforts to anglicize himself, Costa remained associated with 'abroad', the opera house and London – all phenomena that were repugnant to

17 *Musical Times* (1 Jun. 1884), 321–3.

18 Bennett, *Forty Years*, 50. *Musical Times* (1 Oct. 1897), 653.

19 Shaw to *Times* (14 Oct. 1941). Also *Shaw's Music*, vol. 3, 757.

20 *Times* (17 Apr. 1871).

21 Cox, *Musical Recollections*, vol. 2, 323. Kuhe, *Musical Recollections*, 59.

22 *Athenaeum* (3 May 1884), 576. Vaughan Williams in *Grove 2*, 587.

23 Barnett, *Musical Reminiscences and Impressions*, 82.

Figure 8.2 Arditi conducting an open rehearsal at Her Majesty's Theatre (*ILN,* 2 May 1863) (courtesy of Westminster City Libraries)

influential writers such as Thomas Carlyle, William Morris, John Ruskin and Henry Davey.[24]

Costa's personality contributed to the later caricature of a tyrannical reactionary who bore a heavy responsibility for mid-Victorian musical vices. Because of his irascible and unbending nature, many of his professional relationships ended in acrimony. Even before his death, managers and festival committees were showing preference to less inflexible conductors, such as Sullivan (Leeds), Richter (Birmingham) and Arditi (Her Majesty's – Figure 8.2). Although he helped to advance the careers of Sullivan, Hallé and Cowen (and of singers like Adelina Patti and Charles Santley), he was reluctant to share the rostrum with others or to bring on successors.

Because Costa's reforms were of a practical and organizational nature – they were rapidly assimilated by other British conductors and overlaid by subsequent reformers. They were, as a result, taken for granted by later generations, who assumed that centralized conducting and disciplined performance were part of the inevitable progress that characterized their era. Critics wearied of praising Costa's performances for their energy and precision. A typical review of 1877 simply commented: 'to say anything in praise would be to repeat an oft-told story'.[25] A few older writers reminded their readers of what he had done to create respectable orchestras out of 'the coarsest materials'.[26] The *MW* obituary stated:

---

[24] Bennett Zon, '"Loathsome London": Ruskin, Morris and Henry Davey's *History of English Music* (1895)', *Victorian Literature and Culture*, vol. 37 (2009), 359–75.

[25] *Graphic* (30 Jun. 1877).

[26] Chorley, *Musical Recollections*, 84.

> The musical public can have no idea of the state of things which prevailed under the weak management of Sir George Smart and his compeers. It was simple lawlessness, which ashamed and disgusted such men as Spohr, Mendelssohn and Berlioz.[27]

Joseph Bennett commented that Costa's was a case of 'the good is oft interred in their bones'; he drew an analogy between Costa's reforms and those of Carnot, who laid the foundations for the French revolutionary armies but was forgotten in the excitement of the victories that Napoleon achieved with those forces.[28]

His notorious reluctance to promote new music meant that he was easily dismissed by later writers as a dinosaur who, having discovered his niche, lost touch with new trends in music. In terms of repertoire, the writer of his *Musical Times* obituary was probably correct when he observed that Costa 'died in the [bel canto] faith of his youth'.[29] By the 1870s, he was a hang-over from the Mendelssohnian phase of orchestral evolution from which English music was ready to move on. He was associated with musical forms – Italian opera, miscellaneous concerts, oratorios, mammoth festivals – which were losing artistic prestige. In his last three decades, he largely eschewed symphonic conducting, in a climate where 'every lover of the orchestra knows how superior in taste is symphonic music to choral music'.[30] Even in the latter, he was seen by many as reactionary: when *Grove 3* listed the standard Handel editions in 1926, it warned that 'Costa's accompaniments, generally superseded now, are only mentioned where no other edition is available.' He was seen as partly responsible for the tedium and narrow programming of the big state concerts. The fare at the Alexandra Palace, where he conducted the opening concert in June 1875, was described as 'most uninteresting, save to those who delight in a concert made up of operatic shreds and patches, and believe in Sir Michael Costa as much as (by the fact of his name appearing three times in the programme) he appears to believe in himself'.[31]

As a composer, Costa was more successful in his lifetime than for example Smart, Habeneck, Hallé or Jullien. But like most composers who write successfully in the received style of their day, he lacked the originality and melodic flair that are among the ingredients of lasting success. The fading of his own compositions meant that he did not enjoy even the modest immortality of Henry Bishop's 'Home Sweet Home' and Arditi's 'Il Bacio'.In the late 1880s, his ballet scores and the oratorios *Eli* and *Naaman* began to drop out of the repertoire. His style, a melange of Mendelssohn and later-Rossini, had long been superseded. Today his works do

---

27 *MW* (3 May 1884), 274–5

28 Bennett, *Forty Years*, 50 and 53. *Musical Times* (1 Oct. 1897), 653.

29 *Musical Times* (1 Aug. 1884), 443.

30 William Weber, ed., *Musician as Entrepreneur and Opportunist, 1700–1914: Managers, Charlatans and Idealists* (Bloomington: Indiana University Press, 2004), 243 and 272. Nettel, *The Orchestra in England*, 148.

31 *Musical Times,* vol. 17, no. 388 (1 Jun. 1875), 110.

not cry out for revival, though there is a case for another look at his two operas, *Malek Adhel* and *Don Carlos*, his semi-operatic oratorio *Eli* and some of the earlier vocal works written for Malibran and the Old Guard.[32] Costa seems to have realized that composing was not his claim to lasting fame, since he had dropped 'Composer' from his title in the 1881 census – by which time it was possible for a conductor like Richter to have a distinguished career without pretending to be a composer. The verdict of the *Athenaeum* that his compositions entitle him to 'a respectable place in the second rank' of composers seems generous.[33] Because he was not an innovative composer, he fell foul of the late nineteenth-century goal-obsessed narrative in which 'the concept of progress assumes exaggerated importance [and] many works are struck from the historical record on the grounds that they have nothing new to say'.[34]

All of these factors help to explain why Costa did not finish up on a plinth (like the managers Gye and Augustus Harris), in St Paul's (like Arthur Sullivan) or Westminster Abbey (like several less significant figures such as Thomas Greatorex, Samuel Arnold, William Sterndale Bennett and Ebenezer Williams). But Costa's loss of reputation was also due in large part to factors which ensured that virtually all of his generation fell rapidly out of favour by the 1880s. By 1884, nearly all of those associated with the changes of the period 1830–50 had faded away: the composer-conductors – Mendelssohn and Berlioz; the new professionals like Habeneck and Chélard; the 'semi-conductors' – Bishop, Smart and Moscheles; the Old Guard singers; the managers – Laporte, Lumley and Gye; the writers – Chorley, Davison and Hogarth. A new generation of musicians was in the ascendant: composers like Bizet, Dvořàk, Wagner and Brahms, singers like de Reszke, Maurel and Lehmann, and conductors like Richter and von Bülow. Along with Julius Benedict, who died in the same year, Costa was a relic from a different age. The small classical band of his youth, under its string leader, had been replaced by the large modern orchestra under its professional conductor. The gas light and limelight of the 1830s had given way to electric lights (first used at the Paris Opera in 1849). But these shifts of context and mood do not entirely explain the rapidity with which his awesome reputation gave way to disparagement and oblivion.

Costa and the other early conductors lived in a period when their profession was still struggling to establish itself. Apart from Costa (and perhaps Manns, who, however, conducted in suburban Sydenham), no other London-based conductor enjoyed a high metropolitan reputation until the reign of Henry Wood from the 1890s. Two decades after Costa's death, Elgar was lamenting that 'good English conductors as rare as snakes in Ireland'.[35] In the era before the virtuosi like Richter and von Bülow, conductors did not attract attention and often did not even appear on the playbill. This was especially true of opera conductors, who lacked

---

[32] Fuller discussion in Goulden, Chapter 8 and Appendix D.

[33] *Athenaeum* (3 May 1884), 576.

[34] Alex Ross, *The Rest is Noise* (London: Harper, 2007), xvii.

[35] Edward Elgar, 'A Future for English Music', Peyton Lectures (1905–06).

the aesthetic prestige of symphonic conductors. Costa died four years before Edison's first recording, which led to the preservation of the achievements of the next generation.

Three contemporary authorities proved to be particularly influential in damaging Costa's reputation. First, he was attacked by the Wagnerians, who correctly saw him as the heir to the bel canto tradition of Rossini and linked aesthetically (and perhaps racially) to Mendelssohn and Meyerbeer. Although Costa's production of *Lohengrin* at Drury Lane in 1875 was judged 'vastly superior – in almost every respect' – to Covent Garden's, true Wagnerians felt that he did not penetrate the spirit of the score.[36] Stanford contributed amusingly to this theme when he reported seeing Costa in 1877 in Berlin, where he had gone 'to swallow *Tristan and Isolde*' and 'looked as if the meal had disagreed with him'.[37] The Wagner band-waggon had a devastating effect on the prestige of Costa's generation, especially after the first London performance of the *Ring* in 1882. Wagner disparaged the Philharmonic, which he took over from Costa's nine-year tenure in 1855. He saw in it the Mendelssohnian tradition, which he damned in *Das Judenthum in der Musik*: too much *presto* and *mezzoforte* but not enough inspiration (Chapter 5). According to Hueffer, he also blamed Costa for the hostility he encountered there (though their mutual friend Sainton blamed the press).[38]

Second, Costa and his generation also fell foul of the other dominant ideology of late-Victorian music: the English Musical Renaissance. Costa's career was over by the time the 'Renaissance' was launched in the early 1880s. His creative period fell on the wrong side of the dividing line which the *Times* critic Fuller-Maitland drew between before and after 'the Renaissance'. Costa personified the foreign and Italian-operatic ethos of the early Victorian era – a period which the spokesmen of the English Musical Renaissance were anxious to cast as a desert of musical mediocrity in order to highlight the achievements of their protégés.[39] One of its high priests, the *Times* critic and editor of *Grove 3*, H.C. Colles, denigrated Costa in his draft history of the Philharmonic which is annotated in the Society's archive as 'unpublished because of its own inadequacies and because of the inadequacy of demand'.[40] In this mindset, Costa was bound to be compared unfavourably with Manns, who was the protégé of one of the architects of the movement (Grove) and was described by its leading propagandist (Fuller-Maitland) as 'the first streak of the dawn of the renaissance'.

Third, the contradictory material from Berlioz merits close examination because of his influence on the later narrative of the mid-nineteenth century. Berlioz did not feel towards Costa the bitter hostility he showed to Habeneck

---

36 *Examiner* (19 Jun. 1875). Klein, *Thirty Years*, 47.

37 Stanford, *Pages*, 173.

38 Hueffer, *Half a century of Music*, 50–51.

39 Hughes, Meirion, and Stradling, Robert, *The English Musical Renaissance and the Press 1840–1940*, 2nd ed. (Manchester: Manchester University Press, 2001), 4–42.

40 Note of 2 Jan. 1984 on H.C. Colles, *The Royal Philharmonic* (1937), BL RPO MSS 416.

or most of the other Parisian conductors. Some of his early reviews of Costa's conducting were, by his fastidious standards, quite favourable. He commended the Covent Garden orchestra for its power and verve, playing with 'an ensemble, a finish, a precision worthy of the greatest praise'.[41] He compared their productions favourably with those of Her Majesty's. He wrote to a friend that the Philharmonic was 'beyond reproach, and Costa conducts it superbly'.[42] But they had very different personalities and represented different schools, and Berlioz damaged Costa's image in three respects: as a rival concert conductor, as one possible cause of the failure of *Benvenuto Cellini* and as an incorrigible reviser of other composers' scores.

Berlioz had an incentive to disparage Costa as his only serious rival conductor in London. During his five London visits between 1847 and 1855, Berlioz fell in with several of the critics and musicians who supported Her Majesty's Theatre and the New Philharmonic (where Berlioz conducted) and who naturally opposed Costa as the leading musician at the rival Covent Garden company and the old Philharmonic. It was presumably from these sources that he picked up the idea that, contrary to the reviews at the time, Costa had 'ruined' ('éreintée') Beethoven's Symphony no. 9 five years earlier in 1847.[43] He seems to have persuaded himself that he was leading a battle for the new generation against the 'pig-headed old men … these fevered and gout-afflicted individuals', who ran the Philharmonic; and that he had 'every reason to distrust' Costa, whom he wrongly saw as the real power there.[44] He informed Liszt that his appointment to the New Philharmonic in 1852 had stirred up 'Old England', especially Costa.[45] He told his brother-in-law: 'the only opposition I expect is from the followers of Costa, the local Habeneck, who look askance at my arrival in England'.[46] After his first concert, he reported: 'There is dismay in the camp of the *old Philharmonic Society*; Costa and Anderson are drinking their bile by the full glass' (my italics).[47] He wrote gloatingly to his sister Adele that 'I am also a dreadful nuisance to *some other positions*, especially Italian ones.' 'What makes me most feared in a certain very powerful quarter … is my talent as a conductor, which is acclaimed by all musicians.'[48] Although Costa volunteered to share the rostrum for a successful Philharmonic concert in 1853, Berlioz identified him 12 years later in his *Memoirs* as someone (along with

---

41 *Feuilleton* (12 Aug. 1851).

42 Berlioz to Joseph d'Ortigue (15 Mar. 1848). *CG*, 1185.

43 Berlioz to Auguste Morel (10 Feb. 1852). *CG*, 1449.

44 Berlioz to Auguste Morel (24 Apr. 1848), *CG*, 1191. Also Berlioz to Adèle (24 Sep. 1849), *CG*, 1280. Berlioz to Joseph d'Ortigue (15 Mar. 1848), *CG*, 1185.

45 Berlioz to Liszt (2 Mar. 1852), *CG*, 1456. Berlioz to Adèle (16 Jul. 1853), *CG*, 1619.

46 Berlioz to Camille Pal (19 Feb.1852) *CG*, 1453.

47 Berlioz to Ortigue (25 Mar. 1852), *CG*, 1461.

48 Berlioz to Adèle (16 Jul. 1853), *CG*, 1619.

Habeneck and many German conductors) who 'secretly opposes me wherever he can' because he was jealous of Berlioz's prowess on the rostrum.[49]

Berlioz's view of Costa at the opera was shaped by the humiliating failure of Covent Garden's production of *Benvenuto Cellini* in 1853. At the time, they appear to have co-operated well, if warily. Costa correctly offered that Berlioz should conduct the first performances of *Benvenuto Cellini* and corresponded with him 'in a most gracious and even cordial manner'. Berlioz predicted that the London production would be much better than the *Malvenuto* of Paris, since the orchestra was well prepared and everyone was on his side – something that could not have happened without Costa's goodwill.[50] After the debacle, caused by an Italian claque, Berlioz assured Costa of his 'profound gratitude for the care which you took over the rehearsals', adding that the opera's failure was more than compensated by 'the good relations which my brief collaboration with Covent Garden established between us'.[51] But in his *Memoirs* Berlioz recycled and gave some credence to an alleged rumour that Costa was responsible for the opera's hostile reception. 'If it was, as is quite possible, then he is a master of dissembling; his eagerness to be of use to me and to help me during rehearsals allayed any suspicions I may have had.'[52]

Berlioz also portrayed Costa as the prime culprit in England for the crime, which he denounced everywhere, of re-orchestrating the classics.[53] Criticizing a 'tromboned, ophicleided' Mozart production by his friend Michael Balfe at Her Majesty's, he perversely blamed this on Costa because, 'This is the practice in England, wherever the traditions of M. Costa are held in honour.'[54] He accused Costa of 'giving the great masters lessons in instrumentation' by adding a bass drum, cymbals and heavy brass to *Il barbiere di Siviglia*; and similar sins in *Der freischütz* and *Fidelio*.[55] But paradoxically he reported that Costa had performed *Don Giovanni* in a very polished manner, complete with the triple orchestra, which Balfe had omitted.[56] His vivid comment that adding orchestral parts was like slapping a trowelful of mortar on a Raphael painting, which was later used against Costa, was made in the context of a review of a performance by Balfe.[57]

---

[49] Berlioz, *Memoirs*, post scriptum, 476.

[50] Berlioz to Gye (28 Apr. 1853) *CG*,1590; Berlioz to Costa (20 Apr. 1853) *CG*, 1588; and Berlioz to Barbier (10 Jun. 1853), *CG*, 1603.

[51] Berlioz to Costa (7 Jul. 1853), *CG*, 1612. Berlioz to Sainton (7 Jul. 1853), *CG*, 1613. Bennett, *Forty Years*, 156.

[52] Berlioz, *Memoirs*, 466–7.

[53] Berlioz, *Memoirs*, 92.

[54] Addition in first edition (1852) of *Soirées de l'Orchestre* to *Feuilleton* (12 Aug. 1851), omitted from second (1854) edition.

[55] *Feuilleton* (1Jul. 1851). Also Berlioz to Louis-Joseph Le Duc (26 May 1848) *CG*, 1200.

[56] *Feuilleton* (12 Aug. 1851).

[57] *Feuilleton* (1 Jul. 1851).

Against these three prolific sources, the only heavyweight witnesses for the defence were Rossini and Verdi. Rossini had an unusually affectionate relationship with Costa, whom he had probably first met as a boy during his years at the San Carlo (1815–22). In their long correspondence, punctuated by Costa's visits to him in Paris, Rossini treated him as his surrogate son ('Amatissimo figlio').[58] He also went to great lengths to get Costa's oratorio *Naaman* ('our oratorio') performed in Paris. Costa conducted the festival to mark Rossini's death, despite his own illness.[59] But ironically Rossini did Costa's reputation more harm than anyone through a witty comment which became the most quoted 'fact' about Costa after his death: 'Good old Costa has just sent me one of his oratorio scores and a Stilton cheese. The Stilton was very good … '.[60] Rossini's letter of thanks to Costa, by contrast, stressed 'how much I like you and how high is my consideration for your genius and musical expertise. If you were to write another oratorio like the one you sent me, it will add to your growing fame as successor to Handel (the Colossus) and Haydn (the Enchanter). Your sincere friend Rossini.'[61]

Costa's relationship with Verdi began badly. Verdi's arrival to supervise the world premiere of *I masnadieri* at Her Majesty's in 1847 pitched him against Costa and Covent Garden, which at first neglected Verdi's operas.[62] Costa was blamed in the press for humiliating Verdi by rejecting the *Hymn of the Nations* for baritone and chorus, which Verdi had submitted (late and in the wrong form) for the opening of the 1862 Great Exhibition.[63] But Verdi was well-placed to assess Costa, who was the most successful conductor of his operas in England.[64] Arditi recalled that *Rigoletto* at the Lyceum in 1856 was 'superbly conducted by Costa … for all-round excellence it would be hard to surpass even now'.[65] Verdi described him as 'one of the greatest conductors in Europe' and 'un uomo musicale, forte, possente'.[66] He commented to his Paris publisher, Léon Escudier, that 'one single hand, if secure and powerful, can work miracles. You have seen it with Costa in London; you see it even more with Angelo Mariani' (whom Verdi at the time

---

58 Rossini's uniquely affectionate letters to Costa are in Cia Carlini, *Gioacchino Rossini Lettere agli Amici* (Instituto Culturali della Citta di Forli, 1993).

59 *Daily News* (3 May 1869).

60 Henry Davison, *From Mendelssohn to Wagner*, 109. Also Sims Reeves, *My Jubilee or Fifty Years of Artistic Life* (London: Musical Publishing Company, 1889).

61 Rossini to Costa (5 Nov. 1856), RCM letters 2217.

62 Muzio to Barezzi (29 Jun. 1847), in L.A. Garibaldi, ed., *Giuseppe Verdi. nelle lettere di Emanuele Muzio ad Antonio Barezzi* (Milan: Fratelli Treves, 1931).

63 Verdi to Arrivabene (2 May 1862), *Bolletini no. 5 dell' Instituto di Studi Verdiani*, 724. Costa is unlikely to have been the moving figure on a committee which invited Sterndale Bennett to compose a piece to represent England.

64 *Ernani* (1845), *Il due Foscari* (1847), *Nabucco* (1850), *Rigoletto* (1853), *Il trovatore* (1855), *La traviata* (1857), *Un ballo in maschera* (1861), *Don Carlo* (1868).

65 Arditi, *Reminiscences*, 37.

66 Cesari and Luzio, eds, *I copialettere di Giuseppe Verdi* (Milan: 1913), 256; and John Warrack, *Oxford Dictionary of National Biography*, under 'Costa'.

regarded as the finest conductor in Europe). On hearing from Escudier that Costa's production of *Don Carlos* was superior to that of Paris, he wrote:

> So the London production is a success? If it is, what will they say at the Opéra, seeing that in London a work is staged in 40 days whereas they take four months. However you are telling me nothing new when you say that Costa is a great conductor … .[67]

Verdi wrote to Costa explaining that he had not written earlier to thank him for his earlier productions.

> But then, in the early course of my career, I was restrained by the fear that a letter from me full of admiration for you could have been confused with those letters which many have the habit of writing, thus scattering incense in order to receive support and protection. Now that my career is over, or nearly so, such a doubt vanishes and this perhaps false pride falls to the ground. Knowing that I am a great artist and a man of character, I hope that you will understand my pride (*fierezza*) and not be unduly offended by it. Therefore accept with goodwill my sincere thanks for *Don Carlos*, the expression of my highest esteem for your very great genius; and, if unfortunate circumstances or misunderstandings have kept us apart up to now, I hope soon to be able to shake your hand and to see you hasten to accept the greeting from a man who has always had the highest regard for your talent and character. Your devoted G Verdi.[68]

Verdi's private esteem was of little value to Costa in his last decade, especially in relation to the caricature which was being formed by the next generation of critics and music-writers, who held him largely responsible for the musical crimes of the earlier period. Shaw identified him as a leading musical member of 'the Gye-Mapleson-Costa regime', which he blamed for the stagnant repertoire of 'the Donizettian Dark Ages'. Shaw also saw him as the prime culprit in the 'trombonisation' of the classics.[69] Early tamperings with Mozart operas (later corrected) and a heretical re-orchestration of Beethoven's *Missa Solemnis* were frequently quoted against him. It became fashionable for journals like the *Musical Times* and *Athenaeum*, which had praised Costa's reinforcement of Handel's scores as an act of homage, to criticize such treatment in retrospect as 'quite indefensible'

[67] 'Lettres Inédits de G. Verdi à Léon Escudier', *Rivista musicale Italiana*, vol. 35 (1928), 526. Norris, *Stanford*, 175.

[68] Verdi to Costa (6 Jul. 1867), Hans Nathan and Frances Fink, eds, *Autograph Letters of Musicians at Harvard* (Harvard: Music Library Association, 1948), vol. 5. no. 4, Second Series, 483 and 480–81.

[69] *Shaw's Music*, vol. 2, 72.and vol. 2, 218.

and 'unwarranted'.[70] But, as Joseph Bennett pointed out, he was 'only one of many who shared his tastes and practised his methods'.[71] Costa was a mild offender by comparison with most of his contemporaries and was not given posthumous credit for his role in ending the practice of performing operas in shortened double-bills, putting on oratorios in excerpts and transferring arias from one opera to another.[72]

Later writers saw what *New Grove* still refers to as the 'pre-1848 generation of conductors' as falling on the wrong side of the watershed of Richter's seminal Albert Hall performances in 1877, which were felt to have killed off the Mendelssohn tradition and marked the start of first-class orchestral playing in England.[73] By the time of Mendelssohn's centenary in 1909, Ernest Walker wrote that his reputation had sunk so far that, for talented younger musicians, 'Mendelssohn hardly exists'.[74] This was particularly harmful to Costa, who was the main surviving exponent of the 'elegant school' of Mendelssohn, with its strict and rather fast tempo style.[75] Shaw described 'the Costa conception of orchestra conducting' as the antithesis of 'the Richter conception'.[76]

He was also damned, along with Habeneck and most of the early professional conductors, for failing to make the transition from the role of trainer and disciplinarian to that of creative interpreter (Chapter 5). This change of attitude is clear in the contrast between the entry on 'Conducting' in the first two editions of Grove. The 1879–89 edition held out Mendelssohn and Costa as models, observing that the prerequisites were a clear beat and effective communication.[77] The much longer entry by Vaughan Williams in *Grove 2* leans heavily on Wagner's *Über das Dirigieren* and stresses the importance of interpretation.[78]

It is significant that most of those who depicted Costa as a reactionary did so on the basis of his last decade when his reforms, now long in the past, were taken for granted and his activity was largely confined to opera and oratorio rather than orchestral performance. Stanford, who pronounced that 'Costa's heart was

---

70 For praise of re-orchestration see *Musical Times* (1 Feb. 1849), 109–10, *ILN* (15 Mar. 1851), 474 and *Athenaeum* (4 Sep. 1858), 305. For retrospective criticism, *Musical Times* (1 Jun. 1884), 322; *Athenaeum* (3 May 1884), 576–7.

71 *Musical Times* (1 Oct. 1897), 664–6.

72 For praise of unabridged performances see *MW* (15 Jul. 1848), 451, (4 Aug. 1847), 518 and (3 Apr. 1852), 215 and *Morning Post* (14 May 1849); for oratorios, see *ILN* (16 Feb. 1850) and (27 Jul. 1857), 640; *Times* (27 May 1850); and *Musical Times* (Jan. 1884), cited in Scholes, *Mirror of Music*, 68. For fuller discussion see Goulden, Chapter 8.

73 *New Grove 2,* vol. 6, 266. Vaughan Williams in *Grove 2*, vol. 2, 399. Nettle, *The Orchestra in England*, 185.

74 C.L. Graves, *Post-Victorian Music* (London: 1911), 146–9. Ernest Walker, *Free Thought and the Musician* (Oxford: 1946), 30–34.

75 Tovey in *Encyclopaedia Britannica*, 14th ed., vol. 15, 244. Klein, *Musicians and Mummers*, 232.

76 *Shaw's Music*, vol. 1, 525 and vol. 2, 72.

77 *Grove 1*, 390.

78 *Grove 2*, vol. 1, 586.

never in real sympathy with symphonic work', was only two years old when Costa left the Philharmonic and largely ceased to conduct symphonic concerts.[79] Shaw's first reviews date from the late 1870s. Vaughan Williams' semi-critical description of Costa as 'a very fine band-master' reflects the view of a progressive musician who was only 12 when Costa died.[80] Fuller-Maitland, who deprecated 'the old professionals, such as Costa', began his career only in the year of Costa's retirement.[81] Percy Young, who accused Costa of 'the mutilation of the classics' at the Philharmonic, was born 28 years after his death.[82]

But although questionable as sources, their testimony suggests that they lived in a climate where these disparaging views were common currency. Their collective damning of Costa and his generation played to powerful notions of 'progress' and 'modernity' in the late nineteenth-century and the associated tendency to condemn early nineteenth century habits which were coming to be seen as philistine. It helps to explain why Costa's generation attracted at the turn of the century the same almost parricidal hostility that Lytton Strachey later showed to his *Eminent Victorians.* Black's *Dictionary* perversely blamed England's modest musical creativity on 'the great poverty of orchestras'.[83] Most twentieth century writers, following this lead, either ignored him or treated him as a minor footnote, often providing little more than Rossini's damaging joke. It was not until after two generations of deepening neglect that it became possible to reassess Costa's achievement.

---

[79] Stanford, *Pages*, 173. *Interludes records and reflections*, 19.

[80] *Grove 2*, vol. 1, 587.

[81] Fuller Maitland, *A Door-keeper of Music* (London: John Murray, 1929), 87.

[82] Percy Young, 'Orchestral Music', in Nicholas Temperley, ed., *The Romantic Age, 1800–1914* (Oxford: Blackwell, 1988) 369.

[83] For the neglect of English music 'before the English Musical Renaissance', see Simon McVeigh, 'The Society of British Musicians 1834–65 and the Campaign for Native Talent' in Christina Bashford and Leanne Langley, eds, *Music and British Culture, 1785–1914: Essays in honour of Cyril Ehrlich* (Oxford: Oxford University Press, 2000).

Chapter 9
Reassessment

A reassessment of Costa and his contemporaries became possible with the reaction, led by Weingartner and taken up by Toscanini, against the dominance of the Wagnerian ideology of conducting and the 'sensation-mongering' and podium acrobatics of the virtuoso conductors personified by von Bülow.[1] It was coming to be realized that the battle between the 'traditional' (Mendelssohnian) and 'progressive' (Wagner–Lisztian) conducting styles (described in Chapter 5) had been unduly polarized.[2] It underestimated the flexibility in the tempi applied by Mozart and Mendelssohn and exaggerated the liberties advocated by Wagner (who had been careful to stress that tempo variations should be *unmerklich* – 'imperceptible').[3] In this changing climate, it became possible to look again at conductors like Costa and Habeneck, who could be seen as ancestors of Toscanini's doctrine that works should be performed as stated in the score ('come scritto').[4]

In Costa's case, the reassessment began in the middle of the twentieth century, as writers sought to explain the striking advances in musical direction and orchestral efficiency in Britain between about 1830 and 1850. A plausible case was made for seeing Costa as the man who first 'brought unity of purpose into the orchestra' (Nettel), 'the greatest English conductor in the first half of the last century ... the first real conductor permanently settled in this country' (Carse) and 'by far the most experienced and admired conductor resident in London' (Ehrlich). Nettel regretted that more emphasis had not been laid on Costa's early work with the Italian Opera and the Philharmonic Society, which laid the foundations for his successors.[5] By 1973, the conductor Raymond Leppard was describing him as 'the most celebrated conductor in England at the middle of the 19th century; as admired as Beecham and twice the tyrant'.[6] The significance of his reforms was belatedly recognized by the unveiling in 2005, by Antonio Pappano, of a Blue Plaque on his former London residence.

---

1 Felix Weingartner, *On Conducting*, trans. E. Newman (London: Breitkopf and Härtel, 1906).

2 For a fuller discussion of this classification and its deficiencies, see Gunther Schuller, *The Compleat Conductor* (Oxford: Oxford University Press, 1997), Part II and 97.

3 Wagner, *On Conducting*, 89.

4 Rose, 'The Italian Tradition', ed. Bowen, *The Cambridge Companion to Conducting*, 151.

5 Nettel, *The Orchestra in England*, 143–5.

6 Raymond Leppard, 'Music and the conductor', 714.

It is difficult to assess a musical life spanning five decades. Most musicians end their careers out of fashion and out of sympathy with modern trends, as Von Bülow demonstrated with his aversion to the music of Mahler. Conductors in particular are doomed to oblivion or disparagement unless (like Verdi, Berlioz, Liszt and Wagner) their careers yielded major innovations in composition or (like Furtwangler and Walter) their achievements are preserved in recordings. Men of Costa's ilk, who were neither innovatory composers nor recorded conductors, need to be assessed in their proper context. In particular, they need to be seen in the light of the many systems out of which the profession of conductor emerged in the period between 1830 and 1850 (Chapter 3). Seen in context, the transition from the world of Henry Bishop to that of Costa was as significant as that from Costa to Richter and the virtuoso conductors of the late nineteenth century. Those who compared Costa unfavourably with Richter overlooked how far Costa had created the orchestral base for the latter's achievements in England. Nettel commented perceptively that Hallé and Manns built on the foundations Costa had laid and that 'due respect has been unfairly denied to Costa by his successors'. He regretted that Costa's reputation was based unduly on his later career as a choral conductor: 'Costa of the Philharmonic Society is forgotten while Costa of the festivals lives.'[7]

To assess the early conductors in context, it also necessary to set aside aesthetic criteria that were not part of their world. George Bernard Shaw saw musical history as a march of progress from the (shallow) world of bel canto to the (profound) creations of Wagner and Richard Strauss and the interpretative novelties of the virtuoso conductors. But this transition began in England only from the late 1870s. The transition which most challenged musicians, critics and audiences during Costa's career was from Rossini (who ceased composing operas in 1829) to the dramatic and often raw operas of Bellini and Donizetti and thence to the grand operas of Auber, Halévy, Meyerbeer and Verdi. The soprano Grisi, for example, struggled to make the radical adjustment from roles like Rosina, Norma, Anna Bolena and Semiramide to those of Fides (*Les Huguenots*), Alice (*Robert le diable*) and Leonora (*Il trovatore*). Mario made a similar leap with parts like Raoul (*Les Huguenots*) and Alfredo (*La Traviata*). For conductors, too, the switch from bel canto to grand opera presented a serious challenge; Costa was the only conductor in England who surmounted this successfully at the time. It is easy to overlook the length of the journey travelled by Costa from the Naples he left in 1829 to the period of Meyerbeer's pre-eminence and the repertoire which followed in the 1870s, when he was offering creditable performances of *Aida*, *Carmen*, *Lohengrin* and *Faust*.[8] In tackling these new styles, Costa and both opera houses where he conducted showed that they were not totally locked in Shaw's 'Donizettian Dark Ages'.[9]

---

7 Nettel, *The Orchestra in England*, 143 and 148.

8 *Examiner* on *Carmen* (3 May 1879).

9 For fuller discussion of the change of repertoire, see Goulden, Chapter 8.

Some comparative tests of Costa's achievement as a conductor were considered in Chapter 5. These suggest that the orchestra at Her Majesty's was consistently superior under Costa to that of the Philharmonic under other conductors, but inferior to that of Covent Garden when he moved there; that performances of the same orchestra were usually deemed superior under Costa to those under other conductors (except Mendelssohn and Berlioz); and that the profile of the conductor and orchestra rose under Costa to become a important new feature of the opera house. Despite the caveats that must attach to these comparisons, they reinforce the common verdict (shared even by unsympathetic writers like Davison and Grove) that the three main musical bodies in mid-Victorian London – the Opera, the Philharmonic and the SHS – achieved and maintained new levels of discipline and efficiency under Costa's control.

Chapter 5 also indicated that, as a conductor Costa was superior to the previous generation of 'semi-conductors' and to his immediate contemporaries in Britain. He was seen by many as a benchmark for other conductors at home and abroad. In his prime, he had no serious rival as an operatic or choral conductor, though – having largely withdrawn from symphonic work after 1854 – he was overtaken by Manns and Hallé in the concert hall. What can be said with confidence is that Costa was the first conductor in Britain to have a European reputation; and that, until the 1860s, his orchestras and choirs were the only ones to be held up as potential competitors of those abroad.

Comparison with Continental conductors is more difficult. Some recent judgements of Costa seem over-stated: for example Raymond Leppard's placing of him alongside von Bülow, Richter and Mottl; and Ehrlich's with Berlioz and Wagner.[10] He did not measure up, in terms of flair and interpretative creativity, to the greatest Continental conductors of the period (Berlioz, Mendelssohn, Richter, von Bülow and Liszt). But contemporary reviews suggest that many well-known conductors in major music centres were inferior to him: notably Pasdeloup, Hainl and Girard in Paris; Tadolini and Giovanni Bottesini at the Théâtre-Italien; Reissiger, Marschner and Schumann in Germany; and all the Italians until Mariani. Performances at the Birmingham Festival under Max Bruch in 1879 were described as less effective than they had been under Costa.[11] The most intriguing comparison is probably with Habeneck, with whom Costa was often equated. On the European scale, Habeneck's orchestra exercised greater influence, not least for his concentration on symphonic conducting and for the polish that came from superior Conservatoire training and longer rehearsals. But the *Morning Post* rated them as co-equal and Berlioz was less critical of Costa's conducting than of Habeneck's.[12] There are no stories about Costa to match Berlioz's account of Habeneck

10 Raymond Leppard, *On Music: An Anthology of Critical and Autobiographical Writings*, ed. Thomas P. Lewis (White Plains, NY: Pro-Am Musical Resources, 1993), 302. Ehrlich. *First Philharmonic*, 95.

11 *Graphic* (6 Sep. 1879).

12 *Morning Post* (18 Apr. 1843). Article on 'The opera orchestra'.

('that able but limited and unreliable conductor') missing an entry in the *Grande Messe des Morts* because he was taking snuff.[13]

It is not the contention of this book that Costa was a radical innovator. He was not, as sometimes stated, the first baton conductor in London; nor were the ingredients of his system strikingly original. In most of his reforms, he was introducing into England practices which were already being applied piecemeal on the Continent. The system of sending deputies to rehearsals, for example, had already been quashed by Nicolai in Vienna. The revised orchestral lay-out was pioneered by many others, including Weber. His demotion of the leader was first introduced, if only temporarily, by Spohr, who made sure that, when he conducted the Philharmonic in 1843, no leader was named on the programme.[14] The use of female altos in oratorios had long been practised in Berlin. The gargantuan Handel Festivals replicated in many respects the Lower Rhine Musical Festivals. Costa's policy of performing some oratorios in their entirety had earlier been trailed selectively by Smart.[15]

Costa's system needs therefore to be viewed in the context of what other conductors were doing. In a profession that was in its infancy, all conductors were to some extent experimenting and borrowing from each other. There is an interesting parallel between Costa's preoccupations and those of Mendelssohn at Leipzig and Berlin in the same years. Mendelssohn too installed a compliant leader; substantially increased the size of the string section; introduced closed rehearsals during which he made frequent stops for correction; worked hard to secure better salaries for the players; demanded powers which were 'despotic as regards the musicians'; and found himself on 'slippery ground' as he tried to define his role vis-à-vis the managers in Berlin.[16]

There is an even closer parallel, in terms of musical methods, with Habeneck, though the latter was a generation older than Costa and reflected earlier habits – such as conducting with the bow from the violin score. But both were autocratic and exigent. Both raised and sustained high standards of performance for several decades, but tended to over-rehearse and lose spontaneity. Both were seen as personifying their orchestras and were criticized for allowing their orchestras to play too fast and too loud. Both took a literal approach to scores and were eclipsed by the new wave of interpretative conducting. The main difference between them was in their attitude towards the musicians: unlike Habeneck, Costa was never seen as the agent of the management and took pains to conceal rather than expose their errors in performance.[17]

---

13 Berlioz, *Memoirs*, 106, 231 and 476.

14 Foster, *History*, 181.

15 For example, at Liverpool, *Morning Chronicle* (11 Aug. 1836).

16 On interrupted rehearsals, *Morning Post* (14 May 1844). This paragraph draws heavily on Clive Brown, *A Portrait of Mendelssohn* (New Haven, CT: Yale University Press, 2003), 146–201.

17 For a fuller picture of Habeneck see Southon.

In a period when conducting methods were still evolving and subject to experiment, some elements of Costa's system were personal to him and did not prove to be enduring. His edict against public attendance at opera rehearsals appears not to have survived him. Some of his Philharmonic reforms were reversed after he left the Philharmonic, especially the banning of deputies and, to some extent, the side-lining of the leader.[18] His policy of placing weaker players next to stronger ones became unnecessary as musical training improved. His control over the musicians' contracts was ended after his breach with Gye in 1869 and his resignation from the Leeds Festival.[19] The long tenure which he enjoyed was largely abandoned in the next century with the switch to the policy of employing a 'plurality of conductors'.[20]

More generally Costa's system could not survive him intact, because it centralized power unduly on one man and combined ingredients that were incompatible. It was not in the long run possible for a conductor to act as the ally of both managers and musicians. Ultimately, managers had to control the resources that they funded, and the workforce had to defend their pay and conditions collectively. As the music industry diversified and expanded, it ceased to be feasible for a single professional conductor to head so many major institutions at once. Costa's roles were sub-divided between Arditi and others (at the opera), Sterndale Bennett (Philharmonic), Hallé (briefly at the SHS), Sullivan (Leeds), Manns (Handel Festival) and Richter (Birmingham). None of his successors exercised his remarkable concentration of power across the spectrum of opera, concert and oratorio. Manns later enjoyed a similar continuity in the narrower context of the Crystal Palace concerts (1855–1901), as did Jakob Zeugheer at the Liverpool Philharmonic (1843–65), but their powers were never as extensive.

Costa's career thus proved to be a high point of conductorial authority rather than the model for the future of the profession. The music industry was already moving towards a structure in which greater power was gathered in the hands of managers (and their accountants), the technical stage management team, and the agents and trade unions representing the stars and the rank-and-file musicians. Costa was in many ways a transitional figure between the often amateurish regime of 1830 and the centralized, professional structure that gradually became the norm; and between the tentative time-beaters of the 1830s and the interpretative virtuoso-conductors of the later Romantic period.

Given his very modest success as a composer and his shunning of virtuosity on the rostrum, Costa's claim to a recognized place in British musical history rests on his impact on the management and deployment of musical resources. It was here that he had something genuinely important to contribute, which justifies Stephen

---

[18] Ehrlich, *First Philharmonic*, 54 and 101, note 23.

[19] Spark to Sullivan, http://www.leedsfestivalchorus.co.uk/history/conductor-trouble.html (14 Feb. 1880).

[20] Ehrlich, *First Philharmonic*, 179.

Johnson's statement that his career marked 'a clear turning point in the history of the English conductor'.[21]

First, Costa introduced and embedded important orchestral reforms in the main institutions of musical London: the opera, the Philharmonic and the SHS. His lasting achievement was to integrate discrete elements of reform (contracts, rehearsal practice, lay-out, acoustics, women altos) into a coherent system. Collectively, these changes marked the key step between the musical world of 1830 (when there was no professional conductor in Britain) and 1850 (when the *ILN* announced that 'the old style of divided authority between leaders and conductors has exploded').[22] Through these reforms, he raised the standards of orchestral and choral performance and corrected the indiscipline and sloppiness which had characterized English musical performances in the early nineteenth century. As Joseph Bennett remarked, 'Costa – let us give him credit for it – put an end to all that.'[23]

Second, although his system for controlling orchestras and singers was until the 1850s unique to him, it gradually set a template for orchestras across the British Isles. The *MW* credited Costa with using his unique influence to set up 'a standard of efficiency of which every lover of music now reaps the benefit'. Charles Hallé, who made his London debut in 1854 under Costa at the Philharmonic and who employed some members of Costa's orchestra as section leaders in his Manchester orchestra, followed several of his reforms – baton, lay-out, banning of deputies, rehearsal technique and demotion of the violin-leader.[24] Henry Wood adopted Costa's method of writing cues into the score as an aid to rehearsal as well as performance.[25] The arrival of a new norm for directing music was pointedly illustrated when the *Musical Chronicle* berated the Gloucester Festival for appointing a local organist in 1853 instead of Costa:

> Conducting an orchestra is a business per se … This sign of the times is so significant that it is plain the old system is doomed … until they place their festival performances under the control of first-rate leaders they will not have first-rate music … the ability and good intentions of the present class of conductors is fully appreciated, but it is almost a physical impossibility that they should be able to conduct satisfactorily these varied and important performances.[26]

---

21 Stephen Johnson, 'The English Tradition', in ed. Bowen, *Cambridge Companion to Conducting*, 178.

22 *ILN* (21 Sep.1850), 247. Also *MW* (15 Jan. 1853), 31.

23 Bennett, *Forty Years*, 51.

24 Beale, *Charles Hallé,* 61, 64 and 215n. *MW* (3 Jan. 1852). I am indebted to Robert Beale for the information about the link with Costa's London orchestra.

25 Robert Philip, *Performing Music in the Age of Recording* (Yale: Yale University Press, 2004), 78.

26 *Morning Chronicle* (17 Sep. 1853).

Third, the effectiveness of his system, allied to his dominant personality, enabled him to establish the profession of the conductor. There was no tradition of conducting in England until Costa regularized it at the opera house in the mid-1830s and at the Philharmonic and the SHS in the late 1840s. Costa was the first resident conductor to exercise monopoly control over orchestras and choirs by a combination of baton technique, tight management, personality and contractual powers. As the first conductor-manager he became 'the most conspicuous figure of the musical life in England in the last thirty years' (*Athenaeum*), enjoying 'unique success in handling great masses of executants' (*MW*).[27]

Fourth, he was the first musician in England to make his career primarily as a conductor rather than as a composer or instrumentalist. Costa established that the conductor was a major element in the production process – someone who needed to be forewarned and consulted about performances, rather than an employee who was simply told what to perform. Along with Habeneck in Paris, Chélard in Weimar and Mariani (later) in Bologna, he was the first of a new breed of musician: the professional, full-time and authoritative conductor of other men's works. Appearing on the platform as neither player nor composer, they had to build their authority on personality, competence and system. Together they resolved the debate of the 1830s about whether conductors had an essential role. The *Times* registered the change when it observed, after an inept performance by Walter Macfarren, that 'The business of a conductor is a business of itself, only to be learned by long practice and experience. The highest theoretical cultivation would be insufficient to make – for instance – a Costa … .'[28] This 'business' – what Boult later called 'the craft of conducting' and Berlioz 'musical artisanship' – was developed further by a long line of later conductors (Wood, Boult, Walter), distinguished more for their technique than their showmanship or freshness of interpretation.[29]

Finally, he established that a professional conductor could enjoy social and economic status. In the early decades of the century, 'the poor conductor … was a mere harmless and necessary figure in a scheme of attractions in which his drawing capacity was not reckoned'.[30] Costa was the first conductor in Britain who was recognized as a box-office draw and appeared regularly in curtain calls.[31] In a society which could afford to buy the finest talents from abroad – and where success abroad was the seal of approval – he was also the first London-based conductor to find a place at the top of the musical hierarchy. By the late 1860s, his salary at Covent Garden alone was as high as Gye's. He also enjoyed the social status that went with his knighthood – 26 years before Henry Irving received the first theatrical knighthood. George Smart had begun the process of raising the status of the professional musician, albeit with a purchased Irish knighthood and

27 *Athenaeum* (3 May 1884), 576. *MW* (3 May 1884), 276.

28 *Times* (3 Jan. 1845).

29 Stephen Johnson, 'The English Tradition', 184.

30 Kuhe, *Musical Recollections*, 278.

31 Galkin, *A History of Orchestral Conducting*, xxix.

social pretensions which attracted some ridicule. Costa demonstrated, in a society that was still suspicious of the louche world of the opera, an austerely correct lifestyle which was almost a caricature of Victorian respectability. He was thus a key figure in the creation of a climate in which conducting began to be seen as a suitable occupation for English gentlemen.

Because of these achievements, it is reasonable to describe Costa, despite his shortcomings, as England's first conductor in the modern sense of the word. It was Costa who, more than anyone else, marked the direction in which orchestras and choirs were to go. As Joseph Bennett observed, he 'stood at the first parting of the ways in the path of orchestral music amongst us, and though he may not have gone far, he led in the right direction'.[32] His achievement was eased by the growing recognition of the need to raise the standards of English music and by the absence of anyone else with the personality, musical education and long tenure to do so. But bringing English standards and practices up to good Continental standards required more than being what the *Times* described as 'the right man in the right place'.[33] Costa had to break with existing practices and vested interests, often causing pain and outrage in the process. It was for many an unpopular and unwelcome cause, which succeeded only through his unusual energy, persistence and sheer obstinacy.

Conclusion

When looking at the music 'art world' of mid-nineteenth century Britain, the historian constantly comes up against the question raised in the introduction to this volume: how to assess a culture which lacked the composers, ideologists and premieres that were commonly perceived to confer the status of major musical power? Britain did not produce a composer of great originality to compare with Schumann, Liszt, Berlioz or Wagner. It did not have a successful figure in the mainstream tradition, comparable to Mendelssohn, Meyerbeer, Verdi or Brahms. Its repertoire did not include significant revivals, such as marked the rediscovery of Bach in Germany, or premieres of iconic new works like Beethoven's *Missa Solemnis* (St Petersburg, 1824), Berlioz's *Grande Mess des Morts* (Paris, 1837), Wagner's *Tristan und Isolde* (Munich, 1865) or Verdi's *Requiem* (Milan, 1874). Judged by the conventional standards laid down by Continental musicologists – and largely accepted by their British equivalents – music in Britain was derivative, even second rate. Hence the widespread view on the Continent that the country was indeed a 'Land ohne Musik'.

Although British critics and musicians were hyper-sensitive to this slur and protested vehemently that their country was not a Land Without Music, their conservatism tended to confirm the Continental view that the country was behind

32 Bennett, *Forty Years*, 43.

33 *Times* (13 Apr. 1871).

the times and below the standards of other music centres. British critics of Costa's generation almost unanimously misjudged Chopin, Schubert, Schumann, Liszt, Verdi, Berlioz and Wagner. Indeed a comparison of mid-nineteenth-century music reviews with those of, for example, Elgar's conducting around 1910 reveals how much more sophisticated, detached and analytical British musical criticism became in the generation after Costa's death.[34] The efforts of the propagandists of the 'English Musical Renaissance' to push the claims of an English Beethoven merely served to illustrate the puniness of these claims and the inferiority complex which underlay them.[35] Time has not vindicated Fuller Maitland's boast that Mackenzie, Parry, Goring Thomas, Cowen and Stanford 'can be compared with any school that the world of music has seen'.[36] Britain's most obvious claim to musical distinction was the phenomenon of the large-scale festivals; but, although grander than any on the Continent, they lacked aesthetic prestige. The British complex could be cured not by deft propaganda and grandiose performances but by producing a composer or musical events that commanded international respect. That did not begin to be achieved until the turn of the century with *The Dream of Gerontius*.

The fixation with the Great Composer – especially the mould-breaking composer – overshadowed the other achievements of British music in the mid-nineteenth century. As a result, Britain continued to be placed low in the league table of musical esteem. This wounding verdict was a commonplace of foreign comment: 'a musical defect' in the English soul (Nietzsche); 'no ear, either for rhythm or music' (Heine); 'England has no music' (Ralph Waldo Emerson); 'so dreadfully behind the times' (Clara Schumann).[37] Even the well-disposed Mendelssohn commented that 'here they pursue music like a business, calculating, paying, bargaining and truly a great deal is lacking'.[38]

Many British writers privately endorsed these views. Sterndale Bennett told his publisher in Leipzig. 'You know what a dreadful place England is for music.' Haweis wrote, with regret, that 'the English are not a musical people'. Shaw lamented 'two centuries of imitative negligibility' between the death of Purcell in 1695 and the emergence of Elgar. Hueffer acknowledged that there was 'more degenerate taste in England than elsewhere'.[39] The English inferiority complex, which Macfarren traced to 'domestic mistrust' more than to 'foreign depreciation',

---

34 Martin Bird, 'A very good idea at the time: Sir Edward Elgar – Principal Conductor, London Symphony Orchestra', *Elgar Society Journal*, vol. 17, no. 1 (Apr. 2011), 22–36.

35 Henry Davey, *History of English Music* (London: J. Curwen and Sons, 1895), 1.

36 Fuller Maitland, *English Music in the XIXth Century* (London: Grant Richards, 1902) 186.

37 Nietzsche, *Jenseits von Gut und Bose;* Heine, *Lutetia* (1843); Emerson: *English Traits* (1856); Clara Schumann, *An Artist's Life*, ed. Berthold Litzmann, trans. Grace Hadow (Cambridge: Cambridge University Press, 1913), vol. 2, 134.

38 Mendelssohn, *A Life in Letters*, 106.

39 H.R. Haweis, *Music and Morals* (London: Strahan,1871), 124–5. *Shaw's Music*, vol. 3, 415; Hueffer, *Half a Century of Music*, 19; Sterndale Bennett quote from Kistner, cited in Simon McVeigh, 'The Society of British Musicians'.

was not groundless.[40] This was the era in which Bishop (who had no claim to academic eminence) was elected Professor of Music at Oxford; where Smart (who composed very little) became 'composer to the Chapel Royal'; where George Frederic Anderson (an indifferent violinist and non-composer) was Master of the Queen's Music for 22 years. The lively musical scene that had characterized Victoria's court in the first two decades of her reign faded there during the 40 years after Albert's death in 1861.[41] The driving ideology of the mid-Victorian era was to be found not in Romanticism, with its undertones of revolution and turmoil, but in safer and more respectable 'isms': Utilitarianism and Evangelism. Britain's comparative musical backwardness continued to perplex a nation which in so many other respects could claim to be leading the world. This lack of musical prestige mattered in a world where, as Grove pointed out, musical achievement played such an important part in the rise of Germany's self-confidence.[42]

But, in assessing the musical 'art world' of a society, there are other criteria than originality (such as the publication of Berlioz's *Traité*) or iconic events (like the premiere of Wagner's *Ring*). The positivism which shaped late nineteenth century musicological opinion, with its emphasis on national rivalries and claims of innovation, does not tell the whole story. It is arguable that Britain, with its flourishing concert and choral tradition and its openness to a wide range of European music, enjoyed a rich musical culture. It was evidenced in the 21 provincial societies that sent contingents to the Handel Festivals and the audience of 80,000 who attended these serious three-day events. It showed itself in the 50,000 who took part in Ella's Musical Union and the tens of thousands who participated in the tonic sol-fa movement and subscribed to the burgeoning musical press.[43] It was clear from the rising competence of indigenous players and singers and the raised quality of orchestras and choral societies. It can be traced in the growth in musical copyrights from 147 a year (1810s) to 1,313 (1840s) and 4,010 (1870s). In a culture that failed to produce its Beethoven, Berlioz or Verdi, these advances nevertheless showed that a land without composers was not a land without music.[44] In more general terms Victorian Britain became less 'different' – musically as in many other respects – from other European countries. One sign of this was that music was slowly coming to be seen, in influential and much-reissued works like Haweis's *Music and Morals*, as an activity which, far from being foreign, effete or decadent, could promote the national virtues of morality and self-improvement.[45]

---

40 Macfarren, 'The English are not a Musical People', *Cornhill Magazine* (1876), 344.

41 See, for example, Clara Schumann's comments in Joan Chissell, *Clara Schumann* (London: Hamish Hamilton, 1981), 167.

42 Hiller, 'Quasi Fantasia', *Macmillan's Magazine* (1870), cited in E. Graeme, ed., *Beethoven: A Memoir* (London: Griffin, 1870), xx.

43 Ella, *Musical Sketches*, 435

44 This happy phrase is taken from Carnelly, 'George Smart'.

45 Haweis, *Music and Morals*, 87.

These achievements, though widely welcomed for social as well as artistic reasons, were not enough to cure the musical inferiority complex from which many music-lovers suffered. For the ideologues of British music, a good infrastructure was no substitute for the lack of great contemporary composers. The composer-writer Thomas Danvers Worgan summed up this attitude pithily when he described British music as: 'Practically, a mountain, scientifically, a molehill; sensuously, everything, intellectually, nothing.'[46] Chorley echoed the same theme when he regretted that 'the gain in technical performance won by England in the last thirty years' was outweighed by 'the losses to the great world of art'.[47] But in retrospect the creation of a strong musical infrastructure can be seen as a significant achievement of Victorian Britain. It was the fruit of many personal efforts in many fields: educators such as Hullah and Curwen; promoters like Ella and the much-ridiculed Jullien; choral directors like Joseph Barnby; administrators and organizers like Grove, Cole and Bowley; critics and impresarios, especially Lumley, Gye and Mapleson; and publishers, notably Cramer and Novello.

This is the perspective in which it is most appropriate to assess Costa's career and the revolution in musical performance to which he made such a significant contribution. He symbolizes the strengths and weaknesses of English music in this period. He was a man with serious limitations of personality and imagination. His reforms drew heavily on borrowings from foreign conductors. Like most conductors, he reflected the habits of his times, adapting and re-orchestrating scores in a way which was seen later in his career as heretical. Like most composers, he satisfied the conservative tastes of his times, but not those of later generations. His main achievements were performative rather than creative (or, in Henry Davison's apt phrase, 'administrative rather than originative').[48]

Despite these limitations, it is an injustice that, despite the efforts of Carse and others to restore Costa's reputation, he remains the most forgotten of the major figures in nineteenth-century English music. Although not heroic in the Carlylean sense, (which was applied in music almost exclusively to composers), he was a major figure, in the Darwinian sense that he forced a significant evolutionary shift from the defective arrangements that he inherited, creating the basis of highly trained and disciplined performance on which future British and foreign conductors were able to build. He was the main architect of the reform of the main British orchestras and choral societies, which was arguably the country's principal musical achievement in the middle years of the century. Indeed it is hard to imagine that the Victorian revolution in musical performance could have occurred so effectively if he had not arrived in Birmingham to supervise Zingarelli's cantata in 1829.

In the last two decades valuable light has been thrown on what British music did achieve during the 53 years of Costa's career: the creation of canons of orchestral, operatic and choral works; the development of a vibrant concert and

46 Thomas Danvers Worgan, quoted in *MW* (17 Feb. 1842), 49.

47 Chorley, *Musical Recollections*, 396.

48 Davison, *From Mendelssohn to Wagner*, 108.

choral structure across the country; the fostering of a larger and more musically literate audience; the changes in orchestral lay-out and proliferation of concert facilities; the emergence of better standards of musical education, publishing and criticism.[49] These studies provide a sound basis for further elucidating how the disparaged early Victorians laid the foundations of the high performance standards and broad-based musical culture of later decades. They also point to areas where there is scope for further exploration of the musical art-world of Victorian Britain. The project to put together a more complete picture of the genesis and content of concert and opera programming, in the increasingly important provincial centres as well as London, should lead to a more objective assessment of the relative openness of Britain to music of all periods and origins.[50] Was the repertoire of British concert and choral societies significantly narrower than those across Germany, France and (insofar as they existed) Italy? Was the degree of musical participation (in the home and in public) out of line with that in other major cities of Europe and what light does that throw on their relative musical vitality? Specifically, it would be valuable to examine, building on the foundations laid by Daniel Koury, how far orchestral composition and lay-out differed in Britain from those of other music centres.[51]

More generally, there is scope for useful further work to free some of the key players (such as Balfe, Bishop, Moscheles, Smart and Sullivan) from the hagiographies produced after their deaths. The challenge is not to make them the centre of the story or to claim for them merits which they did not possess – occupational hazards among biographers, from which this book is not immune. The target should be to identify their role, within their own limitations and those of the musical culture which they inherited, in creating the infrastructure for the flourishing musical life of the late nineteenth century. One interesting insight into this would be to attempt a comparison of how early conductors tackled the Mount Everest of Beethoven's Symphony no. 9, which would help to illustrate the techniques of Smart, Moscheles, Costa and Sterndale Bennett (and Habeneck, Liszt and Berlioz) and the different constraints under which they operated.

[49] On concert structures and programming, Weber, *The Great Transformation*. On the financial/legal structures which shaped opera and concert repertoires Ringel and Diedricksen. On the cultural politics of London society, Hall-Witt, *Fashionable Acts*. On individual pioneers, Beale, *Charles Hallé*; Bashford, *The Pursuit of High Culture*; Michael Musgrave, *An Audience for Classical Music* and 'Changing Values in Nineteenth-Century Performance: The Work of Michael Costa and August Manns', in Bashford and Langley, eds, *Music and British Culture*. On publishing, Victoria Cooper, *The House of Novello: Practice and Policy of a Victorian Music Publisher, 1829–1866* (Aldershot: Ashgate, 2002). On the broader ideological context, Goehr, *The Imaginary Musical Museum* and Zon, 'Histories of British Music'.

[50] Simon McVeigh, 'The Professional Concert', and 'Calendar of London concerts 1750–1800' (Goldsmiths College, London, n.d.).

[51] Daniel J. Koury, *Orchestral Performance Practices in the Nineteenth Century: Size, Proportions and Seating* (Michigan: University of Rochester Press, 2010).

Underlying all these comparisons are two larger questions. How far is the 'Land Without Music' neurosis merely England's version of one which has been felt in different ways at different times by France (against the influence of Rossini, Beethoven and Wagner), Germany (against the hegemony of French language and Italian music), Italy (against the loss of the primacy of Italian composers and musicians) and Russia (against Western music in general)? And should more be done to liberate music history from the narrative which in the nineteenth century divided the common music tradition of Europe into nationalist and progressive-conservative brands?

Costa and the other mainly executive figures who fashioned Britain's musical infrastructure did not measure up to Carl Dahlhaus's doctrine that genius equates with originality. But, in Johann Gottfried Herder's sense that each nation has its special genius, they embodied the English musical genius of the period more successfully than the middling composers who have received more attention in the dictionaries.[52] At the time, many overlooked the contribution of Costa's generation to what Klein in 1925 called 'the great art-transition which is still actively in progress'.[53] But Herbert Spencer rightly saw the 'progress of musical culture' as 'one of the characteristics of our age'.[54] He was alluding to the great watershed between the largely ad hoc musical arrangements of the early century and the almost industrial infrastructure of the 1850s – a revolution in musical management that, in the contention of this writer, owed more to Costa than to any other figure. In raising the quality, efficiency and scale of musical performance, Costa had a leading role in England's greatest musical achievement in this period: 'the revival of music as a national art'.[55] It was an achievement that did not meet Carlylean or late nineteenth-century German standards of heroism or originality. But it was the fruit of five decades of that dogged striving for progress against adversity, which Francis Galton (drawing on Herbert Spencer) identified as a key attribute of genius.[56]

[52] Herder, cited by Anthony D. Smith in *National Identity* (London: Penguin Books, 1991), 75.

[53] Klein, *Mummers*, viii.

[54] Herbert Spencer, *On the Origin and Function of Music* (1857), quoted in Einstein, *Music in the Romantic Era* (London: Dent, 1947), 342.

[55] Hueffer. *Half a century of Music*, Preface.

[56] Galton, Francis, *Hereditary Genius: An Inquiry into its Laws and Consequences* (London: Macmillan and Co., Ltd, 1914).

Select Bibliography

Original Manuscripts

BL RPS MS Philharmonic archives at the British Library, London.
Davison, J.W., J. W. Davison Papers, Music Collections, British Library, London.
Ella, John, Record of the Musical Union (1845–55), John Ella Collection, Oxford; 1845–80, BL; 1881, RCMA).
—, John Ella Collection, Faculty of Music Library, University of Oxford.
Gye, Frederick, Diaries, ROHC and National Museum of the Performing Arts (this museum has now closed and is part of the Victoria and Albert Museum Collection, London).
Journal of the Society of Arts, The Royal Society for the Encouragement of Arts, Manufactures and Commerce, John Adam Street, London.
Queen Victoria's Journal, Royal Archives, Windsor
Smart, George, Papers, Music Collections, British Library, London.

Other Sources

Adam, Adolfe, *Souvenirs d'un Musicien* (Paris: Lévy, 1868).
Arditi, Luigi, *My Reminiscences* (London: Skeffington, 1897).
Arnold, I.F.K., *Der angehende Muskidirektor* (Erfurt: Henningschen Buchhandlung, 1806).
Bach, C.P.E., *Versuch über die wahre Art das Clavier zu spielen*, trans. William J. Mitchell (Berlin: 1753–62, repr. 1969).
Barbirolli, John, 'The Art of conducting', *Penguin Music Magazine*, vol. 2 (1947), 70
Barnett, John Francis, *Musical Reminiscences and Impressions* (London: Hodder and Stoughton, 1906).
Barrett, William, *Balfe: His Life and Work* (London: Remington 1882).
Bashford, Christina, *Music and British Culture, 1785–1914: Essays in Honour of Cyril Ehrlich*, ed. Christina Bashford and Leanne Langley (Oxford: Oxford University Press, 2000).
—, *The Pursuit of High Culture. John Ella and Chamber Music in Victorian London* (Woodbridge: Boydell Press, 2007).
Beale, Robert, *Charles Hallé, a Musical Life* (Aldershot: Ashgate, 2007).
Becker, Heinz and Gudrun, eds, *Giacomo Meyerbeer, A Life in Letters*, trans. Mark Violette (London: Helm, 1983).

Becker, Howard, *Art Worlds* (Berkeley and Los Angeles: University of California Press, 1982).

Beedell, A.V., *The Decline of the English Musician 1788–1888* (Oxford: Clarendon Press, 1992).

Benedict, Julius, *Sketch of the Life and Works of the Late Felix Mendelssohn-Bartholdy* (London: Murray, 1850).

Bennett, Joseph, *Forty Years of Music: 1865–1905* (London: Methuen, 1908).

Berlioz, Hector, *Grand Traité d'Instrumentation et d'Orchestration Modernes* (Paris: Schonenberger, 1843). (Supplement, 1855), trans. Mary Cowden Clark (London: Novello, 1858).

—, *Correspondence Générale*, ed. Pierre Citron, Yves Gérard and Hugh J. Macdonald (Paris: 1872).

—, *Les Soirées d'Orchestre*, ed. Léon Guichard (Paris: Gründ, 1968).

—, *The Memoirs of Hector Berlioz*, trans. and ed. David Cairns (London: Gollancz, 1969).

Bird, Martin, 'A very good idea at the time: Sir Edward Elgar – Principal Conductor, London Symphony Orchestra', *Elgar Society Journal*, vol. 17, no. 1 (Apr. 2011), 22–36.

Bledsoe, Robert, *Henry Fothergill Chorley* (Aldershot: Ashgate, 1998).

Borland, John E., 'Orchestral and choral balance', *Proceedings of the Musical Association*, vol. xxviii (1901–02), 1–24.

Bowen, Jose Antonio, 'The history of remembered innovation: Tradition and its role in the relationship between musical works and their performances', *The Journal of Musicology*, vol. 11, no. 2 (1993), 139–73.

—, ed., *The Cambridge Companion to Conducting* (Cambridge: Cambridge University Press, 2003).

Bowley, Robert, *Account of the Re-opening of the Crystal Palace* (London: RCM Centre for Musical Performance Collection, n.d.).

—, *The Sacred Harmonic Society: A Thirty-five Year Retrospect* (London: private printing, 1867).

Brown, Clive, *A Portrait of Mendelssohn* (New Haven, CT: Yale University Press, 2003).

Bunn, Alfred, *The Stage, Both Before and Behind the Curtain*, 3 vols (London: Richard Bentley, 1840).

Burney, Charles, *An Account of the Musical Performance in Westminster Abbey* (Dublin: 1785).

Busby, Thomas, *A Complete Dictionary of Music*, 2nd ed. (London: Gillet, 1806; reissue with amendments 1840).

Cairns, David, *Berlioz*, 2 vols (London: Andre Deutsch, 1989 and 1999).

Cambridge History of Nineteenth-Century Music, ed. Jim Samson (Cambridge: Cambridge University Press, 2002).

Carlini, Cia, *Gioacchino Rossini Lettere agli Amici* (Forli: Instituto Culturali della Citta di Forli, 1993).

Carnelley, John, 'Sir George Smart and the evolution of British musical culture 1800–1840' (PhD diss., Goldsmiths College, University of London, 2008).

Carse, Adam, *The Orchestra from Beethoven to Berlioz* (Cambridge: Heffer, 1948).

—, *The Orchestra in the XVIIIth Century* (New York: Broude Bros, 1969, first ed. 1940).

Castil-Blaze, F.H.J., *De l'Opéra en France* (Paris, 1820, Janet et Cotelle).

—, *L'Académie Impériale de Musique* (Paris: Castil-Blaze, 1855).

Charlton, David, 'A maître d'orchestre ... conducts: New and old evidence on French practice', *Early Music*, vol. 21 (1993), 341–53.

Chissell, Joan, *Clara Schumann* (London: Hamish Hamilton, 1983).

Chorley, Henry, *Music and Manners in France and Germany* (London: Longmans, 1841).

—, *Thirty Years of Musical Recollections*, ed. Ernest Newman (London: Alfred A. Knopf, 1926).

Cone, John Frederick, *Adelina Patti, Queen of Hearts* (Aldershot: Scolar Press, 1994).

Cooper, Victoria, *The House of Novello: Practice and Policy of a Victorian Music Publisher, 1829–1866* (Aldershot: Ashgate, 2002).

Cowen, Frederick, *My Art and My Friends* (London: Arnold, 1913).

Cowgill, Rachel and Gabriella Dideriksen, 'Opera orchestras in Georgian and early Victorian London', in Niels Martin Jensen and Franco Piperno (eds) *The Opera Orchestra in 18th and 19th century Europe*, vol. 1 (Berlin: B.W.V., 2008).

Cox, H.B. and Cox, C.L.E., eds, *Leaves from the Journals of Sir G. Smart* (London: Longmans, Green and Co., 1907).

Cox, John Edmund, *Musical Recollections of the Last Half-Century* (London: Lensley Bros,1872).

Crotch, William, ed., *G. F. Handel, Anthems for the Coronation of King George IV* (London: Handel Society, 1844).

Crowest, F.J., *Musician's Wit, Humour and Anecdote* (London: Scott, 1902).

Damrosch, Walter, *My Musical Life* (New York: 1923).

Davey, Henry, *History of English Music* (London: J. Curwen and Sons, 1895).

Davison, Henry, *From Mendelssohn to Wagner, Being the Memoirs of J. W. Davison, Forty Years Music Critic of 'The Times'* (London: Wm Reeves, 1912).

Deldevez, E.M.E., *L'Art du Chef d'Orchestre* (Paris: Firmin, 1878).

Deutsche 'Biedermann', *Wahrheiten die Musik betreffend* (Truths about music) (Frankfurt: Eichenbergsche Erben, 1779).

Devrient, Eduard, *My Recollections of Felix Mendelssohn-Bartholdy*, trans. N. Macfarren (London: 1869).

Dideriksen, Gabriella, 'Repertory and rivalry: Opera at the second Covent Garden Theatre 1830–56' (PhD diss., University of London, 1997).

Dittersdorf, K. von, *Autobiography*, trans, D. Coleridge (London: Bentley and son, 1896).

Dörffel, Alfred, *Geschichte der Gewandhausconcerte zu Leipzig* (Leipzig: 1884).

Drescher, 'J.F. Reichardt als Leiter der Berliner Hofkapelle', *Basler Jahrbuch fur historische Musikpraxis*, vol. 17 (1993).

Ebers, John, *Seven Years of the King's Theatre* (London: 1828).

Eckardt, J., *Ferdinand David und die Familie Mendelssohn-Bartholdy* (Leipzig:1888).

Edwards, F.G., *Musical Haunts of London* (London: Curwen, 1895).

Edwards, H. Sutherland, *The Prima Donna* (London: Remington, 1888).

Ehrlich, Cyril, *First Philharmonic, A History of the Royal Philharmonic Society* (Oxford: Clarendon Press, 1995).

—, *The Music Profession in Britain since the Eighteenth Century* (Oxford: Clarendon Press, 1995).

Einstein, Alfred, *Music in the Romantic Era* (London: Dent, 1947).

Elgar, Edward, 'A Future for English Music', Peyton Lectures (1905–06).

Elkin, Robert, *Annals of the Royal Philharmonic* (London: Rider and Co., 1946).

Ella, John, *Musical Sketches Abroad and at Home*, 3rd ed., ed. John Belcher (London: W. Reeves, 1878).

Elwart, A.A.E., *Histoire de la Societé des Concerts des Conservatoire Impérial de Musique, avec dessins, musique, plans, portraits, etc.* (Paris: Castel, 1860).

Fétis, Francois-Joseph, 'De l'execution musicale', *Revue Musicale*, 1827–28 vol. 2 (Aug. 1827).

—, *Curiosites Historiques de la Musique* (Paris: Janet et Cotelle, 1830).

—, *Manuel des compositeurs, directeurs de musique, chefs d'orchestre et de musique militaire* (Paris: Schlesinger, 1837), 124–5.

—, `M. Fétis on the state of music in London', *Harmonicon* (1829). Later published as part of *Music Explained to the World* (London: Clarke, 1844).

—, *Music Explained to the World* (Paris: 1844).

Feuilleton du Journal des Débats, http://www.hberlioz.com/feuilletons/debats510701.htm.

Ford, Ernest, *A Short History of Music in England* (London: Sampson Low and Co., 1912).

Foster, Myles Birkett, *History of the Royal Philharmonic Society of London:1813–1912* (London: John Lane, 1912).

Fuller Maitland, J.A., *English Music in the XIXth Century* (London: Grant Richards, 1902).

—, *A Door-keeper of Music* (London: John Murray, 1929).

Galeazzi, F., *Elementi teorico-pratici di musica* (Rome: Cracas, 1791–96).

Galkin, Elliott W., *A History of Orchestral Conducting in Theory and Practice* (New York: Pendragon Press, 1989).

Galton, Francis, *Hereditary Genius: An Inquiry into its Laws and Consequences* (London: Macmillan and Co., Ltd, 1914).

Ganz, A.W., *Berlioz in London* (London: Quality Press 1950).

Gerber, E.L., *Lexikon der Tonkünstler* (Leipzig: 1790–92)

Ghisalberti, Alberto Maria, *Dizionario Biografico degli Italiani* (Roma: Istituto della Enciclopedia Italiana, 1960–), vol. 30 (1984).

Giulini, M.F., *Giuditta Pasta e suoi tempi* (Milan: 1935).

Goehr, Lydia, *The Imaginary Musical Museum* (Oxford: Oxford University Press, 2007).

Goulden, John, 'Michael Costa, England's first conductor: The revolution in musical performance in England 1830–80' (PhD diss., Durham University, 2012).

Graeme, E., ed., *Beethoven: A Memoir* (London: Griffin, 1870).

Graves, Charles L., *The Life and Letters of Sir George Grove* (London: Macmillan, 1903).

—, *Post-Victorian Music* (London: 1911).

Grove, George, ed., *A Dictionary of Music and Musicians* (London: 1879–89, 1904–10, 1927, 1940). *New Grove 1* (1980). *New Grove 2* (2001).

Gruneisen, Charles Lewis, *The Opera and the Press* (London: 1869).

Hall-Witt, Jennifer, 'The refashioning of fashionable society: Opera-going and sociability in Britain 1821–61' (PhD diss., Yale University, 1996).

—, *Fashionable Acts: Opera and Elite Culture in London 1780–1880* (New Hampshire: University Press of New England, 2007).

Hallé, Charles, *The Autobiography of Charles Halle*, ed. Michael Kennedy (London: Paul Elek Books, 1972).

Hauptmann, Moritz, *Briefe von Moritz Hauptmann an Franz Hauser* (Leipzig: 1871).

Haweis, H.R., *Music and Morals* (London: Strahan,1871).

Hensel, Sebastian, *The Mendelssohn Family (1729–1847) from Letters and Journals*, trans. and ed. C Klingermann (London: S. Low, 1882).

Hewlett, Henry, *Henry Fothergill Chorley: Autobiography, Memoir and Letters*, 2 vols (London: Richard Bentley and Son, 1873).

Hiller, Ferdinand, *Mendelssohn, Letters and Recollections,* trans. M.E. von Glehn (London: 1874).

Hogarth, George, *Philharmonic Society of London from its Foundation, 1813, to its 50th Year* (London: Bradbury and Evans, 1862).

Holman, Peter, 'The British Isles: Private and public music', in Julie Anne Sadie (ed.) *Companion to Baroque Music* (Oxford: Oxford University Press, 1998).

Holmes, Edward, *A Ramble Among the Musicians of Germany* (London: 1828).

Hueffer, Francis, *Half a Century of Music in England* (London: Chapman and Hall, 1889).

Hughes, Meirion, and Robert Stradling, *The English Musical Renaissance and the Press 1840–1940*, 2nd ed. (Manchester: Manchester University Press, 2001).

Jacobs, A., 'Spohr and the Baton', *Music and Letters*, vol. 31 (1950), 307–17.

Kastner, G., *Cours d'Instrumentation* (Paris: Meissonnier et Heugel, 1839). *Supplement to Cours d'Instrumentation* (1844).

—, *Manuel générale de musique militaire* (Paris: Firmin-Didot, 1848).

Kennedy, Michael, *The Halle Tradition: A Century of Music* (Manchester: Manchester University Press, 1960).

Klein, Herman, *Thirty Years of Musical Life* (London: Heinemann, 1903).

—, *The Reign of Patti* (London: Fisher Unwin, 1920).

—, *Musicians and Mummers* (London: Cassell, 1925).

—, *The Golden Age of Opera* (London: G. Routledge & Sons, 1933).

Klingemann, Karl, *Felix Mendelssohn Bartholdy: Briefwechsel mit Legationstrat Karl Klingemann in London* (Essen: 1909).

Koch, Heinrich Christoph, *Musikalisches Lexikon, welches die theoretische und praktische Tonkunst, encylopädisch bearbeitet, alle alten und neuen Kunstwörter erklärt, und die alten und neuen Instrumente beschrieben, enthält* (Offenbach am Main: 1802).

Köhler, Joachim, *Richard Wagner, The Last of the Titans* (New Haven, CT: Yale University Press, 2004).

Kolb, Annette, *Mozart*, trans. Phyllis and Trevor Blewett (London: Gollancz, 1939).

Koury, Daniel J., *Orchestral Performance Practices in the Nineteenth Century: Size, Proportions and Seating* (Michigan: University of Rochester Press, 2010).

Kuhe, Wilhelm, *My Musical Recollections* (London: Richard Bentley, 1896).

Lampadius, W.A., *Felix Mendelssohn* (Leipzig: 1886).

Langley, Leanne, 'The musical press in nineteenth-century England', *Music Library Association Notes*, vol. 46 (1990), 583–92.

Lawrence, Vera Brodsky, *Strong on Music, Vol. 2: Reverberations* (Chicago: University of Chicago Press, 1995).

Ledger-Thomas, Michael, '"Lyra Germanica": German sacred music in mid-Victorian England', *German Historical Institute London Bulletin*, vol. 29, no. 2 (Nov. 2007), 8–43.

Leppard, Raymond, 'Music and the conductor', *Journal of the Royal Society of Arts*, vol. 121, no. 5207 (Oct. 1973), 707–16.

—, *On Music, An Anthology of Critical and Autobiographical Writings*, ed. Thomas P. Lewis (White Plains, NY: Pro-Am Music Resources, 1993).

Leppert, Richard, 'Cultural contradiction, idolatry, and the piano virtuoso: Franz Liszt', in *The Sight of Sound: Music, Representation, and the History of the Body* (Berkley: University of California Press, 1993).

Lumley, Benjamin, *The Earl of Dudley, Mr Lumley and Her Majesty's Theatre: A Narrative of Facts Addressed to the Patrons of the Opera, his Friends and the Public Generally* (London: Bosworth and Harrison, 1863).

—, *Reminiscences of the Opera* (London: Hurst and Blackett, 1864).

Macfarren, Walter, *Memories, An Autobiography* (London: Walter Scott, 1905).

Mackenzie, Alexander, *A Musician's Narrative* (London: 1927).

Mandler, Peter, *The English National Character* (New Haven: Yale University Press 2006).

Mapleson, J.H., *The Mapleson Memoirs: The Career of an Operatic Impresario 1858–88*, ed. Harold Rosenthal (New York: Appleton-Century, 1888).

Mathieson, Holly, 'Embodying music: The visuality of three iconic conductors in London, 1840–1940' (MusB thesis, University of Otago, New Zealand, 2010).

McVeigh, Simon, 'The professional concert and rival subscription series in London, 1783–1793', *Royal Musical Association Research Chronicle*, no. 22 (1989), 1–135.

—, 'The benefit concert in nineteenth-century London: From "tax on the nobility" to "monstrous nuisance"', in Bennett Zon, ed., *Nineteenth-Century British Music Studies*, vol. 1 (Aldershot: Ashgate, 1999).

—, 'The Society of British Musicians 1834–65 and the campaign for native talent', in Bashford and Langley, eds, *Music and British Culture, 1785–1914: Essays in Honour of Cyril Ehrlich* (Oxford: Oxford University Press, 2000).

—, 'Calendar of London concerts 1750–1800' (Goldsmiths College, London, n.d.).

Mendelssohn, Felix, *Letters of Felix Mendelssohn-Bartholdy from Italy and Switzerland*, trans. G Wallace (New York: Leypoldt and Holt, 1866).

—, *Letters of Felix Mendelssohn-Bartholdy, 1833–47*, ed. Joseph Rietz (Boston: Oliver Ditson and Co., 1869).

—, *Felix Mendelssohn's Letters*, ed. Paul Elek (London: Cole, 1946).

—, *Felix Mendelssohn, A Life in Letters*, ed. Rudolf Elvers, trans. Craig Tomlinson (New York: Fromm International Publishing, 1986).

Moscheles, Charlotte, *Life of Moscheles* (London: Hurst and Blakett, 1873).

Moscheles, Ignaz, *Recent Music and Musicians as Described in the Diaries and Correspondence*, ed. his wife, trans, A.D. Coleridge (New York: Da Capo, 1970).

Mount-Edgcumbe, Robert, *Musical Reminiscences* (London: John Andrews, 1834).

Mozart, Wolfgang, *The Letters of Mozart to his Family*, trans. E. Anderson (London: Macmillan, 1985).

Murray, John, *The World of London* (London: Murray, 1851).

Musgrave, Michael, *The Musical Life of the Crystal Palace* (Cambridge: Cambridge University Press, 1995).

—, *An Audience for Classical Music: The Achievement of August Manns at the Crystal Palace*, Inaugural Professorial Lecture, Goldsmith's College (7 May 1996).

—, 'Changing Values in Nineteenth-Century Performance: The Work of Michael Costa and August Manns', in Bashford and Langley, eds, *Music and British Culture, 1785–1914: Essays in Honour of Cyril Ehrlich* (Oxford: Oxford University Press, 2000).

Nathan, Hans and Frances Fink, eds, *Autograph Letters of Musicians at Harvard* (Harvard: Music Library Association, 1948).

Nettel, R., *The Orchestra in England* (London: Cape, 1946).

Nicholson, Charles, *School for the Flute* (New York and London: William Hall and Son, 1836).

Norris, Gerald, *Stanford, the Cambridge Jubilee and Tchaikovsky* (Newton Abbot: David and Charles, 1980).

Pallua, Ulrich, *Eurocentrism, Racism, Colonialism in the Victorian and Edwardian Age: Changing Images of Africa(Ns) in Scientific and Literary Texts* (Heidleberg: Universitätsverlag, 2006).

Palmer, Fiona, *Dragonetti in England (1794–1846): The Career of a Double Bass Virtuoso* (Oxford: Clarendon Press, 1997).

Parke, William Thomas, *Musical Memoirs*, 2 vols (London, 1830).

Peacock, Thomas Love, 'Mangled operas and the Star System', in *Dramatic Criticisms and Translations, & Other Essays*, vol. 10 (London: Constable and Co., 1926).

Peyser, Joan, ed., *The Orchestra, Origins and Transformations* (New York: Watson-Guptill, 2004).

Philip, Robert, *Performing Music in the Age of Recording* (Yale: Yale University Press, 2004).

Phillips, Henry, *Musical and Personal Recollections during Half a Century* (London: C.J. Skeat, 1864).

Planché, J.R., *Recollections and Reflections of J.R. Planché* (London: Sampson and Low, 1901, first ed. 1872).

Plumb, J.H., *The Commercialisation of Leisure in Eighteenth Century England* (Reading: University of Reading, 1973).

Pritchard, Brian, 'The music festival and choral societies in England in the 18th and 19th centuries' (PhD thesis, University of Birmingham, 1986), vol. 2, section C.

Quantz, J.S., *Versuch einer Anweisung die Flote traversiere ze spielen*, trans. E.R. Reilly (London: Faber & Faber, 1966). Facsimile of 1752 edition (Paris: Zurfluh, 1975).

Ramann , L., ed., *Franz Liszt als Kunstler und Mensch*, trans. E. Cowdrey, 3 vols (London: 1882).

Reeves, Sims, *My Jubilee or Fifty Years of Artistic Life* (London: Musical Publishing Company, 1889).

Ringel, Matthew L. and Didericksen, Gabriella, 'Frederick Gye and "the Dreadful Business of Opera Management"', *Nineteenth-Century Music*, vol. 19, no. 1 (Summer 1995), 3–30.

—, 'Opera in the Donizettian Dark Ages: Management, competition and artistic policy in London 1861–70' (PhD diss., University of London, 1996).

Rohr, Deborah, *The Careers of British Musicians 1750–1850: A Profession of Artisans* (Cambridge: Cambridge University Press, 2001).

Rosenthal, Harold, *Two Centuries of Opera at Covent Garden* (London: Putnam, 1958).

Ross, Alex, *The Rest is Noise* (London: Harper, 2007).

Rousseau, J.-J., *Dictionnaire de Musique* (Paris: Duchesne, 1768).

Ryan, Thomas, *Recollections of an Old Musician* (New York: E.P. Dutton, 1899).

Samson, Jim, ed., *The Cambridge History of Nineteenth-century Music* (Cambridge: Cambridge University Press, 2001).

Santley, Charles, *Student and Singer: The Reminiscences of Charles Santley* (London: Edward Arnold, 1892).

Scholes, Percy, *The Mirror of Music 1844–1944* (London: Novello, 1947).

Schuller, Gunther, *The Compleat Conductor* (Oxford: Oxford University Press, 1997).

Schumann, Clara, *An Artist's Life*, ed. Berthold Litzmann, trans. Grace Hadow (Cambridge: Cambridge University Press, 1913).

Schumann, Robert, *Music and Musicians*, trans. Fanny Raymond Ritter (London: 1891).

Scruton, Roger, *The Aesthetics of Music* (Oxford: Clarendon Press, 1999).

Shaw, George Bernard, *Shaw's Music*, ed. Dan H. Lawrence, 3 vols (London: Bodley Head, 1981).

Smither, Howard E., *The Oratorio in the Nineteenth and Twentieth Century* (Chapel Hill: University of North Carolina Press, 2000).

Southon, Nicolas, 'L'émergence de la figure du chef d'orchestre et ses composantes socio-artistiques: François-Antoine Habeneck (1781–1849). La naissance du professionnalisme musical' (PhD diss., University Francois Rabelais, Tours, 2008).

Spark, William, *Musical Memories*, 3rd ed. (London: W Reeves, 1909).

Speyer, E., *Wilhelm Speyer der Liederkomponist* (Munich: 1925).

Spitzer, John, 'The entrepreneur-conductors and their orchestras', *Nineteenth-Century Music Review*, vol. 5, no. 1 (2008).

Spitzer, John and Neal Zaslaw, *The Birth of the Orchestra* (Oxford: Oxford University Press, 2005).

Spohr, Louis, *Autobiography* (London: Longmans, 1865).

Stanford, Charles Villiers, *Pages from an Unwritten Diary* (London: Edward Arnold, 1914).

—, *Interludes Records and Reflections* (London: John Murray, 1921).

Sterndale Bennett, James Robert, *Life of William Sterndale Bennett by his Son* (Cambridge: Cambridge University Press, 1907).

Strakosch, Maurice, *Souvenirs d'un Impresario* (Paris: Ollendorf, 1887).

Strauss, Richard, *Recollections and Reflections*, ed. Willi Schuh, trans. L.J. Lawrence (London: 1953).

Sutherland Edwards, H., *The Prima Donna* (London: Emington and Co., 1888).

Taruskin, Richard, *Music in the 19th Century* (Oxford: Oxford University Press, 2010).

Temperley, Nicholas, ed., *The Romantic Age 1800–1914* (Oxford: Blackwell, 1988).

—, 'Xenophilia in British musical history', in Bennett Zon, ed., *Nineteenth-Century British Musical Studies*, vol. 1 (Aldershot: Ashgate, 1999).

Tetens, Kristan, 'Continental opera in the London of William IV: Thomas Monck Mason and the King's Theatre, Haymarket, 1832', unpublished paper delivered at the Fifth Conference on Music in Nineteenth-Century Britain at the University of Nottingham (2005).

Thackeray, W.M., *Miscellaneous Prose and Verse* (London: Bradbury and Evans, 1835).

Todd, Larry, *Mendelssohn a Life in Music* (Oxford: Oxford University Press 2003).

Wagner, Richard, *My Life*, trans. anon. (London: Constable 1911).

—, *On Conducting* (*Über das Dirigieren*, 1870), in Robert L. Jacobs (trans.) *Three Wagner Essays* (London: Eulenberg Books, 1979).

—, *Selected Letters*, ed. Stewart Spencer and Barry Millington (London: J.M. Dent and Sons, 1987).

Walker, Alan, *Hans von Bülow: A Life and Times* (Oxford: Oxford University Press, 2010).

Walker, Ernest, *Free Thought and the Musician* (Oxford: 1946).

Walter, Bruno, *Theme and Variations*, trans. J.A. Galston (New York: 1946).

Warrack, John, *Carl Maria von Weber* (London: Hamish Hamilton, 1868).

Weber, William, *The Rise of Musical Classics in Eighteenth Century England: A Study in Canon, Ritual and Ideology* (New York: Pendragon Press, 2000).

—, *Music and the Middle Class: The Social Structure of Concert Life in London, Paris and Vienna between 1830 and 1848* (Aldershot: Ashgate, 2004).

—, ed., *Musician as Entrepreneur and Opportunist, 1700–1914: Managers, Charlatans and Idealists* (Bloomington: Indiana University Press, 2004).

—, *The Great Transformation of Musical Taste. Concert Programming from Haydn to Brahms* (Cambridge: Cambridge University Press, 2008).

Weingartner, Felix, *On Conducting*, trans. E. Newman (London: Breitkopf and Härtel, 1906).

Weinstock, Herbert, *Vincenzo Bellini* (London: Weidenfeld and Nicolson, 1971).

Werner, Eric, *Mendelssohn: A New Image of the Composer and His Age* (New York: Free Press of Glencoe, 1963).

Willeby, Charles, *Masters of English Music* (London: Osgood, 1893).

Willets, Pamela J., *Beethoven and England* (London: British Museum, 1970).

Williams, Alistair, *Constructing Musicology* (Aldershot: Ashgate, 2001).

Wooldridge, David, *Conductor's World* (London: Barrie and Rockliff, 1970).

Yates, Edmund, *His Recollections and Experiences* (London: Bentley, 1884).

Young, Percy, *Beethoven: A Victorian Tribute* (London: Denis Dobson, 1976).

—, *George Grove* (London: Macmillan, 1980).

Zavadini, G., *Donizetti: Vita – Musiche – Epistolare* (Bergamo: 1948).

Zon, Bennett, '"Loathsome London": Ruskin, Morris, and Henry Davey's *History of English Music* (1895)', *Victorian Literature and Culture*, vol. 37 (2009), 359–75.

—, 'Histories of British Music and the land without music: National identity and the idea of the hero', in Emma Hornby and David Maw, eds, *Essays on the History of English Music in Honour of John Caldwell: Style, Performance, Historiography* (Woodbridge: Boydell & Brewer, 2010).

Index

Note: Page numbers in **bold** refer to Illustrations.